Podcasting for Learning in Universities

Podcasting for Learning in Universities

Edited by Gilly Salmon and Palitha Edirisingha

Open University Press
McGraw-Hill Education
McGraw-Hill House
Shoppenhangers Road
Maidenhead
Berkshire
England
SL6 2QL

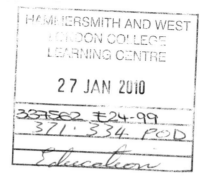
email: enquiries@openup.co.uk
world wide web: www.openup.co.uk

and Two Penn Plaza, New York, NY 10121–2289, USA

First published 2008

Reprinted 2009

Copyright © Gilly Salmon and Palitha Edirisingha 2008

A catalogue record of this book is available from the British Library

ISBN-10 0 335 23429 1 (pb)   0 335 23428 3 (hb)
ISBN-13: 978 0 335 23429 5 (pb)   978 0 335 23428 8 (hb)

Library of Congress Cataloging-in-Publication Data
CIP data has been applied for

Typeset by RefineCatch Limited, Bungay, Suffolk
Printed in the UK by Bell and Bain Ltd, Glasgow

Fictitious names of companies, products, people, characters and/or data that may be
used herein (in case studies or in examples) are not intended to represent any real
individual, company, product or event.

The **McGraw·Hill** Companies

For Lauren, Freya and Samuel, podcasters of the future.

Contents

Figures

Figures cont.

Tables

Boxes

Contributors

Marialuisa Aliotta is a Lecturer at the University of Edinburgh, and supervises undergraduate final year projects in topics related to Physics Education.
email: m.aliotta@ed.ac.uk
web: ph.ed.ac.uk/~maliotta

Simon Bates is a Director of Teaching and a Senior Lecturer at the School of Physics, University of Edinburgh. He is a member of the Institute of Physics Higher Education Group, the JISC Pedagogy Experts group and the Higher Education Academy Physical Sciences Centre Advisory Committee.
email: s.p.bates@ed.ac.uk
web: ph.ed.ac.uk/~spb01

David Bell is a Senior Lecturer in Critical Human Geography. He is also leader of the Urban Cultures and Consumption research cluster at the School of Geography, University of Leeds.
email: d.j.bell@leeds.ac.uk
web: geog.leeds.ac.uk/people/d.bell/

Keith Brunton is an E-learning Developer, School of Physics, University of Edinburgh, and a member of the University's E-learning Forum Committee.
email: kbrunton@uun.ed.ac.uk
web: ph.ed.ac.uk/elearning

Chris Cane is a Teaching Fellow at the Department of Genetics, University of Leicester.
email: crc@le.ac.uk
web: le.ac.uk/genetics/

Annette Cashmore is a Director of the Centre for Excellence in Teaching and Learning in Genetics (Genie), and is Sub-Dean of the Medical School, at the University of Leicester.

email: amc19@le.ac.uk
web: le.ac.uk/genetics/pages/staff/staff_pages/cashmore.html

Claire Chambers is the E-Learning Co-ordinator for the School of Geography at the University of Nottingham. She was previously with the Mathematics Electronic Learning Environment for Engineers and Scientists (MELEES) within the School of Mathematical Sciences.
email: claire.chambers@nottingham.ac.uk
web: nottingham.ac.uk/-lgzwww/contacts/a-z/index.phtml?name=chambers

Brian Cox is a Multimedia Developer in the Electronic Media Unit, Royal Veterinary College, at the University of London, and specializes in video, audio and images.
email: bcox@rvc.ac.uk
web: www.rvc.ac.uk/emedia

Chris Dennett is a Lecturer in Mobile Computing at the School of Computing and Information Technology, University of Wolverhampton, and is the technology chair for the mLearn2008 conference.
email: c.dennett@wlv.ac.uk
web: wlv.ac.uk

Stuart Downward is a Senior Lecturer in Physical Geography, School of Earth Sciences and Geography at the Kingston University. He has research interests in river restoration and water resources management.
email: s.downward@kingston.ac.uk
web: kingston.ac.uk/esg/staff/downward.htm

Palitha Edirisingha is a Lecturer in E-learning, Beyond Distance Research Alliance at the University of Leicester. He was research leader for IMPALA.
email: palitha.edirisingha@le.ac.uk
web: www.le.ac.uk/beyonddistance

John Fothergill is a Professor of Engineering and is currently a Pro-Vice-Chancellor at the University of Leicester. He is a Fellow of the IET (Chartered Engineer), a member of the Institute of Physics (Chartered Physicist) and a Fellow of the IEEE.
email: John.Fothergill@leicester.ac.uk
web: le.ac.uk/eg/jcf/

Derek France is a Senior Lecturer in Geography, Senior Teaching Fellow and E-learning Co-ordinator for the School of Social Science at the University of Chester.
email: d.france@chester.ac.uk
web: chester.ac.uk/geography/dfrance.html

Martin Jenkins is Academic Manager for the Centre for Active Learning (CeAL) at the University of Gloucestershire. He is also a National Teaching Fellow.
email: mjenkins@glos.ac.uk
web: glos.ac.uk/ceal/contacts/martinjenkins.cfm

Mark J.W. Lee is an Adjunct Lecturer at the School of Education, Charles Sturt University. He is also an Honorary Research Fellow at the School of Information Technology and Mathematical Sciences, University of Ballarat, Australia.
email: malee@csu.edu.au
web: csusap.csu.edu.au/~malee/

David Livingstone is a Senior Lecturer in Information Systems at the Centre for Applied Research in Information Systems, Kingston University.
e-mail: d.livingstone@kingston.ac.uk
web: dircweb.king.ac.uk/cism/Queries/Pages/home_page.asp?authorID=253

Jo Lonsdale is a Postgraduate Researcher at the Centre for Active Learning (CeAL), University of Gloucestershire.
email: jlonsdale@glos.ac.uk
web: glos.ac.uk/ceal/contacts/jolonsdale.cfm

Kenny Lynch is Senior Lecturer in Geography at the Department of Natural and Social Sciences, and Deputy Head of the Pedagogic Research and Scholarship Institute, University of Gloucestershire.
email: klynch@glos.ac.uk
web: glos.ac.uk/faculties/ehs/sciences/staff/lynch.cfm

Raymond Macharia is a Lecturer at the Royal Veterinary College, University of London. He became a Fellow of the Higher Education Academy in 2007.
email: rmacharia@rvc.ac.uk
web: rvc.ac.uk/AboutUs/Staff/rmacharia

Matthew Mobbs is a Learning Technologist for the Beyond Distance Research Alliance and the Student Support and Development Services at the University of Leicester. He ran workshops and assisted academic staff in the recording of podcasts for IMPALA.
email: mjm33@le.ac.uk
web: www.le.ac.uk/beyonddistance

Richard Mobbs is Head of Web Design and E-learning Services in the IT Services Department at the University of Leicester. He is responsible for the University's web design team, technical support staff and the VLE.
email: rjm1@le.ac.uk
web: le.ac.uk/cc/rjm1/

Nick Mount is a Lecturer in GIS and Physical Geography at the School of Geography, University of Nottingham. He won the Lord Dearing Award for teaching and learning in 2007.
email: nick.mount@nottingham.ac.uk
Web: nottingham.ac.uk/geography/contacts/points/teaching.phtml?name =mount

Dick Ng'ambi is Research Co-ordinator at the Centre for Educational Technology, University of Cape Town.
email: Dick.Ngambi@uct.ac.za
web: cet.uct.ac.za/DickNgambi

Ming Nie is Research Associate in E-learning, Beyond Distance Research Alliance at the University of Leicester. She worked on IMPALA, IMPALA 2 and 3.
email: mn79@le.ac.uk
web: www.impala.ac.uk

Chris Ribchester is a Senior Lecturer in Geography, and is programme leader for BSc Single Honours Geography at the University of Chester.
email: c.ribchester@chester.ac.uk
web: chester.ac.uk/geography/cribchester.html

Libby Rothwell is Principal Lecturer in English Language and Communication at Kingston University, and is Learning and Teaching Strategy Coordinator for the Faculty of Arts and Social Sciences and co-manager of the Faculty's Academic Skills Centre.
email: l.rothwell@kingston.ac.uk
web: fass.kingston.ac.uk/staff/cv.php?staffnum=97

Gilly Salmon is Professor of E-learning and Learning Technologies at the University of Leicester. She is also National Teaching Fellow and Head of the Beyond Distance Research Alliance. She was principal investigator for the IMPALA project (www.impala.ac.uk).
email: gilly.salmon@le.ac.uk
Web mail: www.le.ac.uk/beyonddistance

Nick Short is a vet who is Head of the Electronic Media Unit, and is responsible for all e-learning activities at the Royal Veterinary College, University of London.
email: nshort@rvc.ac.uk
web: rvc.ac.uk/AboutUs/Staff/nshort/index.cfm

Adam Stevens has a Physics degree and is now training as a teacher at the Moray House School of Education, University of Edinburgh.
email: adamhstevens@gmail.com
web: physicsbase.net/about.html

John Traxler is Reader in Mobile Technology in E-learning. He is also Director of the Learning Lab at the University of Wolverhampton, and author of recent books on mobile learning.
email: John.Traxler@wlv.ac.uk
web: pers-www.wlv.ac.uk/~cm1990/

Belinda Tynan is an Associate Professor and Leader of the Academic Development Unit at the Teaching and Learning Centre, University of New England, NSW, Australia. She is also Associate Editor for the *Higher Education Research and Development Journal.*
email: belinda.tynan@une.edu.au
web: une.edu.au/tlc

Kim Whittlestone is a Senior Lecturer in Independent Learning at the Royal Veterinary College, University of London. He is a vet with many years' experience in e-learning for veterinary and medical education.
email: kwhittlestone@rvc.ac.uk
web: live.ac.uk/html/team_whit.html

Foreword

This book is a timely and authoritative guide to the burgeoning interest in the use of podcasting as an aid to learning and teaching. As Director of Research and Evaluation at the Higher Education Academy in the UK, I am delighted that this excellent book has emerged from the 2006 round of Academy-funded e-learning projects, which has also been instrumental in building a podcasting for learning community.

The fruits of the project set out in this admirable resource has helped a wide range of university teachers to try out the benefits of podcasting for their own teaching and with their own students. Podcasting is one of the most accessible of the Web 2.0 technologies and one of the easiest to try out and adapt. The book offers research-based models of practice and useful guidelines.

This book, which emphasizes research into practice, is grounded in learning (rather than technology) and helps to demystify e-learning developments. It reflects the Higher Education Academy ethos by being highly collaborative and focusing on the student experience and enhancement of learning. The book provides a wealth of empirical data from over 1000 students in higher education.

The project and this fine outcome is an exemplar of excellent use of resources provided through the Academy's e-learning programme.

Professor Lee Harvey
Director of Research and Evaluation
Higher Education Academy
January 2008

Acknowledgements

We would like to thank over 1000 students in 10 universities who tried out many 'first attempts' at pedagogical podcasts and gave their feedback in a way we could get better at podcasting.

Thank you and our admiration to the 30 members of university staff who, initially on a wing and a prayer, became, sometimes to their surprise, successful podcast creators, and have written up their experiences in the spirit of sharing for learning improvement in this book. They were well grounded in both the empirical research and practice. They learned from and helped each other. From little beginnings, the IMPALA (Informal Mobile Podcasting And Learning Adaptation, impala.ac.uk) project partners and the wider international community became a force for good in the complex world of the marriage of teaching and technology. We salute you here in print and a bit more through podcasts on the book's website (www.podcastingforlearning.com).

A big thank you to all those who took part in our national and international IMPALA workshops at Barcelona, Berlin, Edinburgh, Leicester, Nairobi and Naples. Your input helped us to test the transferability of pedagogical podcasting models across disciplines and contexts.

We would like to thank the Higher Education Academy (HEA) in the UK for putting their faith in our vision and for funding the first IMPALA research project from June 2006. And for the HEA's Geography, Earth and Environmental Sciences subject centre (gees.ac.uk) and the Genetics Education Networking for Innovation and Excellence at the University of Leicester (le.ac.uk/cetl/genie.html) for enabling us to continue into 2008.

The Media Zoo at the University of Leicester (le.ac.uk/beyonddistance/ mediazoo and on Second Life) and the Media Zookeeper, Matthew Wheeler, constantly provided a supportive and collaborative dissemination environment.

This book would not have happened without two key individuals to help it. Dr Ming Nie worked as the researcher on the IMPALA project throughout. She undertook most of the empirical data collection and analysis and has kept us organized throughout this book's development, with commitment and smiles. Professor David Hawkridge has provided support, editing and advisory services throughout the book's development. He tells us off so nicely if we fail to meet deadlines. Any mistakes are due to our not taking his advice well enough!

This is our first book for McGraw-Hill and we would like to thank Shona Mullen for her ongoing support and encouragement.

Our personal thanks to Rod (from Gilly) and to Hung-Ju (from Palitha) for their amazing encouragement and tolerance, even when the book threatened to 'take over'.

This book is dedicated to:

- The staff and students of the University of Leicester in the UK in its 50th anniversary year in 2008. We hope its success in innovation in research *and* teaching will continue for many more years to come.
- Impalas – the animals – are medium-sized African antelope, who are adaptable and active day and night – just like podcasts!

Notes from the editors

We both work at the Beyond Distance Research Alliance at the University of Leicester, a research unit bringing together teachers and researchers, who are interested in the field of innovation in teaching and learning (le.ac.uk/beyonddistance). Our collaboration, and dissemination of research-to-practice processes in teaching and learning are focused around the physical, web and virtual presences of the Media Zoo (see www.le.ac.uk/beyond-distance/mediazoo and on Second Life.

Much of the work reported in this book emerged from a research project called IMPALA – Informal Mobile Podcasting And Learning Adaptation, which is also one of the animals in our technological zoo! You can access both the project website at impala.ac.uk and the book website podcastingforlearning.com, where you will find links and examples of some real podcasts.

Our audience

This book is one of the first academic texts that examines the topic of podcasting across a broad area of Higher Education (HE). It aims to be an introduction, a guide and a key resource that will help you to explore podcasting as an exciting area of pedagogical development.

We believe that it will interest the following groups of practitioners:

- lecturers, tutors, university teachers, instructors – with teaching, facilitation, assessment and student support responsibilities in any institution, study level, subject discipline and country context;
- members of staff development units – with responsibility for training and continuing professional development;
- learning technologists and learning resources centre staff – who provide technological, resources and archiving support and advice for academics who are considering developing podcasts;

- senior managers and heads of department who scan the scope of emerging learning technologies to enhance the quality of teaching, learning and assessment;
- researchers who are investigating emerging technologies for teaching and learning.

There is probably another set of you from colleges and corporate training who might like to see what we are up to in HE.

We would add that this is not a book about the technology of podcasting as such. If you are of a technical inclination, the book will interest you more from the perspective of podcasting's use and application by university teachers than the latest technology. However, we do attempt a basic explanation of the technology for non-technical readers in Chapter 3.

The book describes research-based podcast applications to support student learning in the UK, Australia and South Africa. Most of the work of developing and evaluating the use of podcasts was carried out under a research-into-practice project called IMPALA (www.impala.ac.uk) funded by the UK Higher Education Academy (HEA). Other work was chosen for the book because of the soundness of the authors' rationales for developing podcasts and the rigorous methods they used to evaluate students' learning through podcasts. The book also offers an examination of the contexts of podcasting, how and why practitioners developed their podcasts, offers a model and guidelines, some thoughts about the future and a critique.

Routes through the book

As you can see, we have tried to produce the book to meet a wide range of interests, so some guidance on its structure might be helpful. The index on p. 219 will also help you. We would really like you to work through the book chapter by chapter, but each one does 'stand alone', so here are some other routes.

New to podcasting?

Probably best to work through the chapters in order, though you could first try chapters 1 and then 15.

Some experience of educational podcasting?

You might like to compare the model in Chapter 15 with your own experience.

Experienced in podcasting?

We suggest that you could dip into Chapters 4 to 14 for some new ideas, and also speculate and plan for 'what's next?' with Chapter 16.

Researcher?

Chapter 2 places podcasting within the academic literature on mobile learning, Chapter 17 considers podcasting and society, and there is also a note about methodology later in this section.

Sceptic?

If you are not yet convinced by the potential of podcasting, then we suggest that you start at the end with Chapter 17, and then move back to Chapter 1 (and on . . .).

Interested in a discipline specific case study?

We offer law (Chapter 9), physics (Chapter 4), geography (Chapters 5, 6 and 7), veterinary science (Chapter 10), engineering (Chapter 8), computer and information science (Chapters 9 and 13), English language and communication (Chapter 12), genetics and bio-sciences (Chapter 14), and across social and natural sciences (including geography, human geography, environmental management, landscape architecture, heritage, community development, biology, psychology and sociology, Chapter 11).

Facing a particular teaching and learning challenge?

Here we offer podcasting ideas to enhance understanding of difficult concepts (Chapter 4), developing 3-D learning (Chapter 10), promoting active learning (Chapter 11), reflective learning (Chapter 13), supporting software teaching and learning (Chapter 5), field-based learning (Chapter 6), online learning (Chapter 8), distance learning (Chapter 9), incorporating students, voices and perspectives (Chapters 12 and 14).

Addressing the technology and 'how to'?

Start with the Appendix and Chapter 3.

Missions and markets?

Administrators and managers with an interest in podcasting or its potential could scan a couple of chapters among the 11 case studies (Chapters 4–14), where you might find some 'sparks' to help inspire your colleagues, Chapter 3 to gain an insight into the technology, Chapter 2 for positioning of podcasting within the mobile learning literature and Chapter 16 on the future.

Staff development or supporting others?

The model in Chapter 15 and the instructions in the Appendix are the result of practical experience and grounded research and work well for use in workshops.

Collecting the evidence

IMPALA was a collaborative effort (Leicester, Kingston, Gloucestershire, Royal Veterinary College and Nottingham) representing a wide range of universities in the UK.

The examples that were independent of the IMPALA study add to this diversity: Edinburgh, Chester, Charles Sturt University and University of New South Wales (Australia), and University of Cape Town (South Africa).

The IMPALA programme was implemented through a pilot study, a pedagogical design process and the development of discipline-specific podcast applications and research into learning experiences over two academic years, within an action research framework. The pilot study was undertaken at the University of Leicester in an undergraduate engineering module that integrated podcasting and e-tivities based on Salmon's 5-stage model (Salmon 2004). Using the results of the pilot study, IMPALA developed a set of guidelines and a framework (see more in Chapter 15). IMPALA project partners then explored these guidelines and frameworks for their own podcast applications through workshops and developed a range of new approaches to using podcasts for specific pedagogic purposes. More than 500 students and 20 academic staff took part in IMPALA during academic years 2006 and 2007.

The impact on the students' learning of podcasting was studied through qualitative and quantitative data collection. Quantitative data was collected through a beginning-of-semester questionnaire designed to identify students' profiles, the availability of technology to access podcasts, and students' familiarity with new learning technologies (internet and Web 2.0 tools). At the end of the semester another questionnaire gathered data on students' patterns of listening to podcasts, their reasons for not listening, the learning benefits of listening to podcasts and their recommendations for podcasts. The data was analysed using spreadsheet analysis.

The qualitative methods used included focus groups (two groups of six students from each module) in mid-semester and personal interviews with 6–10 students from each module and with the lecturers who developed the podcasts. Student interviews were conducted using a semi-structured schedule developed to explore how student learning was supported by podcasts and whether students were prepared to use personal entertainment devices for learning. Initial findings from the focus groups were discussed with academic colleagues to explore ways of improving podcast design and use. Staff experience of developing podcasts was first gathered informally through email and telephone and later through a formal interview. Information gathered included the pedagogical rationale for each podcast, how podcasts were integrated with other learning activities and learning resources, and issues encountered. All formal interviews were recorded and transcribed verbatim for content analysis to identify key themes and issues related to patterns of use of podcasts, learning outcomes from podcasts and issues related to using MP3 players for academic learning. Each of the IMPALA chapters (5, 6, 8, 10, 11, 12 and 14) provides an overview of evaluation results.

The podcasting projects independent of the IMPALA study (Chapters 4, 7, 9 and 13) used their own methodologies for developing and evaluating student learning from podcasts. Common to all of them, and in line with the aims of the IMPALA project, was a sound analysis of teaching and learning issues that could be addressed through podcasts, and an evaluation methodology to capture student learning and positive and negative experiences of pedagogical podcasting. Each chapter provides an account of how the individual authors went about developing and evaluating their own research.

Our moment in time

Chapter 15 and the Appendix offer you a very practical but research-based approach to developing your own podcasts. Chapters 1, 2, 16 and 17 recognize that our work to date is our 'first shot' and there is much more to say and do. Over to you . . . please report back! We are easy to find through the book's website www.podcastingforlearning.com.

Gilly Salmon and Palitha Edirisingha

1

Doubling the life of iPods

Gilly Salmon and Ming Nie

Summary

Podcasting is capturing the attention of teachers from many sectors of education, but podcasting for teaching and learning in universities is in its infancy. Here we report early studies and the potential benefits for learning in universities.

Introduction

Podcasting for learning in Higher Education (HE) moved over our horizon early in 2006. We both work at the Beyond Distance Research Alliance at the University of Leicester. We noticed a strong surge of interest from university teachers from different disciplines in the use of downloadable audio files. And we watched hundreds of students walking around campus, sitting on the buses, or lying on the grass in the park, with MP3 players 'glued' to their ears. What previously appeared to be a somewhat 'techie' approach to playing music suddenly looked, to us anyway, like something that might have high value and low cost for learning.

Then the UK Higher Education Academy (HEA) funded us to carry out a pedagogical podcasting research project – Informal Mobile Podcasting And Learning Adaptation (IMPALA www.impala.ac.uk), so we got the chance of obtaining some empirical data to find out whether podcasting was 'worth it' for students. Around 20 university teachers and 500 students across six topics, subjects and disciplines and different modes of learning were involved.

It was and it is still worth it! Staff and students appreciated our efforts. It is pretty easy to podcast and have an impact on learning. We hope this book will inspire you to try it.

A winding pathway led us to 'podcast alley'. As with most attempts to exploit new technologies for learning, there are complex histories – and preparing for the future is a little messy and uncertain (We will discuss more about the future later in the book). Out of the melee and the myriad of possibilities, we wanted some well-grounded models and examples from practice to light the way. Critically, though, we were able to draw on some previous journeys.

We benefited from a pilot using podcasts in an undergraduate engineering course. Within a module in electrical engineering (Optical Fibre Communication Systems) at the University of Leicester, podcasts provide students with guidance on weekly learning activities and help to motivate them by including news and fun items (Fothergill 2007). Our first write-up from the pilot concluded (Edirisingha et al. 2007a: 134):

> Our pilot study highlighted how 'profcasting' contributed to student learning: supporting organizational aspects of learning; developing positive attitudes towards the lecturer, bringing in an informality and fun to formal learning; helping with independent learning; enabling deep engagement with learning material; providing access while being mobile. The study also emphasized that listening to educational material is different from listening for entertainment; therefore, podcasts must be integrated with other learning activities . . .

We concluded that students' MP3 players can have a double life – one for entertainment and another for learning.

At the time the IMPALA project started, there was, and perhaps still is, concern that students would be unwilling or unable to separate their learning from entertainment, or be reluctant to use their personal devices for university work, so we addressed those issues in our research. We are happy to report that they were largely unfounded fears, and in the Web 2.0 climate, some evidence that students prefer to use devices of their own choice (Dennett and Traxler 2007).

A renaissance for audio in learning

A British Market Research Bureau survey in 2007 revealed that 32 per cent of UK adults owned an MP3 player; the figure was even higher – 69 per cent – among the 16–24 age group (BMRB 2007). Nineteen per cent of UK internet users (73 per cent of the adult population) downloaded a podcast in the period September 2006–February 2007. About four million UK adults used their phones as MP3 players in 2007. One in ten US adults owned an iPod or an MP3 player; 67 per cent of Pennsylvania State University students owned an MP3 player (PSU 2006). In Europe, more than 7 per cent of the population owned and used a dedicated portable music player in 2006, compared with 2 per cent in 2004 (BBC NEWS 2006).

The IMPALA data showed that over 70 per cent of the students who took part owned an MP3 player of some kind in 2006–7. Around this time commentators began to predict a renaissance of audio products for education because of the spread of portable audio players, broadband internet and free software tools for creation and distribution of audio files (Schlosser and Burmeister 2006).

From 2005, podcasting started to capture the attention of teachers, especially in HE. At Duke University in the USA, first year students were given iPods and academics were encouraged to develop applications (www.duke.-edu/ddi/). Early uses at Duke included course content, classroom recordings, field recordings, study support, file storage and transfer (Belanger 2005). At Stanford University, students can subscribe to Stanford on iTunesU (www.itunes.stanford.edu), and download courses, faculty lectures and interviews and listen to them from their iPods. Another early pilot was Georgia College and State University (GCSU 2006). They began to introduce the iPod to a range of courses in Liberal Arts from 2002. Their iPod project was considered positive and successful. Since 2006, podcasting initiatives have begun to span academic disciplines and student university life in HE in many countries.

The rationale for using audio

Although you will see later, we argue that podcasting for learning in universities is pretty easy and cheap – a true 'high-value, low-cost' approach – we feel the need to show you that there is a wide range of intrinsic advantages in trying it. Most of these examples are based on small samples, and early adopters although we are happy to report some 'scaling up' of pedagogical podcasting and the extension of the research agenda very recently.

1. Flexibility and learner control

Flexibility is a key consideration in designing for learning. Collis and Moonen define flexible learning as:

> a movement away from a situation in which key decisions about learning are made in advance by the instructor or institution, towards a situation where the learner has a range of options from which to choose with respect to these key dimensions (2002: 218).

Early podcasting studies identified time, place and pacing as the three key flexibility dimensions on offer. 'The time-shifting capability of podcasting allows students to listen over and over again at any time and any place' (Huann and Thong 2006: 8). Winterbottom (2007) reports on a study of delivering lectures using podcasting technology for a second-year environmental science module. Students' feedback showed that they enjoyed the flexibility that podcasting brought to their study, 'as they could then view the lectures at the time of the day most suited to their learning styles, rather than be constrained by lecture times' (p. 8).

Most of the studies reported in this book see flexibility as a key feature of students' podcasting experience, and its essential relationship with learners' choice and control. Students confirm that they could and did listen to podcasts at a time and place of their choosing and that the pause and rewind facilities offer them control over the pacing of their learning. In addition, some studies identify new flexibility dimensions. For example, students appreciate access to lecture material when they cannot attend the campus but also like podcasts that offer learning material that enriches and supplements existing learning resources. They also mention the benefits of different formats that appeal to them.

To summarize, the IMPALA research confirmed that podcasting can offer a wide range of flexibility in:

- time of studying (of students' choice);
- location of studying (location of students' choice);
- pace and sequence of studying (faster . . . slower . . . repeatability);
- fresh, topical material (news, content contributed by peers);
- alternative 'channels' (many students liked to listen, rather than observe or read);
- fresh forms of communication (such as receiving feedback from teachers).

Of course, many students may not own an iPod and even fewer own video iPods, but many have MP3 players and all could open the podcasts on their university's Virtual Learning Environment (VLE) via desktops and laptops.

2. Learner motivation and engagement

Audio has been used in distance learning for many years, and its motivational benefits have been well reported. In her studies of audio and radio programmes created at the UK Open University, Durbridge (1984) found that students benefited from learning from audio because they liked:

- responding to sound, as in understanding spoken language, analysing music or hearing the professor's voice;
- listening in on conversations, perhaps about some part of their course;
- being 'talked through' tasks in the lab or workshop;
- hearing facts, discussions and opinions from experts in their field;
- gaining encouragement from the voice of somebody they knew and respected.

Spoken words can communicate emotions and create a sense of intimacy; they can enable learners to identify and interpret personalized content in ways that print material cannot (Power 1990). McIntosh et al. (2003) evaluated a voice tool for learning and found that students who were shy to record their voices eventually overcame their shyness and the majority perceived the use of voice as supporting a non-threatening environment that improved their speaking and listening skills.

In 2007 we saw a gradual growth of voice use on some web-based social networking sites. The emergence of these applications is largely due to the demand for personalized communication between people connecting from different geographic locations. It also adds fun to the sites and motivates more people to take part. You can visit a friend's MySpace website and leave voice messages through the VoiceComments™ widget (www.Snapvine.com). Other popular social networking sites that offer voice technologies embedded in the application are Facebook, Friendster and Hi5. More companies are offering free and paid provision of online voice recording services such as Odeo, Evoca, MyChingo, SayNow and Supcast.

The human and personal features of voices can convey to listeners a richer understanding about the speakers and make learners who are studying online courses feel less isolated (Manning 2005). Short informal audio clips help to increase the sense of belonging to a learning community and increase retention of distance learners (Crockett and Pettersons 1990; Chan and Lee 2005; Lee and Chan 2007b).

The human and personal features of podcasting make it particularly suitable for integration with some subjects, such as language learning. Podcasts bring an authentic cultural experience to students who are learning foreign languages (Chinnery 2006). Stevens and Hewer (1998) found that a majority of their students perceived the audio conferencing activities in their course as critically important for language learning – more votes for voice over text.

Other studies established the types of learning applications suitable for audio. For example, audio files with personalized content, with short, focused stories and memorable, personalized points can help to engage learners (Clark and Walsh 2004).

> Audio is an extremely powerful medium for conveying feelings, attitudes and atmosphere. It is less good at conveying detail and facts. In other words, you will not remember very many facts and figures after listening to a 30-minute audiotape. You will, however, be able to remember general opinions and arguments (Scottish Council for Educational Technology 1994: 24–25).

The human voice increases the sense of the lecturer 'being there' (a social presence) and adds a richness and humanness that was sometimes felt to be lost by early uses of text-based technologies (Reeves and Nass 1996; Kim 2005; Ice et al. 2007).

IMPALA and the other studies in this book confirm that audio does seem to improve the emotional aspects of learning. Chapters 7, 8, 9, 10 and 12 highlight the potential of podcasting to bring immediacy, engagement and stimulation, convey more personalized and individualized content and enable students to experience better quality contact with their lecturers. For us the most unexpected finding of our studies of podcasting was that it helped to improve teacher–student communication and relationships. Many students felt that their lecturer cared about whether they learned, and they appreciated the time and energy their lecturers invested in developing the podcasts.

3. Cognition and learning

Another educational advantage of audio is its ability to influence cognition through clarity of instructions (Durbridge 1984). Early podcasting studies reported that podcasted lectures gave students an opportunity to go back to the learning and teaching material to gain a better understanding of the course (Brittain et al. 2006; Lane 2006; Atkinson et al. 2007; Winterbottom 2007). A study of using podcasts within a first semester Information Systems course at an Australian university reports on students who were given access to a series of podcast episodes that focused on discussion of key concepts in each lecture (Newnham and Miller 2007). Students were expected to use these podcasts to revisit concepts that they found difficult to grasp or for revision and exam preparation. The results indicated that listening to podcasts increased students' understanding of the lecture material. Our IMPALA research confirmed that a key value of repeated listening is in reinforcing and enhancing students' understanding of subject-related material.

We also found that podcasts' repeatability and mobility improved learning. Easy access to portable audio offers learners the opportunity to revisit learning materials at times and places of their own choosing – of course, this is particularly popular at assessment and exam time, but students may also be at home or away on a reading week. Many students pointed out the advantages of being able to listen to a podcast more than once, to understand the concepts better and to clarify and confirm knowledge previously covered, at a time they were feeling receptive, or had 'some peace'.

Early studies of podcasting also revealed that students used it as a back-up tool (Brittain et al. 2006; Lane 2006; Atkinson et al. 2007; Winterbottom 2007). Results showed that students used podcast lectures mainly to catch up on missed classes, revise for exams and take better notes. These services are particularly popular with part-time students, students with English as a second language and students in law subjects (Atkinson et al. 2007).

Results from our studies confirmed this finding: many students mentioned that being able to stop and replay the podcast helped them to take notes, catch up on the missed parts in the lecture and go through the podcast at their own pace. They also appreciated the opportunity of hearing podcasts of visiting lecturers if they had missed the face-to-face event; for example, their train to campus was late or they missed the train.

Some lecturers worry that recording lectures in their entirety and making them available to students will mean that their students will become reluctant to attend lectures and pay full attention. While we think there is a great deal more that we can do with podcasting than recording lectures, we can confirm that this concern was not fulfilled. IMPALA showed that students who regularly attend lectures are also the students who are revisiting the online materials. Student interviews also indicated that students attended face-to-face lectures to pick up interactions with the lecturer and their peers, whereas most of them visited the podcast lectures during revision periods to enhance their understanding of lecture materials or to check if they had missed something.

4. Novel way of presenting information and instruction

Podcasting enables educational content to be presented in an alternative format that may sometimes 'work' better than traditional text-based information. For example, Chapter 5 introduces video podcasts to provide visual instructions on how to use software. Students' feedback shows that video podcasting dramatically improves students' practical-based learning. Visual information helps students to understand software and how to use it, more than do conventional text-based instructions and screenshots.

Chapter 10 introduces an example of using video podcasting for learning about anatomical specimens in veterinary science, by demonstrating structures and tissues in the head system. Students' feedback shows that the podcasts help to develop student understanding through 'three-dimensional' learning. Students commented that they found it much easier to watch the dissections from a 3D podcast than a 2D image from a textbook. They also reported that the podcasts helped their independence. Students can review the podcasts at the time and place of their choice instead of visiting the anatomical museum physically, when they need a member of staff to 'go through' the specimens with them.

5. Learning locations

The widespread availability and falling costs of mobile technology have resulted in considerable interest in off-campus learning (Maskall et al. 2007). You can read more about the wider context of mobile learning in Chapter 2. Podcasting can be used across learning spaces and can support knowledge continuity and transfer from the classroom to the field. We found considerable interest in our IMPALA work from the Geography, Earth and Environmental Sciences (GEES) disciplines, where lecturers use podcasting to provide information and instructions to support fieldwork, a crucial component of teaching and learning in these subjects. For example, Downward et al. (2007) created a way of recording student field trips and making them available through podcasting to prepare the next cohort of students.

Another way to use podcasts is to provide fieldwork instructions. Hand-held technology can be successfully integrated into field experiences as a data collection tool and reference guide (Guertin 2006). Thomas (2006) reports on an experiment in providing audio instructions to support student field trips in a GEES course. Students listened to instructions provided as MP3 audio files and completed three field trips in their own time. In another study, field instructors delivered PowerPoint presentations, instructional DVDs and CD-ROMs to students on a bus while they were travelling to the field site, via a portable audio and video system (Elkins and Elkins 2006).

Podcasting technology can be lent to students for them to produce their own podcasts in the field. For example, Downward et al. (2007) introduced a way of using student-developed video podcasts based on field trips as a means of student assessment, replacing their text-based field trip reports. Chapter 6 extends these ideas and focuses on podcasting for fieldwork.

There is growing interest in the use of telling stories through the use of digital devices. Murray and Sandars (2007) report successfully using this method to engage medical students in reflection on learning and professional practice. Jenkins and Lynch (2006) describe an experiment in using digital story telling. During an induction week, new students were given the mobile devices and were engaged in two days' fieldwork that introduced them to active learning. This experience is reported in Chapter 11.

6. Fostering learning discussions

Huann and Thong (2006) took up Vygotsky's (1978) socio-cultural learning perspective in emphasizing the potential of podcasting for promoting collaborative learning through voice interaction. They showed that students who were involved in producing a podcast in a group can improve their communication, time management and problem-solving skills. Chapter 14 provides an example of student-created podcasts.

We noted that IMPALA podcasts that included the voices of tutors and students often used an appealing conversational and discussion style. Involvement in the design of a podcast encouraged students to obtain advice from their tutors and encouraged them to listen and 'capture' the views and experiences of their peers.

Podcasts have the potential to capture important informal tacit knowledge that can be reused and made available to wider student cohorts. Tacit knowledge is defined as knowledge that resides in individuals' experience and actions (Shin et al. 2001). It is a form of knowledge often acquired 'on the job' (Sternberg and Caruso 1985: 146). Podcasting enables learners to gain access to the tacit knowledge and experience of peers and senior students.

Chapters 9, 12 and 14 particularly emphasize how podcasting can foster a learning community and offer opportunities for learning through discussion.

Learning occurs in formal settings such as universities, but also informally in social structures such as friendship groups (Sefton-Green 2004). Informal learning has gained attention associated with research into mobile learning (Sharples 2000, 2002; Kukulska-Hulme and Traxler 2005, 2007; Traxler

2007a). IMPALA showed that podcasting has potential for enhancing informal learning as well as supporting formal and structured learning experiences. Students said that, compared to attending formally scheduled lectures and reading books, listening to a podcast was an informal way of learning with appealing benefits. Many IMPALA students appreciated the possibility of listening to podcasts at home, indicating that they saw the potential of podcasts for doing their formal learning in a more relaxed and informal environment. They said that listening to podcasts was a mix between entertainment and learning, and emphasized that they benefited from this 'less serious learning': podcasts could deliver formal learning through informal channels. Informality can lie in the voice of the lecturer, as well as in contributions from students and other people, in varied forms of conversation and discussion.

Some students were amazed at how easy and motivational learning can be when they were using podcasts to listen to other people's experiences and to share other people's perspectives. An informal tone helped to raise students' emotional expectations for learning. Students reported that listening to podcasts made their lecturers feel 'more friendly', inviting and personal than in class.

Words used by students to describe their podcasting for learning were 'new experience', 'another way of learning', 'new learning', 'a kind of entertainment', 'relaxing', 'not too serious learning' and 'learning just happens'.

Chapters 12 and 14 focus on podcasting as a way of informal knowledge acquisition through more entertaining and relaxed ways of conversation, discussion and debate. Chapters 8 and 12 show how a friendly and informal tone appeals to students.

7. Contributing students

There are several ways that students' contributions can be integrated into the learning process (Collis and Moonen 2002). We found two approaches that are particularly suitable for students to contribute to podcasts:

- searching for additional information or examples and making these available for others;
- participating in a discussion and leaving a record of key aspects of the discussion for revisiting and use by others.

Chapters 12 and 14 illustrate student contribution examples.

Learner-developed podcasts encourage students to reflect on their own learning, improve on their performance during content creation as well as reconsider and modify their ideas (Hargis and Wilson 2005; Huann and Thong 2006). Chapter 13 emphasizes podcasting to facilitate reflection.

8. Accommodating 'different strokes'

Listening is easier than reading: 'listening is instinctual, reading and writing are not' wrote Clark and Walsh (2004: 5). Some learners prefer learning through listening (Cebeci and Tekdal 2006). Auditory learners 'learn best through verbal lectures, discussion, talking things through and listening to what others have to say . . . For these learners, written information may have little meaning until it is heard' (Sun et al. 2003: 4). Podcasting caters well for their preferences. There is also growing interest in podcasting's benefits for students with visual impairment (Manning 2005) and with dyslexia (Barton et al. 2007). Riordan's (2007) recent study showed that dyslexic students who had access to podcasts were less likely to fall behind their learning set.

Compared to reading textbooks, many students pointed out that they found listening easier than reading (Chapters 7 and 12). Is the popularity of lectures based on nothing more?

9. Moving from entertainment to learning

IMPALA revealed issues related to switching from entertainment to learning. For example, answers to our questionnaires showed that students either did nothing else or took notes while listening to (or watching) podcasts. Interviews with students yielded a similar result: most students preferred focusing on just listening or watching the podcast, or taking some notes as well if necessary. Their answers indicate that students perceived listening to podcasts as a learning activity and different from listening to music, which is often 'background' only.

Our analysis also showed that most students involved in IMPALA owned at least one kind of MP3 player (iPod, another brand of MP3 player, or as a feature of their mobile phones). But most of them reported that they had previously used their MP3 players only for listening to music. Only a few said they had used them to download and listen to educational material.

And so . . . challenges for students

From our IMPALA interviews we found that students said increased concentration was required to listen to educational content compared to listening to music. Some found this level of concentration difficult, especially if they were on the move. Some preferred not to use their podcasts while travelling as they liked to take notes. Some preferred to separate time for study and time for entertainment. Of course, listening to educational podcasts may not fit young people's lifestyles if they may perceive it as 'uncool', but most of our respondents were enthusiastic.

Start here for doubling the life of iPods

We hope now that you will read the rest of this book for inspiration. If you want to get going yourself as an educational podcaster immediately, please move to Chapter 15 and the Appendix. If you have no time even for that today, it should be noted that podcasts for learning in HE should be integrated with other learning activities, so that students' iPods can have a double life – one for entertainment and another for learning.

For this valuable transformation to occur, we propose five basic guidelines:

- Integrate podcasts into online courses with strong links to other activities and resources, especially if they encourage active learning and/or collaboration with others.
- Record them afresh each week and include up-to-date news and feedback.
- Make them partly reusable and recyclable by including some sections that are not dependent on news or feedback from that week.
- Make sure the file size is small enough so that they are downloadable onto any mobile device offering MP3 playback, as well as tethered computers.
- Follow a 'radio magazine' style rather than a lecture.

2

Podcasting in context

John Traxler

Summary

This chapter looks at mobile devices and podcasting in their educational contexts, within mobile learning. Underpinning the discussion are the relationships between technology, e-learning and society, which David Bell addresses in our closing Chapter 17.

Personal mobile devices

There is no stable definition of personal mobile devices nor any definitive list but they include:

- mobile phones;
- camera phones;
- personal media players;
- personal digital assistants (PDAs);
- digital camera;
- games consoles;
- and a host of other gadgets.

Their functions include:

- personal organization/information management (capturing, storing);
- displaying data such as calendars and contacts (tasks that can then be reconciled or backed up with similar data on a PC or server);
- processing and behaving as handheld computers (playing games, mapping ideas, doing arithmetic, doing word-processing);
- capturing, storing, transmitting and retrieving digital data (audio, images, video, position, motion and many other formats);
- connecting and transmitting to other devices or networks (via infrared, Wi-Fi, Bluetooth, phone networks, data cards, USB cables);

- enabling interaction with users of other similar devices (by voice input, virtual keyboard, stylus).

Increasingly, devices are optimized to perform one function as well as possible: iPods play media files, BlackBerrys communicate, digital cameras take pictures and Playstations play games. Most mobile devices perform some other functions too, either well or not quite so well. The balance of functions and performance of any given device is less about technology and more about its marketing, branding and image.

Mobile learning

Pedagogical podcasting straddles a variety of educational disciplines and theories but owing to its canonical technology, the iPod, the most obvious of these is mobile learning. Mobile learning is not merely the conjunction of 'mobile' and 'learning'; it has moved on from its roots as 'e-learning made mobile' and acquired a distinct ethos and identity of its own. Mobile and wireless technologies, including personal mobile media players such as iPods, are becoming ubiquitous in most parts of the world and have led to the development of mobile learning as a distinctive entity (see, for example, the reviews by Naismith et al. 2004 and Cobcroft 2006).

Early attempts at defining mobile learning focused on technology and were technocentric and unstable; for example, 'any educational provision where the sole or dominant technologies are handheld or palmtop devices' (Traxler 2005: 1). Or they stressed the mobility of the technology, describing mobile learning as 'e-learning through mobile computational devices: Palms, Windows CE machines, even your digital cell phone' (Quinn 2000: 1).

Definitions such as these put mobile learning somewhere on e-learning's spectrum of portability: ubiquitous, pervasive and wearable learning. Whether laptops and tablet PCs deliver mobile learning is still considered uncertain because of the lack of spontaneity in carrying them and starting them up. These examples illustrate the difficulty with technological definitions, and the same issues and debates recur with podcasting. The challenge lies in conceptualizing podcasting in a way that recognizes its origins and practices in a specific technology, but is also abstract enough to be durable and to act as a stable platform for theorizing about learning.

There have also been attempts to define mobile learning by distinguishing it from 'tethered' e-learning (to use Gilly Salmon's telling phrase), in terms of the learners' experiences. One view of mobile learning says it involves 'any sort of learning that happens when the learner is not at a fixed, predetermined location, or learning that happens when the learner takes advantage of learning opportunities offered by mobile technologies' (O'Malley et al. 2003: 6).

Another definition illuminates words such as 'personal', 'spontaneous', 'disruptive', 'opportunistic', 'informal', 'pervasive', 'situated', 'private', 'context-aware', 'bite-sized' and 'portable'. These are contrasted with words from the literature of conventional e-learning such as 'structured', 'media-rich', 'broadband', 'interactive', 'intelligent' and 'usable' (Traxler 2005).

These words help to draw a blurred distinction between mobile learning and e-learning. E-learning has benefited by the power and investment in both learning technology and 'adoption' from everyday life (the 'double life' referred to in Chapter 1). Mobile devices have similar virtues as market forces drive improvements in interface design, processor speed, battery life and bandwidth connectivity. Looking at mobile learning, including podcasting, in this way, focuses in on the learners' experiences and emphasizes ownership, informality, spontaneity, portability and context. These special qualities distinguish mobile learning from e-learning. In the UK Higher Education (HE) sector there is a high level of interest in the student learning experience but, by 2008, little mention of mobile learning generally or podcasting specifically (Sharpe et al. 2006). Chapter 16 explores some research questions.

There are other ways we can view mobile learning including personalization, lifelong learning, strategic shortage subjects, basic skills and inclusion. These will continue to be major determinants of development funding and hence of the direction that is taken by pedagogical podcasting in the medium term. An understanding of and an alignment with key issues is crucial to the continued funding and development of podcasting as a mobile learning activity in HE. There is also a need for a continued supply of devices for students to use for ongoing research. Universities have not yet addressed the challenge of resourcing mobile learning – including podcasting via mobile devices – to provide educational experiences that are rich, sustainable and equitable.

There are further dilemmas:

- New and more functional mobile devices are expensive and transient.
- Institutions have a system focused on a three-year cycle of mass procurement, deployment, support and maintenance of computer hardware based around multiple criteria, not just function.
- Most students – but not all – own new and highly functional devices, but many of them are different.
- Mobile devices are not characterized by any underlying common hardware, operating systems, interfaces, applications or standards.

These dilemmas are inhibiting the sustained and large-scale adoption of mobile learning. They do not arise, however, when podcasts are delivered via networked PCs and Institutional VLEs (see Chapter 3, p. 25).

Mobile learning is now sufficiently mature to have given rise to:

- a major textbook though as it was written in late 2004, podcasting is not mentioned (Kukulska-Hulme and Traxler 2005);
- a second book with a distinctly American perspective on mobile learning (Metcalf 2006);
- prestigious international conferences including International Association

for the Development of the Information Society (IADIS) Mobile Learning in Europe, mLearn (globally the leader), the Institute of Electrical and Electronic Engineers' (IEEE's) Wireless and Mobile Technologies in Education (WMTE) workshop in Asia Pacific and Handheld Learning in the UK school sector;
- increasing clarity about the significant issues, as defined, for example, by Sharples (2006);
- a defined research agenda (see, for example, Arnedillo-Sánchez et al. 2007).

Mobile learning now faces significant challenges in terms of:

- scale;
- sustainability;
- inclusion, in different forms;
- equity, in different forms;
- context, in all its possibilities;
- personalization, in all its possibilities;
- blending with other media.

Podcasting, when viewed as a constituent of mobile learning, will face similar issues as it moves beyond its small-scale and fixed-term pilots and trials, and as it tracks the changes in technology and fashion.

To date, developments in mobile learning are driven by pedagogic necessity, technological innovation, funding opportunity and the perceived inadequacies of conventional e-learning. These developments have taken place within relatively narrow educational discourses (see Traxler and Kukulska-Hulme 2005 and Kukulska-Hulme and Traxler 2007 for analyses of a sample) and the same is true for pedagogical podcasting at this stage in its development.

During the first decade of the 21st century, mobile learning publications (JISC 2005; Kukulska-Hulme et al. 2005) and conference proceedings (for example Attewell and Savill-Smith 2004) have put case studies and their evaluations into the public domain – and increasingly these feature podcasting. In looking at these case studies, Kukulska-Hulme and Traxler (2007) see emergent categories:

- Technology-driven mobile learning – a specific technological innovation is deployed to demonstrate technical feasibility and pedagogic possibility, perhaps the new iPhone.
- Miniature but portable e-learning – mobile, wireless and handheld technologies are used to re-enact approaches and solutions found in 'conventional' e-learning, perhaps by importing an established e-learning technology such as a Virtual Learning Environment (VLE) onto mobile devices.
- Connected classroom learning – the same technologies are used in a classroom setting to support static collaborative learning perhaps connected to other classroom technologies; personal response systems, graphing

calculators, personal digital assistants (PDAs) linked to interactive white-boards.

- Mobile training/performance support – the technologies are used to improve the productivity and efficiency of mobile workers by delivering information and support just-in-time and in context for their immediate priorities.
- Large-scale implementation – the deployment of mobile technologies at an institutional or departmental level to learn about organizational issues; for example, Mobiles Enhancing Learning and Support (MELaS, www.wlv.ac.uk/celt/MELaS) funded by the Joint Information Systems Committee (JISC).
- Inclusion, enabling and diversity – using assorted mobile and wireless technologies to enhance wider educational access and participation; for example, personal information management for students with dyslexia.
- Informal, personalized, situated mobile learning – the same core tech-nologies are enhanced with additional unique functionality, for example location awareness or video capture, and deployed to deliver educational experiences that would otherwise be difficult or impossible; informal context-aware information in museum spaces.
- Remote/rural development mobile learning – the technologies are used to address environmental and infrastructural challenges to deliver and support education where 'conventional' e-learning technologies would fail; for example, Short Message Service (SMS) forums for trainee primary teachers in Kenya (Traxler 2007b).

This classification is not purely theoretical or academic; it attempts to define mobile learning by organizing experiences with mobile learning to date. In relation to podcasting, this classification has two roles. First, we can look at podcasting pilots and trials like those in this book and ask if they too map onto this classification and thus help us to understand podcasting. Second, we can ask whether mapping these podcasting trials and pilots onto the classification points to untried podcasting opportunities. Have we thought of trying podcasting in rural settings or large-scale podcasting, for example?

Another classification of mobile learning by Naismith et al. (2004) sug-gests that mobile technologies can relate to six types of learning, examples of which related to podcasting can be found throughout this book.

- *Behaviourist-type* activity: the quick feedback or reinforcement element, facilitated by mobile devices.
- *Constructivist* activity: mobile devices enable immersive experiences such as those provided by mobile field enquiries or games.
- *Situated* activity: mobile devices enable learning in authentic contexts such as field sites or specially equipped locations such as a museum (these are known as 'context-aware locations').
- *Collaborative* learning: mobile devices provide a handy additional means of communication and electronic information-sharing.
- *Informal and lifelong* learning: mobile devices accompany learners in their

everyday experiences. They become a convenient source of information or communication that assists with learning or records it.

- *Support or co-ordination* of learning and resources: improved by mobile technologies at all times for monitoring attendance or progress, checking schedules and dates, reviewing and managing – activities that teachers and students engage in at numerous times during the day.

The pedagogical model developed by the Informal Mobile Podcasting And Learning Adaptation (IMPALA) project (Chapter 15) shows that podcasting is neither an undifferentiated experience for students nor a one-dimensional one, and that some podcasts give student experiences similar to conventional e-learning: structured, scheduled and integrated into a blended learning experience. Others are part of varieties of mobile learning: short, free-standing and informal.

The communities of practice cohering around mobile learning and educational podcasting may feel the need for a theory of mobile learning; for example, for its ability to define a research agenda or produce useful predictions and generalizations. There are attempts to devise theories of mobile learning distinct from those of conventional e-learning; for example, the 'connectivism' (Siemens 2005: 5) and 'navigationism' (T.H. Brown 2005). People are now learning 'through communities of practice, personal networks, and through completion of work-related tasks' in an environment in which 'know-how and know-what is being supplemented with know-where (the understanding of where to find knowledge needed)' (Siemens 2005: 5). This is 'connectivism', 'the integration of principles explored by chaos, network, and complexity and self-organization theories' (Siemens 2005: 5), and it is clearly describing learning situations where mobile-connected technologies are major components.

'Navigationism' similarly seeks to provide a successor or a complement to theories of e-learning based around social constructivism and the affordances of networked PCs and as T.H. Brown (2005: 9) states:

> in a navigationist learning paradigm, learners should be able to find, identify, manipulate and evaluate information and knowledge, to integrate this knowledge in their world of work and life, to solve problems and to communicate this knowledge to others.

We should also mention Laurillard's recognition of the impact of mobility and mobile technologies on the conversational framework and her discussion of the possibilities of increasing interaction between the learner and the environment. Interaction of this kind may be more problematic or unproductive in informal or unsupervised learning, such as in museum spaces and where a teacher is neither in a position to set appropriate tasks nor to provide meaningful feedback. The conversational framework can support:

> a rigorous approach to working out how to support all the component learning activities, in remote locations, with learners guided only by the

tasks set, the information available online, the characteristics of the world they are in, and peer support (Laurillard 2007: 173).

Some argue that in a postmodern era the role of theory as an informing construct is under threat; 'theory' is one of the meta (grand) narratives subject to Lyotard's incredulity (1999). A theory for mobile learning may be particularly problematic since portable learning and podcasting with mobile devices are inherently 'noisy' phenomenon where context is everything and confounding variables abound. E-learning has gained credibility and status from the work of, for example, Laurillard (2002) and Salmon (2004) but there is currently insufficient work in either mobile learning generally or podcasting in particular to underpin theory-building. Instead, we can look at the geographical and cultural spread of podcasting for learning and recognize that any theories that attempt to reason about it will grow out of the dominant pedagogic discourses.

The wider social context of podcasting highlights distinctions between e-learning and mobile learning. E-learning usually takes places in times and spaces allocated to learning, by students or by their teacher. Mobile learning, however, has the potential, because its technologies are familiar, personal, universal, non-intrusive, lightweight and cheap, to be woven into every waking moment, among a myriad of other activities and in all manner of social settings and groups. There is a growing interest in this in the literature of mobilities discussed by David Bell in this book's closing chapter (17).

Most of the literature focuses on the impact of mobile phones on communities and cultures around the developed world but the increasingly rich functionality and connectivity of these devices and other personal mobile devices means that these results are of a wider significance to podcasting. One particularly relevant piece (Bull 2005) explores the relationships between the use of iPods and notions of public and private time and space, while interestingly a much older classic (du Gay et al. 1997) looks at the Walkman in a similar fashion. Even in the limited context of educational podcasting this is relevant work, since mobile devices now take podcasting into informal, virtual spaces.

Conclusion

This chapter has made the case that podcasting using personal mobile devices can be understood within the emerging frameworks, practices and concepts of mobile learning. There are, of course, alternative and complementary frameworks, practices and concepts, most obviously those of conventional e-learning. The basis of this distinction could be clearly and simply the technology of delivery, but this obvious distinction has all sorts of consequences in terms of podcasting within the institution as against podcasting within the community; podcasting in structured blended learning versus informal and opportunistic podcasting. These alternatives are equally valid and each is an appropriate response to circumstances, resources and the environment; each is generating its own research agenda and community of practice, and each has its own relationship with social change and technological progress.

3

Podcasting technology

Gilly Salmon, Richard Mobbs, Palitha Edirisingha and Chris Dennett

Summary

This chapter explains the technology and terminology – for non-technical readers – that enable podcasts and podcasting to happen. It also clarifies the technical characteristics that have made podcasting attractive for learning in universities.

Definitions

The terms 'podcast' and 'podcasting' are new and evolving, but there are working definitions that we use in this book.

We are treating 'podcast' as a noun. A podcast is a digital media file that:

- plays audio (sound) or audio and vision (sound and something to view); with vision, the term 'vodcast' is sometimes used;
- is made available from a website;
- can be opened and/or downloaded (taken from the website offering it and placed on something of your own) and played on a computer; and/or
- is downloaded from a website to be played on a small portable player designed to play the sound and/or vision.

We are treating the term 'podcasting' as a verb. Podcasting is the action of:

- creating the podcast; and
- distributing the podcast.

Most audio podcasts are put into a format called 'MP3'. MP3 stands for MPEG Audio Layer III, a standard for compressing the file to make it more usable. Most podcasts with vision are put into a format called 'MP4'. This is a bit like saying '.doc' for a Microsoft Word document or '.ppt' for PowerPoint files. Just as you would need a piece of software on your computer for using the .doc document or the .ppt one, so you need a media 'player' software for your MP3 and MP4 files. Most of the software is available as free downloads or provided with your computer.

The Sony Walkman was probably the first device designed for personal and portable audio listening but the iPod, and its associated iTunes software, was the first small personal portable device that provided for downloading and playing podcasts. There are now many other providers of personal players at low to high prices. We suggest you look at Amazon or any review site to see the wide range of options. They are usually called 'MP3' or 'MP4' players. Used in this way, the term means the small portable device rather than the software.

The birth of pedagogical podcasting

Podcasts and podcasting were born early in the millennium. Podcasting developed because new web-based technologies could distribute and provide mass access to ('cast') audio files, and because small personal devices for playing audio were becoming widely available at a declining cost. The visual aspects came a little later.

Internet radio show hosts were quick to embrace the technologies as well as the practice of creating, distributing and accessing what were at first known as 'audio-blogs' (sound-based web-logs). To start with there was limited interest and podcasting had humble beginnings: the public was unaware of either the word or the activity. Early in 2004 the word 'podcasting' was coined by Ben Hammersley writing in *The Guardian*, a UK-based newspaper: he used it to identify the emerging practice of 'portable listening to audio-blogs' on the most popular and available audio player at the time: the iPod (Hammersley 2004). In September 2004, the word 'podcast' attracted only 24 hits on Google, but by 2005 *The New Oxford American Dictionary* recognized podcasting as the 'word of the year'. By 2007, podcasting was recognized as a 'low-threshold' technology with the start of its exploration as a learning technology (Ramsden 2007).

So podcasts and podcasting began as entertainment and information. The technologies involved were not designed or intended as learning technologies but, attracted by the simplicity and increasing student ownership of iPods and other makes of player, universities became interested. Duke University in the USA was one of the first into the field. Duke gave iPods to new students in October 2004 and encouraged its academic staff to explore learning and teaching applications of podcasting (Belanger 2005).

In the UK, individual academics such as Dr Bill Ashraf at Bradford University first hit the news media for podcasting his lectures in 2006 (BBC 2006). We believe that the Informal Mobile Podcasting And Learning Adaptation (IMPALA) project, which commenced in June 2006, was the first funded research project to address podcasting for pedagogical purposes in the UK. The Association of Learning Technologies Conference in September 2007 included 12 papers and posters specifically about podcasting and many more where podcasts were mentioned as part of Web 2.0.

Types of podcasts

There are three categories of podcast: audio, video and enhanced. These categories refer to the type of media file contained in the podcast.

- Audio podcasts contain sound only.
- Video podcasts contain sound and imagery, such as moving and still pictures.
- Enhanced podcasts are an extended version of audio podcasts capable of displaying additional information such as still images, weblinks and chapter markers.

Each type has its own special qualities, requirements and benefits. For learning and teaching, deciding which to use may be based on some or all of a variety of interrelated elements and you can read much more about the choices in Chapter 15. Meanwhile, here are some of the characteristics of and differences between the three categories.

Audio podcasts

Audio podcasts are the simplest of the three to create, requiring only a microphone plus recording and possibly editing software. (The Appendix shows you what the wave format software looks like when you are working with it.)

Of the three, an audio-only podcast takes up the smallest storage space on the computer that provides it for downloading, and on the personal devices that make it portable. Conversion utilities, which are small pieces of software, are sometimes used to reduce the size of the podcast file, thus increasing the speed of transmission and lowering the amount of storage space required. These utilities enable users to store more podcasts on their personal device.

There is a choice of recording and editing software for creating podcasts. You can choose depending on which is best for the operating system on your computer, the cost of the software and its ease of use. Very powerful free programmes are available for all the most commonly used operating systems, including Linux, Microsoft Windows and Apple computers.

Audio podcasts are available in an array of formats. The commonest one, called MP3 (Koenen 2002), works on most personal players and is therefore usually the most accessible format. You will often hear devices for playing audio called MP3 players. You will hear about other formats too – Windows Media Audio (.WMA) from Microsoft (Microsoft 2004) and Advanced Audio Coding (.AAC) from Apple (ISMA 2005).

There are choices to be made because the better the quality of the sound reproduction, the greater the file size. The process by which raw audio is stored as digital information on a computer involves taking 'samples' of the analogue waveform. The more samples taken per second, the more

Table 3.1 File size and sound quality

File format	File size	Example application
Raw audio data	125.7Mb	Not for podcasting
.mp3 128kbit/sec Stereo	2.6MB	Good quality music for distribution to various personal devices
.mp3 56kbit/sec Stereo	1.1MB	Voice
.m4a Automatic iTunes conversion at 128kbit/sec	2.6MB	Good quality video for distribution to iPods

accurate the representation of the original sound 'waveform' and the larger the file size on the computer. Formats such as MP3 use algorithms of various qualities and efficiencies to reduce the size of these files, with little effect on sound quality. The conversion utilities mentioned earlier reduce the size of MP3 sound files by setting the amount of information permitted per second. This setting is referred to as the 'bit-rate' of the file and you will probably hear the term used about the quality of sound files.

Video podcasts

Video podcasts include sound and video materials. They are often called vodcasts and vodcasting (De Waard et al. 2007). Originally, video podcasts were intended to be played on devices with larger displays, such as PCs. Earlier, the smaller devices had poor screen resolution and limited file storage. Mobile video players are now becoming popular and as you can see in Chapter 2, movie play features are integrated into other devices such as Personal Digital Assistants (PDAs).

Video podcasts are more complicated, time-consuming and therefore a little more expensive to create. You will need:

- *Digital video cameras* come in a variety of formats, prices and output qualities and you will need one for recording your video. You can even use a webcam which is an inexpensive, simple video camera, that sits on top of your computer monitor. The cost of webcam equipment is quite low but the video quality may be poor. Professional cameras in professional hands of course produce the best results.
- *Software for editing* is essential for editing your recording, to get it to look and sound how you want. Professional video editing software is expensive and complicated, but there is some good licensed software for both Microsoft Windows and Apple computers within both their operating systems (see below).

If you decide video podcasts might be useful for your teaching and learning, you could experiment with minimal financial outlay for basic equipment.

- *The file size and format* you choose for your video podcast is more critical than for audio podcasts. Video is stored in a similar way to audio, but much more digital information is needed to include colour, brightness and contrast. The commonest format is called MP4, though there are many others, the names of some of which look similar.
- *Access* to software and players is essential for your students so they can access MP4 files. Since MP4 files tend to be much larger than audio files, students will require high-speed broadband internet access for downloading them.

Enhanced podcasts

Enhanced podcasts are audio podcasts with additional 'built-in' functions to aid the listener. One example of a built-in function is a small slide-show with its own audio commentary. Another example is podcasts split into 'chapters' by offering points within the audio track for students to 'jump to' to aid their 'navigation' and replay certain sections.

If you have some experience of creating audio podcasts and want to offer more support to your learners, enhancing podcasts is a fairly easy and cheap way of adding value. But currently there are some software and technical restrictions for creating and playing back enhanced podcasts.

Enhanced podcasts are usually produced using Apple computers, equipped with appropriate software, such as GarageBand. For playing them your students must have access to Apple's Quicktime player or iTunes software and an actual iPod, not any other make of MP3 player.

Microsoft are responding to Apple with their own 'solution' to enhance podcasting. Currently, audio and video files can be synchronized with Microsoft Producer, which is a free add-on for Microsoft PowerPoint. An alternative is to use Microsoft Movie Maker which is part of the Windows operating system. Movie Maker allows for the integration of images at pre-defined points on an imported pre-recorded audio file. Both Producer and Movie Maker produce output files with the limitation that they are only viewable using Microsoft Internet Explorer software.

Microsoft Windows Media files can be viewed on PDAs running the Windows Mobile operating system but are inaccessible via other devices such as the iPod. However, free software from Videora (videora.com) converts most of the popular multi-media files to formats suitable for viewing on the iPod.

Commercial software is available for producing enhanced podcasts from Kudlian Soft (kudlian.net). 'Podcaster' software is available for both the Apple and Microsoft operating systems and cost less than $30; it requires no more additional hardware than that discussed above. 'Podcaster' allows the addition of subtitles to images, to improve accessibility, and hyperlinks can be embedded to direct students to documents on the institutional Virtual Learning Environment (VLE), web pages on the internet or to other podcasts.

We expect that some of these restrictions will be removed before long, so it is worth checking the current position when you are ready to give enhancing a try.

Creating enhanced podcasts is only slightly more complicated than doing so for audio podcasts. Recording the audio part is the same as usual. Adding graphics involves 'dragging and dropping' slides, photographs or other static material into your chosen software tool, matching the image on screen to the right point in the audio track and typing in subtitles and hyperlinks in a separate area. The cost of creating enhanced podcasts is therefore a little more than audio, but you may feel that the podcasts become better paced and can be more easily embedded in other learning materials.

Publishing and accessing podcasts

There are two main ways in which the creator of a podcast can make them available for people to use, which is called publishing the podcast. The website that has the original podcast on it is called the 'host site'. The host site can be a university provided VLE or an open website. Similarly, there are two main ways that people receiving the podcast can get to know that it is ready and available for them: either as a direct notification such as an email or an announcement on the front page of the VLE, or via an internet 'feed'.

VLE hosting and direct publishing

If you are starting out as a podcast producer, the quickest and least technical way to publish your podcasts is to put them into your module on your VLE. We call this 'direct publishing' and it is very easy. They can be attached as an MP3 file in the same way as you attach your Word documents or PowerPoint slides.

Using the VLE means that the podcasts are delivered within a password-protected institutionally supported web service where access is enabled through an authentication process. This was the approach taken by all the IMPALA project partners and the other models reported in this book, except Mark Lee and Belinda Tynan, who offer both alternatives (Chapter 9). However, with a VLE, you will then need to let your students know the podcasts are available one way or another. By the way, if your podcasts are in a series, sticking to a regular day of the week works well (for example John Fothergill's approach in Chapter 8).

Internet hosting

If, however, you want to use the internet, outside the VLE, then read on. Internet 'feeds' for podcasts are available from most websites that offer current or changing content. Feeds allow the listener to see when websites have added something new. Feeds are known by the term 'RSS', which stands for 'Really Simple Syndication'. There are three main feed technologies in use but the commonest is RSS 2.0 (RSS Advisory Board 2007).

An RSS feed is a web file that groups information by themes on a web page and sends this information to people who have asked for updated information on specific topics. Such people are called 'subscribers'. You can think of this process rather like 'subscribing' to receive your favourite magazine or newspaper regularly for a period although RSS feeds are usually free.

Figure 3.1 RSS icon on a website

If a website is offering an RSS feed it will have the icon, with an orange background and white lines and a white dot as shown in Figure 3.1.

The RSS feed does not contain the content but provides links back to the original website where the material can be read (news article), viewed (TV/video) or downloaded and listened to – a podcast! The best ones to try first are news providers such as the BBC (bbc.co.uk) or *The Times* newspaper's sites (timesonline.co.uk). Both of these offers free RSS feed services and will help you to get the idea.

An RSS feed requires a piece of software called a 'reader'. Reader software checks the feeds and informs you of any new information such as a news item or podcast from the BBC. Clicking on the link in the Reader automatically connects you to the hosting service and the article is downloaded, letting you read the new article or listen to the podcast.

There are many different types of RSS readers: some are included with most web browsers and some are downloadable applications. With browser-based readers you can access your RSS feed subscriptions from your computer. Web browsers like Internet Explorer and Firefox both support the RSS feed readers where RSS feeds are stored in a similar way to 'favourites' within a browser.

Downloadable RSS readers are available for all PCs and the RSS feed will automatically update when you are connected to the internet. For example, the iTunes software checks the feed and downloads automatically any new material linked to the feed directly onto the subscriber's local computer.

Placing RSS feed readers onto a personal computer limits their use to that machine. People who want to access their feeds from various locations like to use web 'dashboard tools': one such example is Google Reader (google .com/reader) if you would like to try it out. Some people subscribe to many RSS feeds. They use tools that can manage and organize a large number of feeds. Two examples, iGoogle (www.google.com/ig/) and Netvibes (www.netvibes.com), are available free of charge.

Many of your students may be familiar with these methods for download-ing their music.

Mixed hosting

Creating a feed can be daunting for the novice podcast creator, though it becomes quite easy with a bit of practice. But before we leave these issues, we should report that some feed services are now becoming available through VLEs. In Blackboard, for example, a feed service is provided by third-party software written by Learning Objects (learningobjects.com). This means that students can be alerted and linked to the new podcast. In this way, you can combine the advantages of posting course-specific podcasts on a password-protected VLE module and the subscribing and alerting services in common use on the internet.

It is not just a technical choice about where podcasts are stored and how they are distributed. Some lecturers are very happy for their words to be heard by anyone and storage of podcasts on internet services, such as iTunes, is then appropriate. Others prefer to distribute their podcast via the protec-tion of institutional VLEs. And there are copyright issues that you can read more about in Chapter 15 and the Appendix.

Meanwhile, as we mentioned, not all institutional VLEs have RSS feed facilities but this is changing. It does not matter as long as you tell your students that a podcast is ready for them – see them flock in to fetch it.

Podcasting as a learning technology

Table 3.2 shows seven technological aspects of podcasts that support learn-ing. Here we compare them with pre-podcasting approaches.

Content capture

Developing conventional audio and video materials for learning and teach-ing purposes demands the booking of expensive sound and video recording studios and relies on the expertise of a range of technicians. Although the finished product of such a process is typically professional and of 'broadcast' quality, the cost, the time and other resources involved means that most academics are not able to make optimum use of such technology for their educational programmes.

By comparison, capturing and recording content for podcasts is a much simpler process and can be learned quickly by non-experts. The costs of provision and access are low. The simplicity of the technology was evident in the IMPALA project podcast development process. In IMPALA workshops, academics who had never used recorded sound and video for teaching were

Table 3.2 Technical features of podcasting to support learning

Characteristic or feature to support learning	Earlier approaches	Podcasting approach
1. Content capture	Specialized equipment Recording studios	Computers, digital sound recorders Cheap equipment Free software and tools
2. Distribution mechanisms	Duplication/copying Postal services	RSS feeders – free and easy to use VLE delivery
3. Learner access	Postal services Collecting personally	RSS aggregators Downloads
4. Learner-owned personal devices	Cassette player Walkman	Portable mobile devices: MP3, MP4, phones, PDAs Wireless-enabled laptops
5. Technical skills	Training programmes Instructional texts and videos	Owners (students) already familiar with operations of devices
6. Context of learning and use	Bulky tapes, limitations, lack of flexibility	Ease of use, flexibility, mobility, near unlimited storage
7. Content contributors	Teachers, institutions	Teachers, students, alumni, non-specialists

able to learn the basic technology of recording content, editing, finalizing and publishing podcasts. The longest workshops were about three hours and covered pedagogical and technological aspects of podcasting. The equipment involved was often their personal laptops that they also used for general academic work. If they had a digital sound recorder they could use it. Free software was downloaded from the internet – see this book's website for links (podcastingforlearning.com). Often the only extra hardware needed was a microphone and these are very cheap.

Most of the authors of the chapters in this book either made their own podcasts and/or provided a small amount of support and training so that their students could create their own on locations away from the university. Development of video-based podcasts (Chapters 5 and 10) required more technical support. Even then, however, the process of development was simpler and less resource-intensive than developing conventional video and audio-vision programmes.

So our experience is that the technology is simple enough to put fairly quickly and easily into the hands of most university teachers. This transfer of power from technical specialists to the novice teacher makes a positive contribution to developing resources for student learning. As John Fothergill explains in Chapter 8, the simple technology enables a university teacher to create podcasts at a time and locations suitable for him or her. John told us that he composed most of his podcasts during a weekend in his kitchen or sitting room, just after watching an afternoon football game! Flexibility in terms of time and location enables lecturers to be informal and creative in the process of podcast development.

Distribution and access to podcasts

We explained the different distribution methods above (pp. 25–27).

Receiving podcasts through a subscription service such as iTunes enables students to receive new audio material directly onto their desktop computers. Once the subscription service is started, the podcasts arrive automatically each time something new is available, until the learner cancels the service. Alternatively RSS aggregators (for example Google Reader) can make students aware that new podcasts are available to download. The Appendix provides a list of popular podcast subscription services.

If the VLE is used students are required to log into the course area when the podcasts are made available and manually download them onto their computer and/or their digital media player devices.

For novice academic podcasting, we endorse this simplified approach. As John Fothergill says in Chapter 8, students are now increasingly getting used to visiting daily their course sites on the VLE, most of them more than once a day. Accessing podcasts manually will not hinder their use. If students are used to visiting the VLE regularly, and if the content is relevant, students will download and use them. Our questionnaire surveys of students who used IMPALA podcasts revealed that an overwhelming majority of them have access to the internet at their term-time accommodation, with nearly 90 per cent on high-speed broadband connections with unlimited access and the remainder split between pay-as-you-use high-speed and dial-up access. Only about 5 per cent of the students indicated that they did not have access to the internet in their term-time accommodation, but all have access to it at their university facilities. Interviews with students showed that they have sufficient access at university facilities so that they can transfer relevant files onto storage devices such as memory sticks, MP3 players and their laptops, to work on in their accommodation. Students will access and use podcasts that are purposeful, useful and relevant.

Learner-owned personal devices

IMPALA surveys in 2006 and 2007 confirmed that 90 per cent of students entering UK universities were equipped with one or more types of MP3 playback device. Nearly 30 per cent of these students had mobile phones with MP3 playback facility, 30 per cent had an iPod and a further 35 per cent had other brands of MP3 player. Podcasts can be played back on desktop and laptop computers that students have already bought for course-related and recreational purposes. Our IMPALA surveys revealed that a significant majority of students have their own laptop or a desktop computer. At one UK university 86 per cent of undergraduate students had access to a laptop computer and 11 per cent to desktop computers.

Mobile phones are being upgraded year by year with new features, so soon most students entering universities will have access to more than one type of device that can play back MP3 and/or MP4 files.

The characteristics of MP3 and MP4 players that make them appealing to large numbers of users also increase their potential for use for learning as well as entertainment. The IMPALA case studies confirmed that both learners and teachers valued the very large storage capacity on MP3 and MP4 players (and the storage can be extended by small additional storage cards), and they were aware that prices were dropping fast.

Most of the students' laptops come with software to enable access to the internet from wireless locations, further enhancing the potential for their use outside the formal classroom, including via wireless access points throughout the campus and while travelling.

Technical skills

The use of personally owned devices means that students are already familiar with their basic technical operation. It is rarely necessary to train them, as it is with other learning technologies such as VLEs. However, as David Bell highlights in Chapter 17, the transfer from using personal devices for entertainment to learning needs other kinds of motivation and support. We hope the rest of this book gives you deep insights into these.

Context of learning and use

The portability of podcasting offers the potential for students to access easy-to-use academic content and support from many locations:

- outside of the lecture theatre and seminar room in informal settings such as at home or in the library;
- away from the campus but in relevant locations for learning such as on the 'dig', in the field or at work;
- while carrying out everyday activities;
- while travelling.

A major factor that determines the context of using podcasts is whether they have been designed to be used along with formal learning activities or not. For example, Geographic Information System (GIS) podcasts reported in Chapter 5 are typically used in practical classes whereas study skills podcasts reported in Chapter 12 are not directly linked to any classroom activity;

therefore, they could be listened to at a time and place suitable to the learner.

Interviews with students who listened to podcasts outside classrooms revealed that they preferred to listen in the evenings when they were relaxing at home or in term-time accommodation. They were able to listen to podcasts without doing other learning-related activities such as taking notes. Student choice and the flexibility offered by podcasts was a key feature of podcasts that surfaced again and again in interviews with students who listened to podcasts. These students' accounts feature in later chapters. Unlike learning from a lecture in a classroom full of students, podcasts can shift the control over the pacing of learning activities from the teacher to the student, offering many options for flexibility.

Content contributors

The ease in creating podcasts makes a unique contribution to their use as learning resources. Podcasting promotes contributions from a wide range of groups and individuals. Beyond the obvious developers, such as university teachers, contributors may include:

- experts in the field;
- other academics;
- students;
- alumni;
- non-specialists;
- members of local or international communities.

By contrast, for the traditional use of audio and video in education the content was generated by subject specialists directly employed by and/or affiliated to the educational institution. Wide and creative contributions for knowledge-sharing, engagement and interest is a main feature of Web 2.0 technologies, of which podcasts are a part.

Glossary

AAC Advanced Audio Coding, file format supported by Apple.
Audio podcasts podcasts containing sound only.

Enhanced podcasts an extended version of audio podcasts capable of displaying additional information such as still images, weblinks and chapter markers.

GIS Geographic Information System.

iPod an Apple designed portable media player.

MP3   (MPEG Audio Layer III) a digital audio encoding format.
MP4   (MPEG-4 Part 14) a digital audio and video encoding format.
MPEG   Moving Picture Experts Group, established in 1988.

PDA   Personal Digital Assistant. A handheld device offering some functionality of a computer and may contain additional features such as a mobile phone, a music and/or video player and a camera.
Podcast   a digital media file available via a website.
Podcasting   the act of creating and distributing a podcast.

RSS   (Really Simple Syndication) a web feed format used to inform readers, listeners or viewers of new web content.

VLE   Virtual Learning Environment.
Vodcast/video podcast   a digital media file containing audio and video available via a website.
Vodcasting   the act of creating and distributing a vodcast.

Windows   a PC operating system developed and marketed by Microsoft.
Windows Mobile   a compact operating system developed by Microsoft and specifically designed to run on small handheld devices (PDAs).
WMA   Windows Media Audio file format.

4

Podcasts and lectures

Marialuisa Aliotta, Simon Bates, Keith Brunton and Adam Stevens

Summary

This chapter discusses students listening to podcasts before lectures to help them understand conceptually difficult topics in elementary undergraduate physics. We carried out a controlled experiment to assess the podcasts' effectiveness by follow-up in-lecture questions. Student responses to these questions were recorded using personal response system handsets. We found that their listening to the podcasts had a small, yet consistent, positive influence on the proportion of students answering correctly a series of conceptual questions. We discuss using such strategies in undergraduate science teaching, and the outlook for them.

Our aims

Much effort is being devoted to the production of lectures as podcasts: students can download them if they miss lectures or listen to them later for revision purposes. Both Stanford University and the University of California at Berkeley have Apple-sponsored podcast directories. The broader pedagogical possibilities offered by podcasts, going far beyond the simple act of digitally recording a lecture, are discussed by Nie (2006). They are exemplified by case studies illustrating supplementary materials (Edirisingha et al. 2006), and orientating students to in-class activities (Woodward 2007). Draper and Maguire describe podcasting as a 'learner-led educational technology' and conclude that the educational benefit of their use 'requires further and stronger investigation' (Draper and Maguire 2007: 58).

In our study, we had four aims. We wanted to investigate whether or not:

1. Podcasts before lectures could help students understand conceptually difficult topics in elementary first-year undergraduate physics, and how much.
2. Podcasts in audio alone could enhance student understanding of these

concepts, in a subject context that traditionally relies on visual representation in teaching concepts.
3. Podcasts could, as well as providing an introduction to selected conceptually challenging topics, provoke students to reflect on their understanding of these topics, based on previous study of the subject at school.
4. Podcasts created specifically for enhancing conceptual understanding would contradict Mayer's (2001) suggestion that additional instruction via supplementary material can have a detrimental effect on learning.

The first-year physics course at the University of Edinburgh has an extensive online component to complement face-to-face teaching: the pedagogical design has been reported elsewhere together with details of students' behaviour in using the online support materials to aid their learning (Bates et al. 2005; Hardy et al. 2005). Annually, the course has about 250 students, some 40 per cent of whom are taking it as an elective course in their first year, studying towards degrees other than in physics. Students enter with Scottish Highers, Advanced Highers, A-levels and a minority with other qualifications. The cohort is thus diverse with respect to students' aspirations about the course, but also in their previous study and preparedness.

Choosing podcast content and developing the podcasts

Our experience is that many students enter the physics course holding fundamental misconceptions relating to forces acting on objects and rotational motion. Extensive literature in physics education supports our view (Hestenes and Wells 1992). Hake (1998) has shown, however, that educational strategies falling under the umbrella term of 'interactive engagement' are extremely successful in dislodging such misconceptions. We blend a variety of different activities into the course to support this strategy (see Bates et al. 2006 for more details).

We decided to create two podcasts, targeted respectively at forces acting on objects and rotational motion. Students would listen to them a few days ahead of the topics being covered in lectures, and a few weeks apart. We designed the podcasts to engage our students with the material. We wanted to prompt them to think about what would be covered in the lectures and to question their own understanding about the topics based on any previous learning about them.

The two podcasts were roughly scripted to agree overall structure and content, and we recorded and encoded them using Audacity software. They were more conversational than didactic, with examples to contextualize them (Stevens 2007). Each lasted approximately eight minutes. While we were developing the podcasts we also wrote or selected multiple-choice questions (MCQs) for students to answer in the lecture room via an Electronic Voting System (EVS) supplied by Interwrite PRS.

Both podcasts were delivered to students, by broadcasting through speakers, during face-to-face teaching sessions called workshops. The physics class was divided into two groups according to their days of attendance at these workshops.

Podcast 1 was delivered to Group 1 (N = 85) students at the start of their workshop. Three days later, the whole class answered, via the EVS, a set of MCQs at the start of a lecture. Four weeks later Group 2 (N = 88) received Podcast 2 in their workshops and the whole class was tested three days later. By repeating the experiment in this way, each half of the class acted as a control group for the other half. Issues of equity were addressed because each student received one, and missed one, podcast.

By broadcasting the podcasts, we were making use of a captive audience. Pilot studies at the University of Leicester suggested that most students play podcasts as downloads through a PC (Woodward 2007). We perhaps distorted the concept of a podcast by not offering them for download, but we felt that if we offered the podcasts for optional subscription or download to a selected portion of the class, we would not be sure of uptake and this could have jeopardized the dataset we would have had for analysis. The issue of mobility is not crucial here: we were not seeking to open up new learning avenues by exploiting the fact that the material could be used anywhere. Instead, we were aiming to tap into student self-study time, be that on the move or at a PC. We do recognize that by controlling the experiment in this way, we restricted the students' opportunities to learn from the podcasts.

We wanted to ensure that the two groups of students could be considered equivalent in ability, using data from an online diagnostic test, taken at the start of the course and based on the standard physics concept test, the Force Concept Inventory (Hestenes and Wells 1992). The two groups' mean scores were 18.6 and 18.0 (both out of 33), with standard deviations of 6.1 and 7.1 respectively, and a student T-test value of 0.35 suggested there was no significant difference between the groups (95 per cent confidence level).

Podcast 1 dealt with correctly applying Newton's Laws to everyday situations. Figure 4.1 is a well-used classic question about these laws. We knew from previous years that the vast majority, tending towards 100 per cent, of new students choose answer 2 (a fundamental misunderstanding of Newton's Third Law), whereas answer 3 is correct.

Podcast 1 was designed to address this problem by reinforcing important concepts, providing examples, and encouraging the students to take time before the lecture to do some background reading or just think about some problems. We decided to avoid actually giving an example similar to the one in Figure 4.1.

Podcast 2 was delivered four weeks later, allowing for a period of reflection on what could be improved upon for the next presentation. Several important lessons were learned, following preliminary analysis of the responses to the question in Figure 4.1.

Modifications from both reflection on our own aims and practices and from resources online included the following:

- In Podcast 1, the content was designed loosely around the question. We

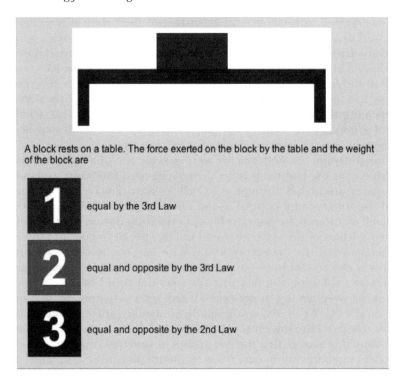

A block rests on a table. The force exerted on the block by the table and the weight of the block are

1   equal by the 3rd Law

2   equal and opposite by the 3rd Law

3   equal and opposite by the 2nd Law

Figure 4.1 Question used for Podcast 1

expectated that students would be able to identify the question three days later. Few students identified the misconception. We were overly optimistic!

- For Podcast 2, content and questions were developed together. An initial question was used as a starting point; one that had seen much use previously and had typically produced a very poor performance. We designed three other questions, each to address a particular misconception about angular momentum. The content of the podcast would then be designed specifically aimed at resolving these misconceptions. More than one such question would enable us to gather a greater amount of data, rather than relying on just one question.

- Informal feedback on Podcast 1's usefulness was sought from students during workshops. They commented that the music made them 'switch off' in between the sections and actually made it less easy to remember. Uninterrupted speech would potentially be even worse than having music intersecting it, so we decided to use two voices to give a conversational tone to the podcast.

- We related the material directly to the lectures by using two 'personalities' who crop up frequently in the course. 'Alison and Billy' (A and B) are used during lectures to concretize abstract algebraic examples.

The questions we used to analyse the effectiveness of podcasting are illustrated in Figure 4.2. Question 1 is designed to lead the students gently, with a very easy and often-stated example. Question 2 is the original question from previous course content, similar to that shown in Figure 4.1, in the sense that a similarly small (often negligible) number of students choose the correct answer (2). The classic misconception in this case is illustrated by choosing answer 1. Questions 3 and 4 are designed to test students' understanding of how different choices of origin and changing velocity influence the angular momentum of the object. The correct answer in both cases is 3. These two questions are similar in scope, and go beyond the concepts tested in Question 2. The total number of respondents to these questions varied between 99 and 105.

1

A satellite orbits the earth with constant speed [v].

If we take our origin as the centre of the earth, which of these is true?

1   The satellite has no angular momentum.
2   The satellite's angular momentum is constant.
3   The satellite's angular momentum increases as it orbits.
4   The satellite's angular momentum decreases as it orbits.

2
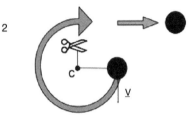

A ball, held on a string whose other end is fixed to a point, C, moves in a circle on a horizontal frictionless surface at a constant speed, [V].

At some point, the string is cut. With respect to the point, C, which of these is true after the string is cut?

1   The ball has no angular momentum.
2   The ball's angular momentum stays constant.
3   The ball's angular momentum increases.
4   The ball's angular momentum decreases to zero.

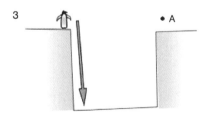

3

A sad little penguin decides to end it all by leaping from an icy cliff.

Alison watches from the top of a cliff opposite. With respect to her reference point, which of these is true?

1   The penguin has no angular momentum.
2   The penguin's angular momentum stays constant.
3   The penguin's angular momentum increases as it falls.
4   The penguin's angular momentum decreases as it falls.

4

A sad little penguin decides to end it all by leaping from an icy cliff.

Billy watches from the bottom of a cliff opposite. With respect to his reference point, which of these is true?

1   The penguin has no angular momentum.
2   The penguin's angular momentum stays constant.
3   The penguin's angular momentum increases as it falls.
4   The penguin's angular momentum decreases as it falls.

Figure 4.2   Questions used to evaluate Podcast 2

Methods of data collection

The main methodological challenge for this study was how to provide clear, systematic and reliable data to support ideas that are, at worst, wholly abstract. The EVS handsets were loaned to students like a library item: because we retained a record of which student had which handset, we could identify responses to an individual. We explained at the start that any data reported would be presented anonymously and that their responses to any questions we asked with these handsets did not count towards their marks for the course.

In analysing the data, we made three pragmatic assumptions:

- Students attended workshop classes on the days they were allocated to attend them.
- Students brought and used their allocated EVS handset in lectures.
- Students answering outside the possible choices (for example number 4 or above for the question shown in Figure 4.1) were discounted.

Although we had a large cohort of over 200 students, only about half answered the in-class questions. Some students did not obtain a handset; others were not registered for workshops, did not attend the relevant lectures or did not answer the questions in the lecture.

Results for Podcast 1 and the 'block on table' question

Figure 4.3 shows the profile of answers to the 'block on table' question in Figure 4.1. The 'haves' listened to the podcast, 'have nots' did not. The

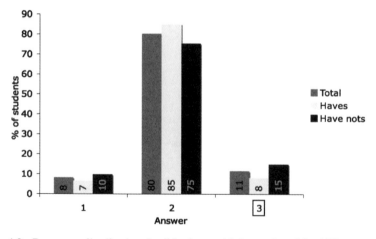

Figure 4.3   Response distribution for 'block on table' question (N = 122)

percentage of students choosing that answer appears at the base of each bar and the black frame indicates the correct answer.

We found the results disappointing: not only did most students still slip on the inevitable banana skin, fewer of the group of students who listened to the podcast ('haves') chose the correct answer. However, with so few students getting a single question correct, it is not possible to draw anything meaningful from this.

Results for Podcast 2 and Questions 1–4

Figures 4.4 and 4.5 illustrate responses to the questions asked following Podcast 2 (Figure 4.2). Question 1 was straightforward, requiring a pre-university level of conceptual understanding of circular motion. The results (Figure 4.4, top) confirm that most students chose the correct answer. Almost all students (98 per cent) who heard the podcast chose the correct answer.

Question 2 addressed a commonly held misconception about angular momentum. What is particularly interesting here (Figure 4.4) is that not only do a slightly larger proportion of those students who heard Podcast 2 choose the correct answer (item 2), appreciably fewer chose the 'classic' incorrect answer (item 1), this latter being associated with a fundamental misunderstanding, paraphrased as 'only things moving in a circle have angular momentum'.

The observed trend of slightly more 'haves' than 'have nots' choosing the correct response is again seen in the responses to Questions 3 and 4,

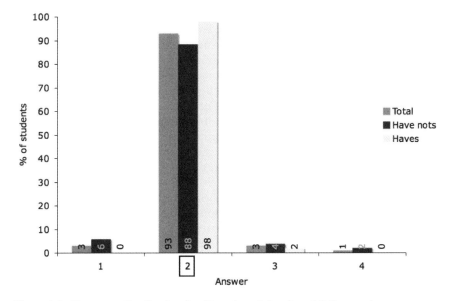

Figure 4.4 Response distribution for Questions 1 (top) and 2 (bottom)

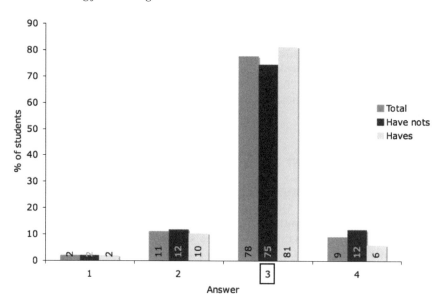

Figure 4.5   Response distribution for Questions 3 (top) and 4 (bottom)

illustrated in Figure 4.5. The differences in the number of correct responses are somewhat marginal, with Question 4 attracting a larger proportion of incorrect answers than Question 3, despite the fact that it is essentially the same question.

The response distributions for all four angular momentum questions after Podcast 2 contain a consistent, if small, trend. In each case, approximately 10 per cent more of the 'haves' get the correct answer than the 'have nots'. We calculated for these questions the number of correct answers for each student (see Figure 4.6). The distributions are similar, with a slight shift for the 'haves' to a higher number of correct questions. This shift is reflected in the mean number of correct answers. For 'have nots' it was 1.9; for those who had it was 2.2. The results should not be over-interpreted because both distributions have large standard deviations and a student t-test does not indicate any statistically significant difference between them (~60 per cent confidence level). The only students to get all four of these questions correct did come from the 'haves'.

Although we heavily constrained the opportunities that our students had to engage with the podcasts, there is some evidence here that their understanding of conceptually challenging material was enhanced. The podcasts' impact seemed to increase when the content was more directed and as our own experience of authoring and integrating them within the course developed. We had, and continue to have, reservations about whether podcasts are the best approach in conveying concepts in physics, an inherently visual subject.

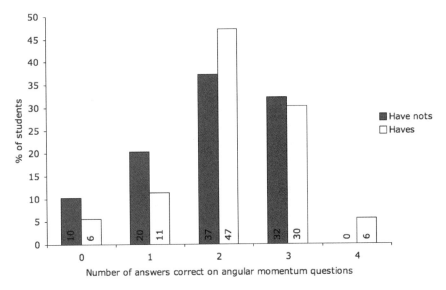

Figure 4.6 Number of correct responses for angular momentum questions

Discussion

Besides Podcasts 1 and 2, we provided supplementary information through three more: these covered initial aspects of course housekeeping and studying at university, making the most of lectures and workshops, and advice on preparation for examinations at the end of the course. Second-year students who had taken the course in the previous year were included as 'voices' in these podcasts, as a way of helping listeners to relate to the people presenting the material (Lee and Chan 2005; McLoughlin et al. 2006).

We included questions on all the podcasts in the end-of-course online questionnaire completed by 113 students. About half said that they had not listened to them: they had problems with technology or felt they preferred learning other ways. Those who had listened said the podcasts were useful, particularly the one on exam and revision strategies. Did students feel that the three later podcasts provided for information only were not sufficiently coupled to, or integrated with, the course itself?

The role of podcasts in science courses needs to be carefully considered: are they providing supplementary (or simply optional) material, or are they essential for the course week to week, as the only medium through which dissemination of information, activities or tasks for students is provided? Undergraduate science curricula have traditionally aimed to cover a rapidly expanding body of knowledge, staff becoming obsessed with content coverage. The problems have been highlighted (Institute of Physics 1990, see 3.2) and less than adequately addressed (Institute of Physics 2001).

Conclusion

This study has investigated whether students listening to podcasts before lectures can be helped to understand conceptually difficult topics in elementary undergraduate physics. We do not claim to have quantitatively demonstrated the unequivocal effectiveness of podcasts in improving conceptual understanding. We used only audio in a subject where exposition via diagrams, sketches and mathematics are believed to be essential to its successful teaching. We addressed widely held (and deep-rooted) misconceptions that have confounded large proportions (sometimes all) of previous cohorts. Finally, we had no previous experience of writing, producing or delivering podcasts for maximum effectiveness, and learned a great deal on the fly.

Our study suggested that we should ensure that podcasts are (i) targeted to the relevant course material, (ii) structured in a logical and engaging way and (iii) possibly incorporate visuals to concretize the concepts being discussed. We recognize that we artificially constrained the learning opportunities within this experiment, by broadcasting episodes, rather than letting students choose an effective way to use them within their learning. Future work will deploy refined, targeted podcasts available to students to use as they wish. We will then have the options of (a) following up patterns and styles of use qualitatively and in depth with some students and/or (b) designing an assessment to be taken by all students, to gather quantitative data, but enable us to discriminate between those who did and did not elect to use the podcasts.

The use of emergent technologies in education seems set to develop apace. The aim should be to engage the learner: 'Science should be taught in whatever way is most likely to engage the active involvement of learners and make them feel willing to take on the serious intellectual work of reconstructing meaning' (Millar et al. 2001: 289).

5

Podcasts and practicals

Nick Mount and Claire Chambers

Summary

In this chapter we consider the use of video podcasting to support the practical teaching of software tools and supplant the traditional, paper-based manuals.

Introduction

The ability to make use of software tools is now a feature of learning outcomes in degree programmes spanning most disciplines. Within the last 50 years, the requirement for student engagement with subject-specific software tools has expanded from early specialist courses in the computer sciences, engineering and mathematical sciences, through wider adoption of computer technology across the full breadth of scientific disciplines, to the more recent development of specialist software to support the arts. Coupled with this subject-specific growth is the rapidly increasing uptake of e-learning technologies requiring students to engage with generic software tools to enhance information access, communication and flexible programme delivery. For almost all contemporary students then, learning to use software tools, both subject-specific and generic, is a feature of their Higher Education (HE) experience. It is, perhaps, surprising that despite the rapid advances in software technology over the last two decades, teaching students how to use software tools often remains locked in the production and use of paper-based manuals, illustrated with screenshots – an approach that has changed little in decades and, arguably, fails to meet the needs of modern, flexible learners. This is despite the opportunities offered by new, rich media approaches including interactive learning objects and video-based manuals delivered as podcasts. We shall briefly review the arguments surrounding rich media and improved learning before considering, in the light of these arguments, experiences of using video podcasts for software teaching and learning in the University of Nottingham's undergraduate modules in geographical information sciences. We shall thus identify and discuss the advantages of using video-based approaches to enhance the student learning experience when confronted with software-based materials.

Current practice: screenshot-illustrated textual manuals

Paper-based or on-screen manuals, illustrated with screenshots, remain the approach of choice within HE. To illustrate this, we did a Google search (search term: 'Introduction to SPSS', conducted on 28 September 2007) for introductory courses to the software package SPSS, a statistical package commonly used in HE. The 10 most relevant websites included UK- and US-based HE institutions. Of these, only one (University of Alabama) provided instructional materials with any degree of interaction – provided through PowerPoint animations of software screenshots. All others were presented as step-by-step textual instructions interspersed with screenshots. From our limited survey, it appears that electronic delivery of software teaching materials has become widely adopted in HE, but the materials are mostly of relatively low media richness. We now live in a media-rich world: new possibilities are available for creation and distribution of advanced, multimedia materials including audio and video podcasts for software teaching. Teachers need to consider whether traditional, text-based manuals enhance their students' learning better than new, media-rich technologies.

The media-richness debates

Given the extensive use of software in HE modules, and the necessity of teaching students how to use it, there is a dearth of literature focusing on benefits and limitations of different types of software tuition materials available (although this may be due to the continued use of broadly similar approaches throughout the sector). This dearth is remarkable given the rapid growth of distance-based programmes, e-learning and blended learning approaches, and the resulting increase in the availability of new, media-rich technologies to support software teaching, such as interactive learning objects (Dolphin and Miller 2002). But the long-running debates concerning the learning benefits of increased media richness in instructional materials (see Clark 2001a for a comprehensive appraisal) remain particularly relevant to the topic.

These debates centre on whether learning is influenced more by content and instructional strategy than the medium of delivery or, indeed, on whether the richness of the media used to deliver instructional material has any learning benefits at all. It seems intuitive that the richness of the media used to deliver teaching materials should have an impact on learning, with increasing media richness resulting in improved learner achievement. But this argument fails to account for the fact that any given teaching method can be designed into a variety of media presentations, and it is the underlying methods, not the media, which ultimately influence the learner. Indeed, the notion of a simplistic, positive causal relationship between media richness and learning has been superseded. More complex questions are being asked about how media should be used to influence learning for particular students, tasks and situations, to influence cognition and the cognitive process.

For example, Mousavi et al. (1995) identify the benefits to learners offered by dual presentation of audio and visual information, particularly for complex scientific concepts. Of particular relevance to software manuals are the problems associated with the integration of multiple sources of information such as text and screenshot illustrations, which must be achieved before the materials can be understood. The effort required to achieve this integration, which is a specific feature of text-based software manuals, can cause difficulties for many learners (Clark 2001b). Similarly, the impact of redundant graphical and textual information in a software manual can result in a negative effect on learners' cognition (Sweller 1999), yet the redundancy effect can be eliminated if the two information forms are fully integrated. The conclusion is that some media modes may lead to more efficient learning for some learners, and that some media may be better suited to some learning tasks than others (Cobb 1997).

The media-richness debates also extend to considerations of student motivation and, particularly where video-based podcasting is of interest, studies investigating the motivational benefits of TV instruction versus print. Once again, a positive relationship between media richness and motivation to learn would appear intuitive. However, evidence from classic educational psychology studies (Salomon 1984) highlights the fact that students' motivation is influenced by their expectations about their chances of learning from a given medium, rather than the medium alone. Many of our HE learners are 'digital natives' (Prensky 2001: 1), therefore it is likely that offering podcast materials to them will result in improved motivation – but it is the learners' expectations rather than the podcasts themselves that are at the heart of any improvement.

The media-richness debates offer important insights for those developing materials for software teaching in HE, particularly those considering replacing text and screenshot-based manuals, delivered electronically or in paper format, with media-rich materials such as video podcasts. The debates have led to an understanding that it is the instructional approach, rather than the media, which improves student learning, and that investment in the production of media-rich materials will not necessarily result in improved learner achievement. Media-rich materials may enhance cognition via improved information integration, reduced information redundancy and improved learner efficiency. And podcasting is likely to improve student motivation because learners expect that podcasts will help them to learn. Given these potential benefits, staff in the School of Geography have invested in the production of video podcast materials for all software tuition in the Level 1 Introduction to Geographic Information Systems (GIS) module, replacing traditional text and screenshot manuals. In the context of the media-richness debates, we shall consider the results of a three-pronged evaluation aimed at identifying the improvements for learners that podcasting has achieved.

The Introduction to Geographic Information Science module

Geographical Information Science (GISc) has been a rapidly developing area of geography since the late 1980s, with large numbers of modules now commonplace in most undergraduate degree programmes. Geographical information scientists are concerned with questions relating to 'where' as well as those relating to 'what'. Working with geographical information requires students to engage with and learn how to use complex specialist software called GIS. The University of Nottingham, like many universities, requires all of its undergraduate students in geography programmes (between 180 and 200 students each year) to complete a compulsory Level 1 module in GIS, to ensure a minimal level of software competence across the student cohort and to equip students for higher-level modules in GISc. The module, lasting 10 weeks, comprises a weekly lecture (about one hour) in which the emphasis is on theory, and a weekly practical (about two hours) that links and embeds theory through practical experience while imparting skills in using and applying GIS software.

Barriers to software learning within the module

For most UK geography students, university study is the first time they encounter the discipline of GISc or GIS software packages; they have little or no innate feel for software designed for processing data with spatial location as the primary attribute. Indeed, while most Nottingham University undergraduates have good general information and communications technology (ICT) skills covering standard software packages such as spreadsheets, word-processing packages and internet browsers, their initial response to the GIS software is commonly one of unfamiliarity, inhibition and a lack of confidence to engage. Some of their reticence can be put down to the unusual and highly specific user interfaces of GIS software, for which the mapping/viewing of spatial data is fundamental. In additions, the large, complex and modular nature of many contemporary GISs may be offputting. Coupled with this, GIS software is dynamic and non-linear with respect to the workflows needed for its successful operation. Successful software manipulation is dependent on students accessing the correct functionality, in the correct order and at the right time. Large numbers of detailed options are associated with the execution of most functions, and while these options may not create a discernible difference in outcome in proximal steps in a workflow (making them hard for students to recognize), they tend to combine in a non-linear manner so that a student's final output may be highly anomalous due to a small operational error early in the workflow. Students therefore require some representation of the workflow dynamism to be present within teaching materials, and a level of descriptive and visual detail that can effectively communicate the correct option selections for software functions and offers a chance to revisit material so that the source of error in outputs can be located.

For some students, these problems present a significant barrier to achieving the learning outcomes of the module, which reflect the importance of attaining competence in using and applying GIS software.

A media-rich strategy to overcoming the learning barriers

Prior to 2006/7, teaching materials for the module were of low media richness, comprising text and screenshot manuals delivered either as paper-based or electronic documents. The module had a reputation among the students for being particularly technical and difficult, with relatively few students sufficiently motivated to progress to higher-level GISc modules. Indeed, student progression to Level 2 was less than 20 per cent on average with as little as 4.5 per cent progressing to Level 3 in 2004/5 (Table 5.1). Student feedback indicated that the module's practical elements were particularly unpopular, with the text-based materials perceived as an over-abstraction of the user/software interaction they attempted to describe. Consequently, the practical exercises were difficult to follow and resulted in students being poorly motivated and lacking confidence about their ability to meet practical learning outcomes.

Table 5.1 Student uptake of Level 2 and Level 3 GIS modules between 2002/3 and 2006/7

Intake year	Level 1	Level 2	Level 3
2002/3	171	30	16
2003/4	171	38	15
2004/5	176	25	8
2005/6	153	25	No data
2006/7 (podcasting is introduced)	186	86	No data

In response to these concerns, we developed a strategy to improve student cognition and motivation for the subject through the use of contemporary and flexible media technologies, centred on video podcasts for all practical classes. To this end, the module was redesigned for 2006/7. We decided to replace all paper-based manuals with narrated screen capture videos, delivered as MP4 files, and available either as streamed video via the WebCT Virtual Learning Environment (VLE), or as downloadable video podcasts. Although we retained the basic instructional methods, we integrated the textual instructions and screenshots of the paper-based manuals into media-rich video podcasts. We produced 24 video podcasts, totalling 136 minutes of viewing. These replaced 60 pages of paper-based manuals and 45 screenshot illustrations. We constructed the podcasts with CamStudio, a freely available package, that allowed the lecturer to undertake each practical exercise in turn, capturing the on-screen manipulation of the software and a synchronous audio commentary explaining the detail and functionality of the software manipulation.

Figure 5.1 summarizes the perceived benefits of the video podcasting. In line with ideas stemming from the media-richness debates, we recognized that the move to media-rich podcasts was not likely to improve learner

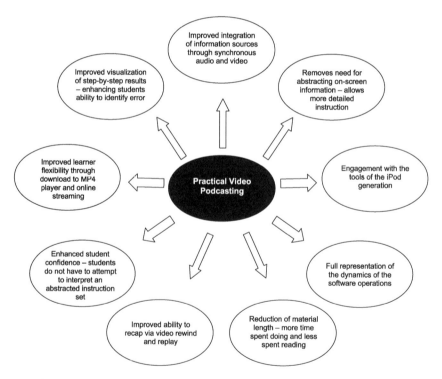

Figure 5.1   Perceived benefits of video podcasting in the practical elements of introduction to GIS

achievement by default as, fundamentally, the instructional approach remained unchanged. Instead, we saw the benefits to learners as centring on:

- improving student cognition through improved information integration, reduced information redundancy and an improved representation of the dynamics of software operation;
- improving teaching material flexibility by offering rewind and recap functionality and the ability to access learning materials flexibly through web-based streaming or as MP4 downloads to PCs or mobile devices;
- improved student motivation through engagement with the mobile devices and podcasting technologies that are now an integrated component of students' lives.

Research methodology and process

The evaluation, by Informal Mobile Podcasting And Learning Adaption (IMPALA) researchers, included qualitative and quantitative methods. The Preface provides an overview of the research methodology and the data analysis. Quantitative data were collected from 96 students through an end-of-semester questionnaire. Qualitative data were captured through four focus groups, each with six students, during mid-semester and personal interviews with nine students at the semester's end. Additionally, WebCT logs of individual student activities and marks were obtained to analyse relationships between frequency of student use of podcasts and performance in assessed items.

Results of the questionnaire

The questionnaire was separated into two sections addressing access to the video podcasts and student usage.

Questions about access to the video podcasts

Responses served to highlight the ubiquitous ownership and use of PCs and MP4 players within the student cohort. Perhaps surprisingly, all students reported having access to a PC beyond those available within the university's computing laboratories, with 85 per cent owning laptops and the rest having a desktop PC or both desktop and laptop. Of the laptops owned, 83 per cent were wireless-enabled, allowing complete flexibility of access to electronic resources when on the university campus. Ubiquitous access to mobile computing was also evident in student ownership of MP4 players, with students reporting having MP4 players available on their mobile phones (21 per cent), or as iPods and other brand players (77 per cent). Only 9 per cent of students said that they lacked access to an MP4 player, an anomalous finding given that all students claimed to have access to a PC, on which MP4 software is freely available.

We were interested too in Level 1 students' access to broadband internet connections for downloading and streaming podcasts. Due to the high percentage of students living in university accommodation, 89 per cent of respondents had broadband access, with a further 9 per cent having dial-up access. This is more evidence of ubiquitous mobile computing technology and MP4 players among our undergraduate students, who are well equipped with hardware necessary to benefit from widespread use of video podcasting, with the university providing a back-up through its computing laboratories.

Students' use of podcasting in the module

All students had to watch all the podcasts at least once in order to complete the module. Where did they watch these podcasts? Of the respondents, 34 per cent said that they watched equally on and off campus, or mainly off campus. Given that practical classes were always taught on campus, this result indicates significant reuse of the podcasts outside allocated teaching time, with the flexibility of delivery making it possible for more than a third of students to engage with the materials in their own time, and off campus. When questioned on their methods for watching the podcasts, however, 79 per cent of respondents said that they streamed the podcasts through the university's VLE (WebCT) without saving, and only 10 per cent actually downloaded them to laptop or MP4 players to watch offline. Given the high proportion of students reporting ownership of MP4 players (77 per cent), we were surprised that students did not take advantage of downloading their own copies of the podcasts; it seems that live streaming of podcasts through a VLE offered students the flexibility and reliability of access they wanted.

Results of student focus groups

Immediately following the module, the focus groups were convened to gather students' views on how the use of podcasts improved their learning. The groups' discussions were recorded. Analysis of the transcripts identified four main reasons why the groups felt they had benefited from podcasts: material flexibility and reuse; promotion of independent learning; cognitive benefits of rich media; and student engagement and motivation.

Material flexibility and reuse

Significant material reuse was indicated by the questionnaire answers and confirmed in the focus groups, with students commenting on their repeated use of podcasts to support coursework and to enable them to undertake practical exercises outside designated practical periods (see comments 1 and 3). Importantly, and in line with the perceived benefits shown in Figure 5.2 (p. 53), students noted the value of being able to fast forward, rewind and recap (comment 2).

Comment 1
'I occasionally missed like, the practical but because all of it was online, you can do it in your own time. And that was quite useful 'cause sometimes if you've had a really busy day, and a two hour practical's a really long time. Erm, and so if you, if like you know, you can squeeze it in another time, that wasn't really a problem.'

Comment 2
'. . . if you had an assignment for mapping and – I couldn't quite remember how to do a specific detail, I'd go to back to an earlier podcast, . . . fast forward to the relevant bit and find what I was looking for and then close it down and carry on . . .'

Comment 3
'Some of the practical ones I'd watch more than once. I've watched them during the practical and then watched them again while I was doing the coursework.'

Promotion of independent learning

Evidence from the focus groups indicated that the video podcasts enabled students to work independently, with the podcasts offering them sufficient information that they did not have to ask further questions or seek additional help (comment 4). Indeed, students were prepared to reuse the podcasts to answer their own questions (comment 5) and this gave students a sense of control over their learning and confidence in the level and accessibility of the materials (comment 6).

Comment 4
'So there was no need to ask questions directly?' '. . . generally speaking, there wasn't, no.'

Comment 5
'. . . we had videos showing us how to use the software . . . I watched quite a few of them again for the coursework . . . I watched again to remember how to deal with those particular bits. Because I couldn't remember the whole of it . . .'

Comment 6
'[Podcasts] made everything more accessible to me and I certainly felt as though it was very much at my level. Sometimes in lectures you feel like

you should have known something beforehand to understand it . . . but . . . podcasting just made sure that everything was really well explained. And that I felt like I was in control like, because I could pause it and fast forward it.'

Cognitive benefits of rich media

The value students attached to the integrated rich media offered by podcasts was a strong theme to emerge from the focus groups, with some highlighting the cognitive benefits of this media over text-based instructions (comment 7). Students also commented on the benefits of dynamic materials that provided a representation of *where* to go, as well as *what* to do (comment 8), and recognized the integrated nature of the materials (comment 9). The video podcasts provided students with instructions of greater clarity (comment 10) and this helped to improve students' motivation through encouraging them to be confident that they were capable of following the instructions, even if their initial attempts were incorrect (comment 11).

Comment 7
'I struggled to sit down and read something . . . Whereas when I'm watching videos, I feel more connected to it . . . it goes in. I remember much more of it . . . video just seemed to be much better at . . . going into my brain, memory much better.'

Comment 8
'The practical [podcasts] were really useful because we had to use software that we'd never used before. And they were . . . much easier to follow when you see someone else doing it on their screen. The alternative is like screenshots on a handout but . . . you end up with lots and lots of screenshots whereas 5 seconds of video can show you what . . . 10 screenshots show. It's much easier to watch a short video . . .'

Comment 9
'It's a visual and audio. So the lecturer will be using the program on the computer, and you can see it and use it. He explains to you what to do and run the program at the same time.'

Comment 10
'And then there are the practical videos . . . . they were really specific: How to do this, How to map wherever. Because none of us are familiar with the GIS programme, I find it a really, really good way of doing it . . . . a lot of people were really positive in their feedback for that.'

Comment 11
'. . . it was motivational because you could actually see [the lecturer] going through it, so he made you realise you could understand it if you just looked again.'

Student engagement and motivation

In addition to the motivational benefits offered through improved information integration, students commented on the freshness of the podcasting approach (comment 12) and it being more engaging (comment 13). In particular, they contrasted podcasts with text-based materials requiring substantial reading (comments 7, 8 and 12).

Comment 12
'It's a different way of learning, it's a fresh way of learning.'

Comment 13
'Watching helps.' 'It's more engaging if [you] watch.'

The user statistics

Individual student user statistics were collected for the total number of podcast downloads, marks for the practical assessment item and the overall mark for the module. Students with incomplete records were deleted from the data along with records containing zero marks (indicating non-completion of assessment), resulting in 179 complete records. Podcast download totals were regressed against practical assessment marks (Figure 5.2) and overall module marks (Figure 5.3) as a measure of the direction and strength of the relationships between them. For Figure 5.2, a low correlation coefficient

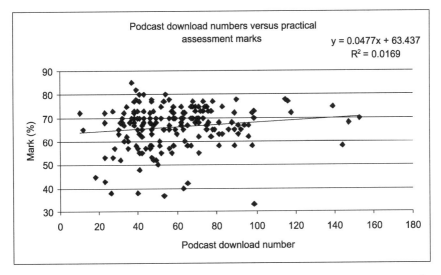

Figure 5.2 Relationship between podcast download and practical assessment marks

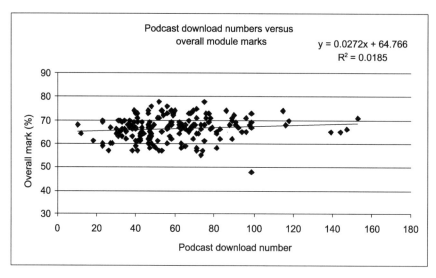

Figure 5.3　Relationship between podcast download and overall module marks

(0.0169) and weakly positive trend indicate no clear relationship. For Figure 5.3, a low correlation coefficient (0.0185) and weak positive trend again indicate no clear relationship.

In both cases, a positive trend in the relationship is evident, with the trend being greatest in the relationship between download numbers and practical assessment, but in both cases it is very weak. Both relationships are also statistically weak with the correlation coefficients indicating that improving marks cannot be explained solely on the basis of podcast downloads in either case. This is an unsurprising finding given the complexity of the learning process, the different learning styles and strategies that might be expected in a group of 179 learners and the fact that the record of a download on WebCT does not necessarily equate to the student watching it.

Placing the evaluation within the media-richness debate

The podcasts are an example of a strategy, based on a significant increase in media richness, designed to improve aspects of teaching and learning skills in the practical use of GIS software. The strategy was informed by the media-richness debates from which three fundamental notions were derived:

- Media richness should not be confused with instructional method and does not directly equate to improved learning – instead learning benefits are likely to be indirect.

- Increasing media richness can improve learner cognition of complex information through improved integration of instructional media (in this case, the integration of text and images into video) and reduced information redundancy.
- Increased media richness does not necessarily equate to enhanced learner motivation unless the learner has expectations that the rich media will be beneficial.

Despite changes to the module for the 2006/7 academic year, including replacement of assessment items and some new and updated practical applications, the instructional methods used in the module remained unchanged by the use of podcasts. Practical sessions continued to be focused on example datasets and applications that aimed to complement the theoretical material of the weekly lectures, while providing linkage to subjects being studied more widely in the student's undergraduate geography programme. However, changes in assessment items in 2006/7 meant that it was not possible to compare directly the difference in achievement between students using paper-based and podcast materials. The user statistics showed that simply downloading the podcasts more (probably increasing the level of engagement with them) did not have a statistically significant impact on learner achievement.

We developed from the student focus group responses a more insightful and evidence-based analysis of the cognitive benefits of increasing media richness. Several students contrasted paper-based and video podcast materials, highlighting the greater efficiency of video podcasts in relaying information and reducing the requirement to memorize and interpret textual instructions. These results, even if anecdotal, support the view that media-rich materials offer improved learner cognition and learner efficiency.

The evaluation also highlights the motivational benefits of video podcasting, with students noting an improved desire to engage with video, a freshness of approach that motivated them in a way that reading did not, and the element of control for their own learning the podcasting offered. Questionnaire data relating to access to computing, MP4 player and broadband technologies highlighted the extent to which our students see these technologies as an integral part of their everyday lives. Such findings indicate the extent to which today's students see engagement with, and investment in, mobile computing technologies as being beneficial for their learning. Consequently, students might also expect teaching materials, designed for and delivered to these technologies, to be beneficial for their learning. Certainly, the doubling of the uptake of Level 2 GIS modules following the introduction of video podcasting (an average of 17 per cent between 2002 and 2005, and 46 per cent in 2006) would strongly suggest improved student motivation.

Summary and implications for teaching practice

This study highlights the value of video podcasting as an instructional tool for those involved in teaching software use. Video podcasting improves learner cognition through better integration of the visual and textual materials found in paper-based manuals, and improves learner efficiency through reduced information redundancy and a less abstract representation of the steps needed for effective software operation. It encourages a more flexible approach to learning, offers a new element of learner independence and control and improves student motivation by directly engaging with contemporary students' expectations about the benefits of mobile technologies for their learning. Video podcasts should be considered a realistic and achievable alternative to paper-based manuals for those involved in the teaching of software use. These podcasts should only be considered where clear evidence exists that students are equipped with the technology and hardware to benefit from them.

Those considering the use of podcasts should recognize that there is no direct causal link existing between media richness and learner achievement. Like any other enriched media, video podcasting is not a 'quick fix' for improving student achievement. Indeed, simply replacing paper-based manuals with podcasts is unlikely to have any significant learner benefits unless it is accompanied by a teaching strategy that considers the limitations of existing media approaches, the nature of the benefits (both direct and indirect) offered by podcasting and the underlying instructional method. Those considering the use of video podcasts should think about how their media richness can be exploited to overcome recognized barriers to learning, through enhanced information integration, improved representation of dynamic information, reduced information redundancy and improved learner efficiency. They should also take into account the learners' expectations, especially how contemporary students integrate mobile devices and learning materials, to produce a more flexible learning approach.

As technology develops, new opportunities for creating media-rich materials are likely to appear, and video podcasts will become outdated. Essential elements in successful use of these new technologies for teaching and learning will be recognition of the value and limitations of media richness and the nature of the relationship between media richness and learner achievement.

6

Podcasts and locations

*Stuart Downward, David Livingstone, Kenny Lynch
and Nick Mount*

Summary

This chapter highlights the experience of lecturers and students in using podcasting to support geography, earth and environmental sciences (GEES) fieldwork activities at three UK universities. We discuss the role of fieldwork in GEES teaching and illuminate the opportunities that podcasting brings in enhancing the student learning experience and in linking learning spaces.

Context

Students studying geography, earth and environmental sciences (GEES) subjects are unique in terms of the variety of physical learning spaces they inhabit: lecture rooms, laboratories, independent (at home) and fieldwork spaces. Fieldwork is an essential element of GEES students' learning experience because it involves learning skills of observation, recording and evaluation of real world phenomena from first-hand experiences. However, these experiences must be contextualized if they are to have full meaning and value. Context can only be gained by integrating the fieldwork experience with knowledge acquired in other learning spaces. Similarly, fieldwork knowledge gained through experience enriches theoretical and practical underpinnings. Key pedagogic skills lie in the lecturer's and the students' ability to engage with these physical learning spaces, to understand how they integrate and to fashion coherent, flexible teaching and learning tools and strategies. Then learning carried out in one space can be linked to, and integrated with, learning carried out in another space (Figure 6.1).

Podcasting offers exciting opportunities for GEES lecturers and students who are looking for ways to support the transmission, linkage and integration of information between physical learning spaces, so enhancing the students' fieldwork experience. As a communication tool, the MP3 player is a portable device for conveying pre-recorded information to students in a

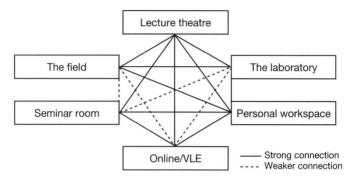

Figure 6.1   Interconnected learning spaces in an undergraduate GEES subject

variety of formats in the fieldwork learning space, and, in turn, for conveying information from the field to the lecture theatre, laboratory or independent learning space. As an integrating process, podcasting is a means of giving feedback that blends the experience students gain, in multiple learning spaces, through instruction, self-reflection and assessment.

Fieldwork in GEES subjects and opportunities for podcasting

Fieldwork activities in GEES subjects are highly varied active learning experiences. These activities can be formal and staff-directed, ranging from short-duration local field site visits, to overseas residential field trips lasting several days or weeks. Depending on the learning aims and objectives, fieldwork activities can be singular in purpose (say, project data collection for a specific investigation or for learning and practising a particular fieldwork method), or can involve several different fieldwork activities with several learning modes. Students can also conduct fieldwork independently from the lecturer, as when collecting field-based information for an individual research project.

GEES subjects tend to be very practically oriented: students must learn important transferable practical skills, acquiring a 'toolbox' of practical expertise they can take to the workplace. An employer of a GEES graduate may rightly expect him or her to have specific skills such as knowing field and laboratory procedures, as well as more general skills of fieldwork project design and management and effective communication of the findings.

As lecturers, we are conscious that fieldwork is one of the most effective modes of experiential teaching and learning, but in comparison to say the lecture room, fieldwork can be expensive and resource-intensive. We want to maximize students' time in the field and ensure synergy between their experiences in other learning spaces. We believe that multi-directional learning in GEES subjects is enhanced when the students' field and laboratory experiences are brought into the lecture theatre, and those in the lecture theatre and laboratory are taken into the field.

In ensuring this learning and synergy, we involve the students in four activities:

- First, in advance of the field trip, we provide them with theoretical settings and background field area information that will underpin fieldwork insights.
- Second, we encourage students to engage fully with their fieldwork by making it stimulating, challenging and rewarding for them. We clearly define the learning aims and objectives, promote careful time management and provide field guides and supplementary teaching in the field.
- Third, as a follow-up, we expect students to reflect critically on their field experiences, to develop their understanding of what they observed. For example, they explore, through laboratory and computational analysis, the data they gathered in the field and they relate their findings to the theoretical and/or geographical context.
- Finally, we assess students' fieldwork formally and summatively, both in the field and on return to the campus, and we give them feedback to encourage self-reflection.

We see podcasting as enhancing, not replacing, traditional fieldwork teaching methods. As indicated below, podcasting can aid each of the four activities. It can also build bridges between learning spaces because it provides a richer and more immediate method of integrating and accessing information across learning spaces in ways that contrast and compliment traditional methods.

Podcasting in GEES subjects is flexible and versatile. Lecturers can tailor podcasts to meet very specific learning objectives and present information to their students. They can produce bespoke podcasts that target very specific users and tasks, or general ones, with wide appeal. They can decide when to release each podcast and to whom. Students can subscribe to podcasts and can receive automatic downloads and notifications (Whitehead et al. 2007) that can help them to integrate the podcast material into their educational, working and recreational lifestyles. Students can view podcasts several times and can choose the order and sequence of play. They can use them for fieldwork in the absence of the lecturer.

Podcasting in audio and/or video formats can promote greater efficiency in how students write up fieldwork notes (such as recorded voice notes) and personally store this knowledge. Evidence reviewed by Grabe and Christopherson (in press) suggests that elements of taught and observed information may soon be forgotten, but podcasting aids the retrieval of information because it can provide an information back-up, a theoretical underpinning perhaps to specific observations at a particular field site. From the lecturer's perspective, improved communication efficiency can add value to a time-limited field trip without adding the number of fieldwork days, so there can be a strong strategic logic to introduce podcasting to support fieldwork activities as well as pedagogic arguments. Long term, podcasts can be time- and cost-effective because they can be used by many more students than might be conventionally taught by one lecturer. Once created, the same podcast can be used and, intellectual property rights permitting, shared by multiple cohorts of GEES students.

Podcasting is also portable. Presentations previously limited to the lecture room can be taken into the field, the 'outdoor wall-less classroom' (So 2004: 5), or any environment of the listeners' choosing (Bryans Bongey et al. 2006) bridging formal and informal learning spaces. Mobile devices (MP3 or MP4 players) can be GPS (Global Positioning System)-enabled so that information can be spatially referenced, and they have the potential to receive streamed information. Podcasts can also be viewed on static computers, in other learning spaces. Their portability can add efficiency by enabling students to use 'dead-time' during, for example, journeys in aircraft and buses between field sites.

Podcasts provide students with a communication tool for aiding the description, evaluation and dissemination of field phenomena. Podcast creation requires careful self-reflection and review of the fieldwork learning aims and objectives. Instructing students to create podcasts is a valuable exercise because it engages them with the technology (in itself a potentially valuable transferable skill). A podcasting community can be set up, offering students active participation in creating learning materials that stimulate reflection.

Fieldwork podcasting in practice

We have experimented with podcasting to support fieldwork at three UK universities (Kingston, Nottingham and Gloucestershire). The examples we present are empirical; we have used podcasting technology in different physical learning spaces and monitored and informally evaluated the student response to determine best practices based on our experience. The methods used and the quality of podcasts produced have varied and are presented in terms of increasing complexity and ambition, from transmitting information between learning spaces to linking and integrating information between learning spaces. We want to illustrate the breadth of possibilities through examples based on our experience. We describe four methods of using podcasts: preparation for fieldwork, the iWalk, instructional podcasts and student-directed podcasts as a means of assessment.

Preparation for fieldwork

Preparation for fieldwork is important because it provides context for the observations and experiments that will be undertaken in the field and it improves students' understanding of the field phenomena. The more students understand the background to the study area and specific field sites, the better they will be at asking appropriate questions in the field.

Preparation may be theoretical, logistical or site-specific. We provide academic structure to the fieldwork, such as conceptual models (for example landform development) that can be deductively tested in the field. We also provide practical logistical advice such as travel schedules, requisite vaccination requirements and so on. In providing information about a particular field area, or about a specific site within the field area, we bear in mind students' abilities and their need to apply theoretical knowledge when observing, recording and evaluating field phenomena, without prior site-specific background.

Traditionally, students get a printed field guide prior to departure. The guide is portable, simple to reproduce and may be easily read and annotated by students, both in the field and before and after the trip. We do not suggest that podcasting will replace this guide, which continues to excel in providing maps, flow charts, questionnaire examples, and so on. However, podcasting provides an alternative and supplementary means of communicating preparatory material to students. Podcasts can provide a rich multi-format extension of the traditional field guide because they can include audio descriptions of field phenomena and video imagery of field sites edited with other graphics and/or the audio signal.

In practice, we created preparatory podcasts using material collected from previous field trips and fieldwork reconnaissance (Figure 6.2). Some

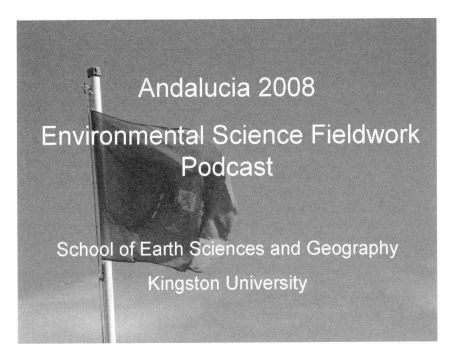

Figure 6.2 The opening title of a podcast-based fieldwork guide

podcasts included audio and video clips of students themselves: we observed that students respond positively to watching the experiences of other students. For example, we included students' descriptions of particular phenomena, students undertaking particular activities and responding to specific questions asked by the lecturer, and, as in an engaging radio broadcast, students' multi-voice narrations, which students found more engaging than a single-voice narration. Hearing and watching other students engaged in different activities is in itself engaging for the students as it creates a sense of ownership in the exercises and reinforces fieldwork as a very active mode of learning.

The flexibility with which podcasts can be created and delivered means that a podcast-based field guide can be produced as a series of short individual podcasts, each specific to a field site or issue, or as a longer 'all-in-one' guide that is divided into chapters. It may be simpler to prepare and edit a series of short guides, and distribution to students may be more straightforward, particularly if the format of the trip changes from year to year.

The iWalk

The concept of the iWalk is simple: the user follows a predetermined route, perhaps from a map, with any number of identified 'stops'. At each stop, podcast information is available that is specific to that location.

The iWalk concept has been used by galleries and museums to provide electronic audio guides to direct and inform visitors, usually via a borrowed headset rather than the user's personal MP3 device. More recently, the opportunity to take the iWalk outdoors has been catching on: the tourism potential of city iWalks is growing in popularity (for example Dublin and Liverpool). In these cases a website provides the portal for downloading the MP3 podcast, each stop on the tour is a separate 'chapter' of the podcast, and a pdf version of a map.

We developed the iWalk to support student learning in the field: students are provided with a map, such as in a paper field guide. They walk between the sites, stopping where indicated to listen to and/or watch a description of each location. We decide whether the students should follow a prescribed route between the specified stops (for example there may be a spatial dimension to the development of the narrative) or explore the stops at random and piece together a conceptual impression for themselves of the field area on completion.

A podcast-based iWalk has an advantage over the fieldwork guide because students can be observing and listening to an audio signal simultaneously. The iWalk need not be used merely in the field: it may also be used at the computer as a desk-based virtual guide to the sites and themes prior to a field visit, or for review following the visit.

For example, Kingston University is developing a River Thames iWalk for its incoming geography students during induction week to orientate them to the Kingston-upon-Thames environment. In this case the River Thames is the central linear theme that unites nine individual sites that introduce students to nine particular geographical themes (Figure 6.3).

Each site of the nine is represented as a separate audio-only 'chapter' in the podcast and the students select the chapter that corresponds to the site on the map. Each chapter is five minutes long; a 'bite-sized' optimum length that we anticipated would be students' concentration limits in the field at any one stop. Production was co-ordinated by a BBC radio producer, who used his expertise in sound-recording and editing to produce an exemplar iWalk. He advised us that interview-based narration of the river themes with experts

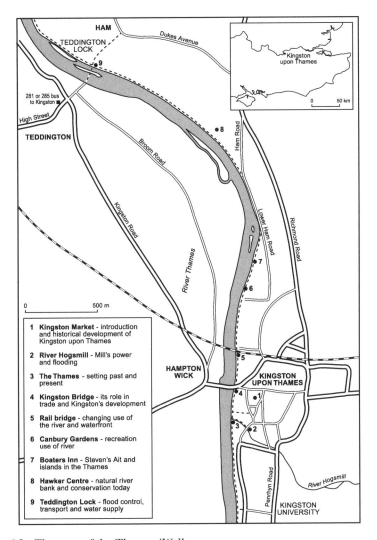

Figure 6.3 The map of the Thames iWalk

in the field would convey a powerful sense of engagement (Bradbury 2006; Shim et al. 2007) and place. For example, background noises such as the sound of running water, crowds or bird songs create atmosphere that enhances the listeners' imagination of the river environment (this is particularly valuable where the iWalk is not used in the field). In this iWalk, the student follows a printed map, but there is no reason why a stylized and simple map could not be edited to the audio signal on the podcast timeline and presented as a simple video podcast, so long as care was taken to ensure the on-screen cartographic image is not compromised by a small-sized display.

The iWalk need not be passive: it can also be used actively. The lecturer can design the iWalk in such a way that students are prompted to undertake particular activities, such as being directed to record particular phenomena at a given stop (for example a field sketch), to promote critical thinking and active engagement in the themes (Barresi 2007).

We envisage two future developments of the iWalk as podcasting converges with other mobile technologies. First, GPS-enabled mobile devices with wireless network connectivity will allow podcasts to be automatically fed and/or selectively streamed to individual students, based on each student's location in the field: this can be called webcasting or synchronous distance learning (Dufour et al. 2007; SPLINT 2007). The lecturer will also be able to audit where and when students visited particular field sites on the iWalk. Second, others mobile technologies such as mobile webcams and text messaging will enable students to report their observations live, direct from the field, to their peers and lecturers. Students will be able to receive guidance if they have queries about phenomena they observe.

Instructional podcasts

Fieldwork often involves using specialist equipment or methods for information sampling and analysis, in the field. Training in using equipment is integral to a GEES student's development. Students are trained usually before a field trip at the university or sometimes a lecturer demonstrates how to use the equipment and methods in the field. Students working independently, or wishing to refresh their memory, can use instructional podcasts for on-the-spot explanations of equipment or methods. The lecturer can pre-record instructional steps that can be revisited in the field with an MP3 player, complementing paper version on instructions. Where video podcasts are used, the visual reference adds considerably to the students' understanding of the method. To illustrate, Figure 6.4 shows an excerpt from a podcast demonstrating the use of a mechanical flow meter to estimate stream flow velocity and discharge: the student can observe how to set up the equipment, determine point sample locations in the stream and visualize the equipment working correctly. The student can also observe the water's movement in the stream – movement providing an enlightened illustration of river flows and

Figure 6.4 An instructional podcast for fieldwork

physical processes. In preparing the video podcasts, care was taken with font style and size to ensure that it is clearly readable on the mobile device. The lecturer has to reduce text-based information to the essentials or use headings and sub-headings presenting 'meta-knowledge' (Churchill and Hedberg in press).

Instructional podcasts can also be produced by students working in groups. For example, they were asked to record for a podcast their own video account of using the methods in the field. Figure 6.5 illustrates how the environmental science students, working in the field in Spain, recorded a description of a field technique on camera. A video like this could just as easily be narrated afterwards. Through making the video podcast, students were challenged to think about and explain the steps of the field methods. All members of the group were engaged. Furthermore, the podcast they made can be used to instruct other groups, in later years, either in preparing for fieldwork or as a reminder in the field.

Student-directed podcasts as a means of assessment

Assessment of field-based learning activities is important to ensure students have attained required levels of understanding. Traditional methods of

Figure 6.5   Environmental science students creating their podcasts

assessment are variable. These include fieldwork mapping, annotated sketching, written reports and oral presentations, role play and essays. In all cases, the student is not simply presenting the findings of his or her field investigation, but is developing communication and dissemination skills to transcribe these findings to a wider audience. These are important transferable skills that GEES lecturers wish to develop in their students. Planning and creation of the podcast help students to evaluate their progress. As with student-created instructional podcasts, the process effectively integrates learning spaces because the production of the podcast is incremental, revisionist and is developed in multiple learning spaces.

Assessing students through their podcasts of a specified field experience is feasible. Technical impediments that limited audio-visual production in the past are 'slowly dissolving, resulting in the opportunity of having non-technical users to author, create and publish materials' (Shim et al. 2007: 588). Our experiments with students working to produce field-based podcast presentations revealed several advantages including developing a strong sense of ownership and engagement with the podcast, resulting from group interaction and from design, information acquisition and production.

Geography students at Kingston University undertook a group-based research project as an integral part of a field trip to South Africa. Each group of three students was challenged to present their research project as a

10-minute video podcast. In theory, this is little different from asking students to present their research project as a PowerPoint presentation: the students will select slides, possibly containing embedded video, and give a live narrative. In the podcast, there is emphasis on the use of video imagery and the narrative is recorded. Otherwise the conceptual processes are essentially the same; providing a coherent introduction and presenting their project aims and objectives, methodology, results and discussion points. Students considered before production what video imagery they required for the presentation and then decided on a programme of image capture while carrying out the project itself. They storyboarded the project in advance, creating a paper-based timeline for the presentational elements (Figure 6.6). Producing a timeline or storyboard relates closely to plans for the project itself including its research context, aims, objectives and research questions and data required. Planning and creating the podcast can help the student to evaluate the project's progress and likely success as it evolves. Indirectly, the process of storyboarding helps co-ordination and co-operation between group members. Because the project outcomes may not be known from the start, there is often the need to acquire much more information than is ever actually used in the podcast, but data storage and redundancy were not a problem in the field.

Students captured video imagery using a digital camera in video mode set to the highest resolution. A 640×280 pixel capture resolution at 30 frames per second was discovered to be perfect for playback on the computer screen for editing. The camera's memory capacity was 1GB providing about eight minutes of recording. Individual captured clips were seldom over 30 seconds and students carried multiple memory cards and/or backed up the video clips to a 60GB iPod operating as a mass storage device. The video readily

Project: River meandering study – R. Towy, UK
Authors: J. Smith and D. Brown, Kingston Univ.
Date: 28 Sept. 2007

Time	Section	Imagery	Narrative
0–10s	Title	Titles	None
10–40s	Introduction	Location map – S. Wales – detail	Introduce research project aims/ objectives
40s– 1m 30s	Study site background	Pan imagery Towy at Llandilo Bridge. Fixed video Towy floodplain. Floodplain to railway embankment.	Description of physical setting – channel and floodplain environment

Figure 6.6 A storyboard with timeline for planning a podcast

copied to the computer without the need to transform file formats. The students were encouraged to archive their imagery carefully and to file it in such a way that selection and retrieval for later video podcast production was straightforward. We discovered that this process, usually undertaken at the end of each day in the field, was a valuable exercise in itself, in revisiting and reviewing information acquired earlier.

The podcast was produced at the university shortly after the field trip. The student groups were tutored in the use of Windows Movie Maker. We chose Move Maker as our preferred video editing software, because of its universal availability on Windows-based PCs and its simple use. The students then independently produced the podcasts. The podcasts were assessed by the lecturers and marks awarded for content and presentation. We were concerned that students would divert time and effort from the scientific elements of their project into the presentation and that content would suffer as a consequence, but our initial results show that this was not the case: the better students who designed, managed and executed good research projects were also the same students who produced the best video podcasts. We hope this is not a coincidence or isolated case but it illustrates how the podcast can support students' reflection and active learning.

The assessment presented interesting results, too: students found that the collection of video imagery, in some cases narrated in the field, provided them with a valuable record of fieldwork that aided their interpretation. For example, one group commented that the video allowed them to visualize particular landforms back at the university much better than photographs, while another group recorded videos of interviews in the field.

Lessons learned

Our experience, and that of our students, yielded guidance for those wishing to support fieldwork activities using podcasting. In addition to the modes of operation we have highlighted, we learned three general lessons.

1. The podcasts' content and production quality must be appropriate. Content quality must be tailored to the fieldwork learning aims and objectives and the intended audience. This will inform the level of complexity required from the podcast and determine whether the podcast will be used as a communication device in an interactive sense, where learning spaces are blended through carefully considered feedback and/or assessment loops. Production quality must be fit for purpose: for example, there is no point in a broadcast quality high-resolution podcast if it is going to be viewed only via MP3 or MP4 players. Lecturers can adapt their podcasts by assessing the students' learning achievements and through student feedback from the podcast experiences.
2. Who is being recorded in the field and who will view the recordings?

Where people are involved it is important that they give their consent to the production of the podcast. Once this permission is obtained, it may be impossible for them to withhold consent for subsequent use, particularly where the podcast may be available to download from the Web. This is an ethical problem for staff and students in fieldwork settings. Who will view the recording has important implications for intellectual property rights. For example, will the podcasts be available only to students within a particular institution by subscription or will the podcast be more widely available, perhaps as a shared archive? (See notes on copyright in the Appendix.)

3. Our experiments to date have been mostly empirical. Feedback is important in guiding podcast creators to develop best-practice guidelines that bridge learning spaces. Savel et al. (2007), for example, describe how members subscribing to a series of medical podcasts are encouraged to provide feedback that will shape future podcast delivery. Absenteeism is not an immediate concern for fieldwork activities for GEES subject lecturers because students have little choice but to participate in fieldwork activities, most of which are directly assessed. However, our view is that podcasting is to support and not necessarily to replace traditional fieldwork activities.

4. Lecturers should take care that no students are disadvantaged. Disabilities are already considered by field trip leaders prior to fieldwork with respect to the range of activities students will undertake. Access to activities also need to be considered. IMPALA's research at Kingston University reported that 78 per cent of students had personal access to MP3 audio devices; we also need to cater for those who do not have access or do not wish to use their personal devices. There may be resource implications regarding the amount and serviceability of sharable hardware. In these cases the lecturer needs strategies to ensure that individuals are not disadvantaged: group-based work, paper-based activities such as storyboarding and careful time management may help.

Conclusions

We have presented scenarios that illustrate how podcasting can contribute to fieldwork teaching and learning for GEES subject students and staff. By blending multiple learning spaces, learning experiences can be enhanced in the field and fieldwork experiences can enrich teaching and learning in the lecture theatre, laboratory and independent spaces. Our experience demonstrates the flexible and adaptive nature of podcasting as a communicating and integrating tool that can be readily developed by staff and students. Future mobile technologies that integrate portable MP3 devices with GPS and live streaming of data will further enrich the integration of learning spaces by promoting real-time feedback of observations and queries between these spaces.

7

Podcasts and feedback

Derek France and Chris Ribchester

Summary

This chapter provides research evidence and observations about the potential of podcasts for enhancing feedback to students.

Introduction

We begin with a brief review to situate, within current thinking, about assessment design, implementation and feedback, how podcasts can provide effective feedback and ameliorate recognized weaknesses of existing practice. We then outline the ways in which podcasted feedback has been used in two modules in the Department of Geography and Development Studies at the University of Chester. The core of the chapter provides empirical evidence, largely from a student perspective, about the experience of receiving digital oral feedback and how this is seen to vary from more commonly used feedback methods. These findings highlight strengths but also identify drawbacks. We conclude by exploring briefly the conditions when podcasted feedback may prove to be particularly effective and worth while.

Assessment and feedback

Assessment is central to students' experience of Higher Education (HE) (Knight 1995; Brown and Glasner 1999; Ramsden 2003). Its centrality is reflected in the large amount of time spent by students on assessment-related activities (Innis and Shaw 1997). 'Assessment frames learning, creates learning activity and orients all aspects of learning behaviour' (Gibbs 2006: 23). The corollary is that, if tutors change their assessment strategies, these changes impact on student learning, for better or worse.

The literature on design and execution of assessment suggests broadly that assessment is likely to be most effective when it is closely aligned with intended learning outcomes, course content and teaching methods (Biggs 2003), ensuring therefore that it is 'fit for purpose' (S. Brown 2005). The value of assessment is enhanced when exercises are designed to promote deep learning through active engagement of students in evaluating and applying ideas and in interpreting meaning. Less valuable are those requiring reproduction of knowledge and superficial, short-term, memorization. Students' engagement and understanding can be promoted through publication of transparent assessment criteria (S. Brown 2005) and discussion of required standards, possibly through using examples. While the availability of such information is helpful, studies suggest that its potency can be augmented by forcing a direct engagement with assessment criteria, not least through peer or self-assessment (Rust et al. 2003; Bloxham and West 2004, 2007). The promotion of such methods is indicative of a push towards more participative, less hierarchal, forms of assessment (Reynolds and Trehan 2000). At a programme level, a diversity of assessment modes is considered to be beneficial (Race 2005), as is the 'spreading out' of assessment deadlines to help ensure that student workloads are seen to be fair and achievable in the time available.

Another critical factor, widely recognized as influencing the depth of learning from assessment, is the feedback provided on completed assignments (Black and William 1998; Hattie and Jaeger 1998). Ramsden (2003: 187) believes that it is 'impossible to overstate the role of effective comments on students' progress in any discussion of effective teaching and assessment' and Race (1999: 27) observes that 'feedback quantity and quality are probably the most important factors in enhancing students' learning'. In this chapter we focus on the nature and quality of feedback comments and the subsequent student interpretation of, and engagement with, the feedback provided. Our own experience is that in this context podcasts can help students.

The nature and quality of feedback comments

Effective feedback is detailed and specific, and refers to published criteria and statements of standards. It reviews the strengths and weaknesses of a piece of work and provides a clear sense of why the final grade was awarded. But feedback also needs to be formative, guiding the student on how to improve, ideally by providing specific examples. For feedback to influence future behaviour it must be timely, giving students a chance to act on it. If they do so, they may have a sense of progression. For some authors, resubmission (after feedback) of work should be used more, as well as feedback on work-in-progress (Boud 2000).

Communicating feedback is not a simple transfer of information from marker to student (Higgins et al. 2001; Carless 2006). Typically, feedback represents an asymmetrical power relationship between tutor (the 'expert') and student (the 'novice'). 'Receiving feedback is also an emotional business'

(Higgins 2000: 7), with significant potential to affect, positively or negatively, an individual's confidence and perception of self-efficacy. Feedback commentaries on performance and learning are important, rather than ones on the student and his or her personal characteristics (Gibbs and Simpson 2005). Comments need to be in a non-authoritarian tone, balancing positive comments with constructive criticism. And 'great delicacy is needed if critical feedback is to have the effect of helping students, especially inexperienced ones, to learn something rather than to become defensive or disheartened' (Ramsden 2003: 188).

Student interpretation of, and engagement with, the feedback

Research on how (if at all) students interpret and engage with tutor feedback indicates that they often consider feedback to be difficult to interpret and that there is significant potential for misunderstanding (Chanock 2000; Higgins et al. 2002; Weaver 2006). There is a gulf between tutor and student perceptions of the usefulness of feedback (Maclellan 2001; Carless 2006; Glover and Brown 2006). Carless (2006: 230) argues that tutor–student 'assessment dialogues', focusing on the principles, operation and process of assessment, would help to close this gap. Similarly, Weaver (2006) stresses the value of more direct guidance on the use of feedback and help with interpreting the academic discourse used by tutors.

Even carefully constructed feedback may be scrutinized closely by only a minority of students. A widely held suspicion, only partly supported by research, is that students' main concern is the mark or grade. Feedback needs to be timely, fitting the overall scheduling of assessment: see Gibbs (2006) for how assessment can be designed and timed to encourage the use of feedback. Encouragement of students to monitor and reflect on their personal progression, perhaps through Personal Development Plans, can push students towards reviewing feedback in more depth. Indeed, Nicol and Macfarlane-Dick (2006: 205) argue strongly that good feedback is defined 'as anything that might strengthen the students' capacity to self-regulate their own performance'.

Such challenges are long-standing, but '[r]esource constraints in conventional universities have led to a reduction in the frequency of assignments, in the quantity and quality of feedback and in the timeliness of this feedback' (Gibbs and Simpson 2005: 9). At the same time, an increasingly diverse student body has added an extra layer of complexity. Rust (2007: 231) observes frankly that 'if the literature suggests we are bad at assessment generally, the evidence is that it is in the area of feedback that we are possibly worst of all'. So, within this context, any innovation (technological or otherwise) that may help tutors achieve the goals of effective assessment deserves careful evaluation. Our case study looks at how using podcasts may help them.

Details of the case study

We tried podcasts for assessment feedback in two geography modules during one academic year. In Semester 1, 26 students took an optional final year (undergraduate Level 6) module, in which audio feedback by podcast was provided on three assignments: an e-postcard (a single PowerPoint slide designed to 'persuade' a world leader to change policy on a key aspect of climate change), a group oral presentation and a fieldwork report. In Semester 2, 24 students took a first year (undergraduate Level 4) module in which audio feedback was provided for two assignments: a mid-module short question-and-answer test and a fieldwork report presented as a website (France and Ribchester 2004).

Two types of podcast were recorded for each assignment. First, the feedback and mark for each student (or student group in the case of the oral presentation) based on the quality of their work. Once this first phase was completed, a second podcast was created providing feedback on the group's performance as a whole and reflecting on general strengths and weaknesses of the students' work. This generic podcast was then edited together with the bespoke feedback for each student. Therefore, within one podcast each student (or group) would have the opportunity to contextualize their own performance within that of the module cohort as a whole. Additionally, brief written feedback and a mark were provided for two of the assignments – the fieldwork report (Level 6) and website (Level 4). The final versions of the podcasts were posted in the feedback section of each student's electronic Progress File (personal development planner), embedded into the University of Chester's intranet system. This system, IBIS, designed 'in-house', is similar to Blackboard. Students received an automatic email as soon as a new podcast became available for them to download. All the commentaries were recorded using a 30GB Apple iPod with a microphone attachment. Editing and file compression was carried out using GarageBand and iTunes.

We evaluated this initiative in three ways, using the same method for both modules. First, all students were given the opportunity within an early teaching session to complete a short questionnaire. This focused mainly on their understanding of podcasting generally, views and experiences of existing methods of feedback, and any expectations they had about feedback via podcasts. The response rate for this initial survey was high: all the enrolled students for the Level 6 module and all but three (88 per cent) at Level 4. Once the modules were completed and feedback and marks returned, a further questionnaire was distributed, asking students to indicate their use of the podcasts and their perceptions of them. A good response of 69 per cent was achieved for this survey at Level 6, but a much lower rate of 29 per cent was obtained at Level 4, reflecting difficulties of contacting students once teaching had formally ended. In summary, our evaluation is based on 72 returned questionnaires (47 pre-feedback and 25 post-feedback). Additionally, two focus groups were held, lasting about two hours shortly after completion of the modules, both facilitated by a tutor previously unknown to the students. Four students volunteered to participate in the Level 6 discussion; five first-year students attended the other. The groups explored student engagement with the feedback in more depth and clarified themes emerging from the questionnaires.

The Level 4 and Level 6 students shared a number of perspectives and the results from the two groups are often combined in the discussion that follows. We use quotes to illustrate points that were made, and identify the respondents by level of study and evaluation method (that is PreQ – pre-feedback questionnaire, PostQ – post-feedback questionnaire, FG – focus group).

Accessing and listening to the feedback

The 'pre' questionnaire identified two cohorts of students who were generally 'confident' in their use of computer-based technology, most (82 per cent) claiming knowledge of podcasting, but far fewer (33 per cent) direct personal experience of listening to or watching a podcast. Students showed a degree of scepticism, particularly about the likely accessibility of the feedback podcasts. Initially, these concerns may have seemed well founded, as technical challenges (including optimizing the volume level of the podcasts) delayed the first phase of feedback during the Level 6 module. However, crucially, there was strong evidence to indicate that most students listened to their podcasted feedback. Though the small return for the Level 4 'post' survey created some uncertainty about the 'take-up' of the feedback for the website assignment, informal discussions with the students indicated a high 'listening rate' for the mid-module test feedback, and it is reasonable to assume that this pattern was repeated for the final assignment.

The students' responses recognized how providing feedback in an electronic format via the university intranet system tended to increase its accessibility. 'Easy to use and obtain feedback off campus – don't have to make special journey to collect feedback' (L6 – PostQ). 'Liked the access from home, even though I live near the University' (L6 – FG). 'There is no time wasted coming down to collect the feedback and it can be easily accessed if you have to leave the Uni, i.e. to go home' (L4 – FG).

Some Level 4 students, who received their first podcast during the Easter vacation, also recognized electronic feedback's potential to reduce the turnaround time between assignment submission and receipt of feedback.

The students seemed to like the podcasts' '24/7' availability, but the podcasts' accessibility seemed to be widely recognized in another, perhaps more important, way. Unexpectedly, nearly half (49 per cent) of the students completing the 'pre' survey commented on how their use of written feedback had been undermined at some point because of their difficulty in reading tutors' handwritten comments, the most basic of barriers to effective feedback. By contrast, the podcast audio commentaries were 'better than trying to read bad handwriting', as one student bluntly observed (L4 – PostQ). The challenge of reading (and deciphering) feedback is all the greater for students with specific learning difficulties, such as dyslexia. Podcasts offer real opportunities to increase the accessibility of feedback to students, though appropriate adjustments must be made for students with hearing difficulties.

Contrary to the tutors' initial expectations, very few students saved their feedback to an MP3 player. This was despite eight students owning an iPod and the availability to borrow them from the department. Instead, most (84 per cent of the post-feedback questionnaire respondents) listened to their feedback directly from a desktop computer or laptop, using freely available software such as RealPlayer, iTunes, QuickTime or Windows Media Player. Students commented that permanent storage of the podcasts within the online Progress File significantly reduced the need to download (as well as making it impossible to mislay the feedback). Interestingly, six indicated their reluctance to download because they preferred to use their MP3 player for listening to music only, reminding us of the need to 'tread carefully' when exploring the use of technology that has a 'high level of social cachet' (Chan et al. 2006: 111). Although, at one level, the use of familiar technology could serve to narrow the perceived 'power gap' between tutor and student, it could also 'be interpreted as an unwanted intrusion into the personal and social (external) life of the individual, and an infringement of norms of behaviour between 'teacher' and 'learner' (Knight 2006: 21).

The nature and content of the feedback

One of our key motivators for engaging with digital audio feedback was the expectation that we would be able to provide more comments than with written feedback. Tutors can usually speak more quickly than they can write or type, therefore can provide more feedback, in the same time. Of course quantity does not automatically equate to quality and we were well aware that, if done poorly, podcasts could actually decrease the transparency of the assessment process and undermine student learning. Reassuringly, the students' responses suggested that this did not happen, but we know that podcasts can just as easily facilitate excessively judgemental, opaque, summative commentaries as they can deliver sensitive, clear, formative feedback.

Students' comments on the nature and content of the podcasted feedback were common: 68 per cent of the post-feedback questionnaire respondents referred, in some way, to greater depth and detail in feedback compared to their previous experiences. These observations are typical: 'there is more quantity of feedback and . . . it is probably more specific and carefully thought through' (L6 – PostQ). 'More constructive, can be targeted to specific points for improvement and gives you a more accurate account of the quality of work and why marks were awarded' (L6 – PostQ). 'You tend to get a lot more feedback than you would with more traditional methods' (L6 – PostQ).

Students said the feedback was more personalized, too. For example, 'This

feedback felt that the work had really been looked at and evaluated personally' (L6 – FG). 'It is done on quite a personal level and in a good amount of
detail for you personally' (L4 – PostQ). 'A lot more personal information.
Felt like I was getting a "one-to-one" (L4 – FG).

Although 'more personal' and 'more detailed' were used interchangeably
by the students, they deemed being 'spoken to' a more direct engagement.
The sensitive microphones did tend to pick up the sound of pages being
turned or mouse buttons being clicked as feedback commentaries were
being constructed and spoken. This background noise provided an almost
tangible sense of a student's individual piece of work being reviewed and
may have added to the perception of more personalized feedback. It was
'like a personal tutorial' according to one student (L4 – FG). Pitts (2005:
223), in her small-scale study of music students' attitudes to feedback style
and content, notes that respondents were 'keen to see evidence of thought
and commitment on the lecturer's part'. Podcasts seem to provide the
potential to do just that. More generally, innovations seen to be of value
can engender a positive attitude towards tutors: 'the feedback was really
useful and it is good that the department is willing to try out new technologies' (L4 – PostQ).

'Given mass higher education, it is perhaps unsurprising that feedback
is often terse; perhaps a solution here is not the 'reform' of direct feedback,
but the use of alternative methods?' (Mutch 2003: 31). The evidence
suggests that podcasting is an 'alternative method' that can counter this
problem.

However, unexpectedly, podcasting also raises the possibility of providing
too much feedback: some students referred to feedback commentaries lasting too long. Across the five assignments, the generic feedback podcasts were
two to seven minutes, the individual podcasts two to eight minutes. The
longest combined podcast (generic and specific feedback) for an individual
student was 14 minutes. Generally, the podcasts for the Semester 2 module
were longer, as tutor confidence and comfort in providing audio feedback
increased. Notably, comments about the length of the feedback were almost
entirely from the Level 4 students in Semester 2, which might indicate that
the longer commentaries that they received had crossed some 'natural
threshold' beyond which attention begins to diminish. Chan et al. (2006)
speculate that the limit for podcasts is three to five minutes, roughly the
length of a typical song. By contrast, the Level 6 focus group suggested that
the length of podcasts should be dictated by 'what needs to be said' and not
some predetermined time limit. Different views also emerged about the
value of the generic commentaries provided within each podcast. The Level
6 students were generally positive about the opportunity to contextualize
their own performance: for example, 'the generic feedback helps to improve
my confidence, especially knowing that others may be struggling with the
same things' (L6 – FG). But the Level 4 students were more inclined to
question its value. The different opinions in the two cohorts may reflect the
Level 4 students' lack of experience and lower levels of engagement in their

first year of study, but possibly lengthy commentaries create uncertainty about the key feedback messages being sent.

Engagement with the feedback

Both student groups thought they received more detailed and personalized feedback. Significantly, both the 'pre' and 'post' evaluations also suggested a greater sensitivity to the spoken word and a sense of immediacy in comparison to written text, particularly in relation to negative comments. For example, 'the impact of the words being spoken [will] be much harder hitting and may be a bit demoralizing' (L6 – PreQ). 'Any criticism will hit home more' (L6 – PreQ). 'May be harder to hear a poor mark, rather than in writing' (L6 – FG). Comments like these emphasized the uneven power relationship between tutor and student (Higgins et al. 2001) and the importance of constructing sensitive commentaries that do not undermine student confidence. Furthermore, students recognized the tutor's tenor as an important factor in enhancing understanding. As one student commented, you can get 'the tone of voice with the words so you could understand the importance of the different bits of feedback' (L6 – PostQ). Both Welham (1999) and Kates (1998) recognize the significance of how words are delivered in their reviews of using tape-recordings for assessment feedback. Even the widest vocabulary in written text cannot replicate the voice's ability to 'adjust intonation, inflexion, phrasing, pacing, volume, loudness and timbre . . . Print does not allow a learner to identify and interpret audible nuances that personalize content because print cannot stimulate the auditory senses' (Power 1990: 45).

Students' appreciation of these subtleties may be affected to some degree by their preferred learning styles, but many commented favourably on audio compared with written feedback. For example, 'Actually took in the feedback, sometimes skim-read written feedback' (L6 – PostQ). 'Don't just briefly read it, you actually listen to it and take it in' (L6 – Post Q). 'Really like this idea, I find listening to things that much easier' (L4 – PostQ).

Students' deeper engagement with the audio feedback is also encouraged by the 'concealed' nature of the final mark, which is not instantly viewable as on a feedback sheet. Instead, it is delivered somewhere within the audio commentary, typically towards the end. It 'makes you listen to all of the feedback not just the mark' (L6 – PostQ), although for some this was clearly a source of frustration and also anxiety, as the podcasts approached their conclusion. One student admitted, 'ignored the feedback at first until I got to the mark, and then went back to the start' (L6 – FG).

Students' engagement with feedback is affected by the context in which it is received. The evaluation yielded interesting findings in this respect. The questionnaire responses showed that most (72 per cent) students accessed and listened to their feedback off campus, on their own and in their own study spaces. Such circumstances can be conducive to careful listening and scrutiny of the feedback, if the student is motivated to do so. By contrast, a whirl of activity can sometimes surround the return of assignments and feedback. For example, there is the 'dash' to the departmental office after the teaching session.

Some drawbacks and challenges

We have been highlighting perceived benefits of podcasts, but we also noted three factors that may impact negatively on student engagement with the feedback. First is the physical separation of the assignment and feedback. Students are inclined to listen to their feedback as soon as possible, even if they have not got immediate access to their assignment. Where applicable, students need to make the effort to collect a hard copy of their submitted work or, probably more commonly, access their own digital copy, to ensure that the feedback is contextualized fully. The more detailed and specific the comments are, the greater the importance of listening to the feedback while reviewing the assignment. Second, there is the loss of annotations on written work. Though much feedback can be provided more efficiently through the spoken word, it is probably quicker to amend a hard copy than describe the necessary changes orally if they are in the fine detail of grammar, punctuation, spelling and referencing. The absence of written comments may, in some circumstances, make less obvious which parts of an assignment are being discussed, although writing reference numbers on the work (to act as discussion points) can avoid this problem, and is advocated in Welham's (1999) discussion of tape-recorded feedback. Third, there was no summary feedback sheet for three assignments in this case study. It is common practice in the Department to provide feedback sheets that include both tick-boxes (ranging from 'first' to 'fail') referenced against the assignment's assessment criteria and qualitative comments. The loss of the feedback sheets was commented on by both focus groups and the extent to which it could still be retained was questioned, 'Podcasting was different, I liked it. It is different to the criteria sheet but I would not replace it. I would like both' (L6 – FG).

Conclusion

Our research shows how podcasting technology enhanced the range of feedback strategies available to tutors. Our findings suggest that podcasts have the potential to increase the detail and accessibility of assessment feedback, provide commentaries that students view as more personalized and understandable, and encourage a deeper engagement with the feedback information. However, tutors need to be wary of providing commentaries that are too lengthy and the possible drawbacks of the reduction in, or possibly complete absence of, written feedback for a particular assignment.

While the case study shows how digital oral feedback has been provided for a number of assessment modes, it really only 'scratches the surface' of possible assignments for which podcasts may be used for feedback. Indeed, we suggest that specific details of an assessment exercise along with its timing and overall position within a programme of study will strongly influence the usefulness (or otherwise) of podcasted feedback. Decisions about implementing feedback podcasts will therefore have to be made at a local level, but practitioners do need to research and share their experiences to help develop a model that highlights circumstances in which podcasted feedback is likely to work most effectively. We suggest that podcasts may offer significant advantages over traditional feedback methods for assignments that do not require detailed annotations on student work or when this is simply not possible, as with artefacts and some electronic based submissions. Podcasts may work particularly well when providing feedback for oral presentations, role plays or drama 'performances'. Even if detailed written feedback is deemed essential, a generic overview feedback podcast can help all students to situate their own performance in relation to others in the group and to be aware of their groups' strengths and weaknesses in a given assignment. Generic podcasts may also be an appropriate strategy for large groups (perhaps above 40 students) when individual podcasts are not a viable option.

More generally, we think that podcasting is more likely to be readily accepted in modules, like the two geography ones, where there is already a technology-enhanced learning component. It is also likely to be embraced more enthusiastically in programmes with a pre-existing e-learning culture reflected in the technical abilities of both students and tutors, and the provision of an adequate hardware infrastructure and technical support. Furthermore, like many e-learning initiatives, podcasted feedback may prove particularly valuable for students learning at a distance.

Acknowledgements

The authors would like to thank Dr Anne Wheeler (University of Wolverhampton) for facilitating the two focus group discussions and Kelly Wakefield for helping to put the finishing touches to the text. This research was supported by a grant from the Higher Education Academy Subject Centre for Geography, Earth and Environmental Sciences (2006) and contributed to the University of Chester HEA/JISC e-learning Pathfinder project.

8

Podcasts and online learning

John Fothergill

Summary

This chapter provides an approach to using podcasts to support students who carry out a significant portion of their studies online. Although students enrolled in campus-based institutions generally carry out their studies through face-to-face methods such as lectures and seminars, the wider penetration of Virtual Learning Environments (VLE) offers the potential to deliver some of the learning content online, offering the students the flexibility of learning at a pace, time and locations suitable to their circumstances. Podcasts can support the online learning of campus-based students and those learning at a distance.

Why bother about podcasting?

Listen to a good academic talking about lecturing (in one of those big rooms with a whiteboard and a screen at the front). They will tell you how rewarding they find this and how motivating both the lecturer and the students find the process. They will tell you how they can continually adapt their lecture's content and style depending on the reactions of the audience. I certainly remember some excellent lecturers and lectures – I might have even given a few myself.

In a course delivered online or at a distance, there are opportunities for enthusing students, and indeed remaining motivated as a tutor, through the various synchronous and asynchronous methods of interaction, from the phone call, and e-tivities (Salmon 2002) to the wiki. Indeed, there are many opportunities that are not available offline. It is difficult, for example, to assess group work offline without considerably more resources than are necessary online. But, as a course tutor, one can still feel that, after three or four years of presentation, the course starts to lose life and lack lustre: the enthusiasm of preparation may wane after repeated presentation. Perhaps this is just perceived. The students, after all, are new to the ideas and perhaps even the methodologies for presentation. But even for the students, if the course material has been honed and frequently asked questions inserted in response to enquiries from previous cohorts, the material may start to look static. Interestingly, a polished course may even lack some of the perceived liveliness of one that is still being developed.

Podcasts may be used to enliven a course. They enable tutors to talk to their students. In this way, they can respond to their students: their level of activity, their opinions, conclusions and their results from assignments. Tutors can give feedback in this way, not instantly, but once a week is quite feasible. They can help to pace their work. Furthermore, they can react to external developments whether it be breaking news or a new scientific discovery. The medium of podcasting, which is now straightforward to use, can bring a course back to life and rekindle some fire in the students.

Podcasts in an online undergraduate engineering course

This chapter reflects on how podcasts have been incorporated into an undergraduate engineering course for cohorts of approximately 50 full-time campus-based students. Unusually perhaps, the course was delivered almost entirely online. A VLE (Blackboard) was used as the framework for this. Most of the assessments were also taken online. Some of the students were second year and they took a slightly different pathway through the course than the other, final- (third- or fourth)-year students. Many of the students did not have English as their first language. While many of the students had used Blackboard, this was the first time they would have experienced it as the primary means of delivery of a course. The course has been delivered four times in this format – it was delivered as a 'conventional' 20-lecture course in one form or another for about 20 years before that.

Much of the content was delivered through short (10–15 minute) online lectures. There are about 40 of these and they comprise an audio-recording of the lecturer, with PowerPoint slides and a transcript. These were first compiled mainly with 'Impatica' (www.impatica.com); an example screen dump, originally in colour of course, is shown in Figure 8.1. More recently, the university has standardized on using Adobe Acrobat Connect (formerly known as Macromedia Breeze; see www.adobe.com/products/acrobatconnect) for this application. The lectures are intended to be available over low bandwidth internet connections and independent of the computer or browser (they produce platform-independent Java script). The lectures are accessible at any time and can be played, paused, 'rewound' and so on, under the control of each student. Indeed, it is tempting to think that students would work mainly during the day and party at night. However, it is clear from the VLE statistics that the students worked more on this course in the evening than in the morning (see Figure 8.2).

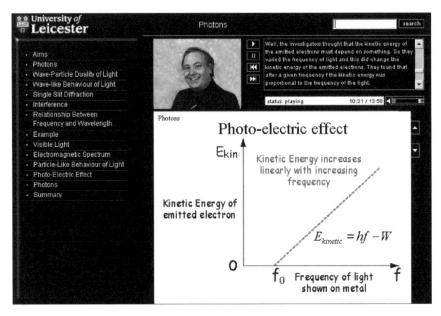

Figure 8.1 A screenshot showing an online lecture

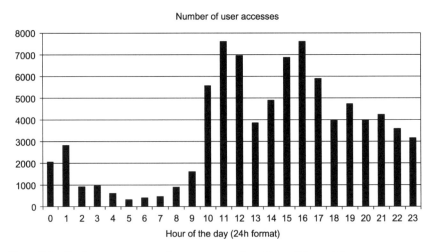

Figure 8.2 Student accesses to the course as a function of time of day

Other online content included video clips and animations, video contributions and lectures from an external lecturer from industry. Many of these modes of delivery could be thought of as podcasts – certainly this is true if MP4 as well as MP3 technology (see Chapter 2) is included in their definition. Indeed, 'zipped' forms of the lectures were available for students to download (on USB flash drives, for example). The lectures have been shown

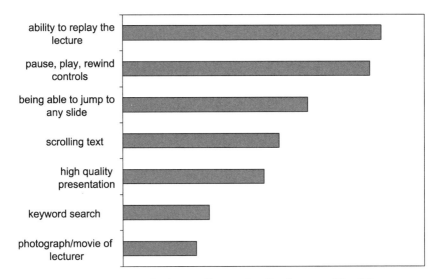

Figure 8.3 Importance ascribed to attributes of online lectures (N = 30)

to be very popular with these engineering students (see Figure 8.3 for details of importance ascribed to attributes of online lectures); perhaps because (real) lectures form a medium that they experience a great deal. Interestingly for them, the 'speaking head' (see Figure 8.1), was the least important feature of these lectures, suggesting that if these were to be optimized for mobile devices, this would not be an important feature to maintain. Indeed, for many of the lectures, the talking head was changed to a photograph, which made recording and editing a lot easier.

Online lectures in the context of online learning have been discussed well elsewhere (Dutton et al. 2001) and so, in this chapter, the discussion of podcasts will be mainly confined to audio-recordings that, at least in this case, were prepared afresh (or at least refreshed) for each presentation of the course. However, as the domain of podcasts expands, it might be worth demonstrating that students did take to this form of 'lecturing'. Although, as campus-based students, they did not want to lose face-to-face interaction in all courses, and stated that they particularly valued blended learning (Cullen and Foster 2007). They were much more positive about substituting 'real' lectures for online lectures than might have been expected (see Box 8.1).

The quotes and statistics presented here come from:

- six students who were interviewed by the IMPALA researchers at the University of Leicester during the course of the semester;
- an end-of-semester survey administered through Blackboard;
- discussion forums led by an external moderator for two of the e-tivites;
- collations of postings on the discussion forums.

The online resources also include 35 formative assessments (known as

---

Box 8.1   Quotes from students regarding online lectures

'I am able to actually listen to a lecture, and just pausing it, and stopping it if there is something you don't understand. In a traditional class setting, you just sit there and listen. If there is something you don't understand and you raise your hands once, ask the question but sometimes you still don't understand even after the explanation. And you don't want to ask again. Therefore you just leave it be.'

'I think that the online lectures are better, because I can do it anytime and any place.'

'So basically if it is a 15 minutes lecture . . . I need one and a half hours to study that 15 minute lecture because I need to take notes from whatever he's saying, so sometimes I need to pause it because he just speaks right so it's like one sentence, 2 sentence comes together so when I'm writing I need to take some time to write and some time to understand the thing because there's no point just writing down all the things – So I pause it or sometimes I go back to the slide before. Again, to get this idea again. So basically it takes 1 hour for a 15 minute section.'

'quizzes' to the students), online summative assignments, links to selected external resources, and a message board for queries (I will not answer general queries on the course content unless they are sent through this message board). The previous year's message board is available for reference, formatted as 'frequently asked questions'. The only elements of the course that are not online are an initial introductory lecture during which the students are introduced to Blackboard, optional problem classes before each summative assessment and a final group assignment. Three summative assignments are taken under examination conditions in a computer laboratory; the final assignment is a group submission.

The mode of delivery of the course benefited the students by providing them with personal experience of e-learning, giving them insight into the role of information technology (IT) in personal development and introducing them to a mode of independent learning. Freeing content delivery from the template of fixed-length lectures allows more flexibility in the length of each Learning Unit rather than having to break only at the end of a lecture slot. Students also benefited from being in control of the pace of their learning and from being able to follow optional pathways through the course, using supplementary materials as required, and from having access to more interactive material and rapid feedback from formative and summative assignments. My duties (as Pro-Vice-Chancellor at the time) within the university resulted in a busy schedule, often taking me away from the campus. A more flexible mode of delivery was therefore useful to both the students and me as the tutor. The rationale for introducing podcasts included enlivening the course, complementing the announcements page ('what you're doing next week', and so on), as a mechanism for providing feedback on work, e-tivities and assignments, and for informal knowledge acquisition in a perhaps more entertaining way.

Typically a podcast was divided into three main sections:

1. 'News'
2. Announcements and feedback
3. Fun ending

The 'news' related the course material to current events. It gave the course context and the students a wider background so that they could situate what they were learning to the world they were in. While not being directly assessed through an understanding of this informal knowledge, they could also use their new-found knowledge in situations not discussed directly elsewhere in the course. The intention of this was that they would reflect on their learning, perhaps even discuss it with colleagues and friends, and gain deeper insights into the material. Because this item was reasonably topical, it was not usually possible simply to recycle podcast news from the previous presentation of the course. However, some discretion is available here, for example the 40th birthday of fibre optics last year became the 41st this year! Giving some history of the subject enabled a discussion of the constraints that needed to be overcome and the specifications required for a communication network. Other news sections included:

- Coping with e-learning. This was the first podcast and started with an interview with a student from the previous year. We discussed the course from the student's perspective, and he provided hints to enable the current cohort to work more effectively. For example, he described how he timetabled his work to help himself to study, how he prepared for assignments, and how he made use of the podcasts. Students reacted positively to this – perhaps it was better for a peer to present his methods of coping and learning than for me, the tutor, to tell them 'how it should be'.
- Fibre optics used in the 'Internet Superhighway' – this followed some news that the backbone of the internet was under pressure from digital broadcasting. It enabled students, early in the course, to realize how vital fibre optics are to our digital environment.
- New uses for light-emitting diodes (LEDs). The semiconductor laser theory that students were taught enabled them to understand how very bright LEDs could now be manufactured for use in other applications from lightweight long-lasting bicycle lamps to Ferrari Formula-1 stop bulbs.
- A lunar eclipse was a good excuse to talk about why the moon was red (during the eclipse) and the sky is blue (during the day). This was then related to some quantum photon theory that they were studying.

- Problems in delivering the internet over the 'final mile' to the house enabled a discussion of jointing fibre optics and their economics in comparison with delivering digital signals down copper cables.

Usually these news sections lasted about five minutes. Enough germane material was required to maintain interest. I found that it was better to include material closely related to the course and, perhaps not so topical, than very topical news that was less closely related. For example, topics on new electronic gadgets were less likely to be well received even though they were in the news and I thought them of interest to the cohort. Audio, then, can support emotional aspects of learning by conveying immediacy and a connection with the teacher. Audio, the core content medium in podcasting, is not new to education; indeed, one could argue that it is the oldest. Durbridge (1984) at the Open University in the UK identified one of audio's educational advantages as its ability to influence cognition through clarity of instructions. It was therefore natural for me to continue the podcast with signposts relating to the course. This second section, which I considered as *announcements and feedback*, would comment, in a general way, on the students' achievements and signpost what they should be doing next. It helped to motivate the students and helped them to pace their work. Second section topics included:

- *An overview of typical amounts of work that I would expect students to do each week.* It was then possible to compare this with how long students had been logged onto the VLE that week. It was also possible to see where students had got to on the course, and to what extent they were making use of the quizzes. This was especially useful at the beginning of the course. (Real slackers were followed up with personal emails as well.)
- *A comparison of the findings of the groups in their 'e-tivities'* (Salmon 2002). For example, one of the e-tivities asked groups, 'Can you find out using the internet what the longest distances are that single fibres can cover without repeaters (which regenerate and amplify the signal)?' There was a wide variety of findings, with one group finding a fibre of several 1000 km while another only found one of about 100 km. By discussing such discrepancies in the podcasts, members of groups were motivated to get involved. Indeed, in many ways, the summarizing that I could do at a group level on the discussion board could subsequently be achieved through the podcast at a whole class level.
- *Comments on the assignment.* Although the results from the assignments were given to individual students, I tried to give students a feel for how they did, and encouraged them to do better, by comparing the performance of their respective groups. It was also possible to give general feedback, so that students could understand where they went wrong and how they were getting on in comparison with the rest of the cohort. An example from such a podcast is given in Box 8.2.
- *Pacing.* I used the podcasts to let students know where they should have got to on the course and what they should be planning to do that week:

'. . . you should be about a third of the way through Section 2 now. Try to aim to finish Learning Unit 2.4 this week. Also, I've posted e-tivity 2 now – this is called, 'How long can a fibre be' . . . It would be good, if you can do that by Tuesday week, i.e. the 27 February.'

- *Further explanations.* It was clear that occasionally groups of students were having difficulty with a particular concept. Normally this was addressed through the discussion boards and/or by referring them to other explanations, for example, through links to other websites. However, I did occasionally attempt descriptions where these were feasible, in the podcast. The nature of the material normally made this difficult, but nevertheless talking about some concepts in a different way appeared to help some students.

Box 8.2   Example from podcast of commentary on an assignment

'Well – how do you think the assignment went?'

'The group with the highest score was group 2 – well above the others with an average score of 72 per cent. Group 3 got a score of 63 per cent and the other two groups got average marks in the high 2(ii)s. The average mark was 31 out of 50, i.e. 62 per cent.'

'You mostly did well in knowing the different types of fibre and you seemed to know what attenuation was – although you didn't always get your decibel calculations correct. You need to make sure you understand the difference between millis, micros, nanos, and kilos, megas, and gigas – if you're not sure then check in the Engineering Data book and learn them.'

'You were a bit more hazy on what dispersion is – which is a pity because it's really the rationale for using lasers as you'll see later in the course. You'll see that lasers have a very narrow bandwidth and so reduce intramodal dispersion. Many of you couldn't answer the question that gave you some data and then said, If the source has a bandwidth of 50 nm, what is the maximum bit rate possible over a 10 km link? This will be quite useful in your final assignment. In particular many of you found it difficult to distinguish between different types of dispersion.'

The last part of the podcast was the 'fun part', and normally consisted of a joke. It was quite difficult to find jokes about optical fibres so they were not always particularly relevant! On one more famous occasion I did a rap, which seemed to capture the imagination of the press (Tysome 2006). Why did I include a fun part at all? When I was considering this course, I looked at the student feedback from my previous lecture course and found that some students enjoyed the humour in the lecture. Again, it kept it alive.

(Of course, some students also complained about the quality of the jokes!) But it seemed reasonable that, if I were to put the course online, it should not lose this aspect. So the podcasts finished with some humour. I also tended to include cartoons on the announcements page, hoping that students would be more motivated to log for a smile. The rationale for this was therefore:

- to encourage students to listen to the podcast;
- to keep students listening to the end;
- to humanize the podcast and make it more informal.

How well did the podcasts work?

The podcasts were reasonably popular – even though they were obviously an 'optional' part of the course. For example, in the last presentation, there were nine podcasts; 92 per cent of the cohort listened to at least one podcast and 59 per cent listened to eight or nine of them (see Figure 8.4).

The podcasts were generally listened to on the computer, rather than students downloading them and listening to them on an MP3 player. This may have been because the recordings were not made available using syndication feeds – these need to be saved to disk and then transferred manually to the MP3 player. Box 8.3 shows some reactions of students to the podcasts. It is clear that they like the ability to listen to them at a time that suits them. They also appear to like the informal nature of the podcasts in that they do not consider listening to them to be course work. They realize that relating the material to 'real life' helps them to understand new concepts. Although they express it in a different way, they also appear to agree that podcasts do bring the course to life.

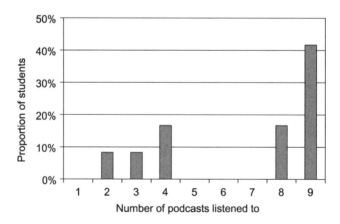

Figure 8.4   The percentage of students who listened to podcasts in the last presentation of the course

Box 8.3   Student reactions to podcasts

'The good thing about podcasts is you can sit in your room and play and listen to them. He is saying things about the module. It is good to listen to them.'

'I listen to them after about 8pm. When they are announced . . . when I don't have anything else to do like course work, I listen to them. When the announcements say that podcasts are available I listen to them. Mostly after I go back home. That is the good thing about the module. You don't have to do it at the same time as others. Go home and listen to them. Sit down and listen.'

'It is really good when he relates information in the lecture to real life. It helps you to understand things.'

'In the beginning I didn't know what podcasts are. I think he is singing in the sixth one, my friend told me, so I'm like "mm, that should be interesting!" [laughter]. Professor has got a really good sense of humour. I really like that. I really like his lectures and podcast. If you are interested in the way the module is taught, then you sit down and study. But if the module is boring or the lecturer is boring you think "oh, I have to study this. But I don't want to."'

'The way the module is taught is interesting. It makes people interested in the module.'

'It is different. It is like, "let's see what joke he has got in this one!" Also there is a lot of information as well.'

'Professor talks about the course, example, topic for the week and explanations relating to the topic studied. I learn other things which sometimes aren't related to the course. It is quite useful, it is just general feedback. He points out where students make mistakes.'

Integrating the podcasts into the course

So how did the podcasts integrate into the course? In an interview a student was asked to describe how he approached the course:

Q: So what do you do after you log in?
A: Everyday he puts up like a cartoon sketch. First thing when you click the optical communication, I go there, I see the picture and try to

understand what it is. Then I go to my group area where there will be some discussion . . . there. So normally there will be some e-tivities that we're supposed to do. So I go to my group area and check if there's new people who have put something down. And if I want, if I can contribute something to whatever they put I'll try to do that. Otherwise normally I'll just keep it like OK, I'll do it later. Then I go to this course material [lectures].

Q: So, what about the multiple choice questions, the quizzes? Do you do them as well?

A: Yeah, yes. Obviously – because that's the main thing. After doing the quizzes it is then if I know I understand that chapter. I try to get massive amounts in the first time – And if it's like some problem questions also I try to do it and, if I get the same answer – Then I'll be happy,

Q: Were there times when you'd done the quiz and gone back to the lecture again?

A: Yes, only a few times because in quizzes it explains basically what's gone wrong and that type of thing, normally it's always there so there is no point to go back to the lecture again. I went only once or twice.

Q: So when you were asked to do these e-tivities what was your feelings, what was your reactions?

A: Well basically it's research isn't it? Like you find out stuff by yourself rather than spoon feeding. So you're actually submitting that information to other people. So we will get feedback from others. So we will know whether we are going the right way or not. So it actually helps me to filter down what to search . . .

Q: What about the podcasts?

A: He talks about the new things happening in this area, like about different fibres, apart from this basic information he's giving a broad idea. So I'll just listen and it is just like, you know, reading a newspaper. Because some things you remember – I mean some things it is like 'catch-able'. Like you don't study the newspaper right? I mean, it is helpful in the way like if you are having a discussion about something like that. Then if the topic comes up like optical communication – you can also say something about it.

To this student, the podcasts were about informal learning. They were not felt, however, to be outside the course. To him, they were just another way of learning – learning that you 'catch' rather than teach yourself.

The end of course survey suggested that podcasts had a variety of uses – in particular they were found to be stimulating and motivating (see Table 8.1).

Interestingly, the only slightly negative comment about podcasts was a technical one (the students were engineers). When asked what could be improved about the course, the only comment relating to podcasts was: 'Higher quality podcasts, the 32 kbps podcasts (1 and 2) were OK to listen to, the 16 kbps podcasts (3–5, 7–9) were very hard to listen to, the 128 kbps

Table 8.1 Student perceptions of benefits of podcasts (N = 30)

Statements	% of cohort agreeing with statement
Podcasts helped me to understand more about e-tivities	58
Podcasts were useful in preparation for assessed work such as tests	50
Podcasts were useful in getting to know our progress as a group	50
Podcasts helped to stimulate my interest in the subject	42
Podcasts provided summaries of e-tivities	42
Podcasts helped me to organize/structure my weekly learning activities	33
Podcasts were motivational	33
Podcasts helped me to stay focused on the course	25
Podcasts helped me to make good use of my time	8

podcast (6) was excellent. We didn't have a 64 kbps podcast, but I think it could be a good compromise.'

Conclusion

A format of podcasts has been developed, which provides informal learning, motivation, pacing, encouragement, feedback and stimulation, and enlivens an online course. While the podcasts could be considered as 'optional' in the sense that the course ran without them for two years and a small proportion of students often do not listen to them, they appear to be considered valuable by the majority of students. The 'three sections' of the podcasts worked well. The first 'news' section enabled them to relate their learning and topical issues, getting a better understanding of both. The second section, commenting on the progress of the class, helped to signpost the way through the course and pace their work. The third 'fun' section encouraged them to engage with the course by making it more human. Clearly, podcasts have many uses, such as for mobile learning; many of these are described elsewhere in this book. It could be argued that the podcasts produced for this course could equally well have been published as text files on the announcements page of the course. However, as well as being more straightforward for the tutor to produce, it appears that the tailored audio track, reacting to the issues raised by the students and providing interesting background contextual information, is attractive to students through enlivening the course. It seems that this could be recommended for other online courses.

9

Podcasts and distance learning

Mark J.W. Lee and Belinda Tynan

Summary

This chapter examines the use of podcasting to support distance learners, with case studies of how it has been implemented and evaluated at two institutions, which are among Australia's largest distance education providers.

Introduction

Australia has a strong tradition of distance education due to its small and geographically dispersed population (Bell et al. 2002). The distance learning cohorts at Charles Sturt University (CSU) (www.csu.edu.au) represent 65 per cent of the university's enrolments. At the University of New England (UNE) (www.une.edu.au) 88 per cent study at a distance. The two universities accounted for nearly 30 per cent of Australia's university distance learning students throughout 2001–6 (Department of Education, Science and Training 2007). Like many tertiary education providers, our universities want to provide distance students with rich, interactive and effective learning experiences. Podcasting, as one technology among many emerging Web 2.0 and other technologies, is an increasingly important aspect of the learning experience at both institutions.

First, we describe the rationale behind the use of podcasting to support distance learning. Second, we present the two case studies at our universities as a starting point for locating current initiatives involving podcasting in distance learning contexts. Third, we discuss themes drawn from the two cases, focusing on distance students' experience of podcasting, and considerations in introducing podcasting for them.

Podcasting in distance education

The use of audio-based educational technologies for distance learning and teaching is certainly not new. From the beginnings of radio, this type of medium was used in distance education, sometimes in combination with print materials, face-to-face tuition and group learning. Cassette tapes, and more recently, compact discs (CDs), have been used where radio airtime is simply not readily available or when learners are distributed over too large an area (World Bank 2000).

In recent decades, however, audio has been somewhat neglected as a teaching and learning medium (Romero-Gwynn and Marshall 1990; Scottish Council for Educational Technology 1994). Web-based distance learning systems have tended to focus on text as the primary medium. Barnes (1995) points out that, despite all the capabilities of the cyber classroom, one element that is still missing is non-verbal communication such as facial expressions and bodily cues. Voice-based communication technologies have potential to address these shortcomings, since 'spoken words through heightened intonations or subtle nuances can communicate . . . emotions and create a sense of intimacy at the same time . . . allow[ing] a learner to identify . . . [and] interpret audible nuances that personalize content' (Power 1990). As a result of 'a renaissance fuelled by the ubiquity of portable audio players, broadband internet, and software tools that allow the relatively easy creation and distribution of audio files' (Schlosser and Burmeister 2006), distance educators now have access to a vastly expanded toolkit of digital audio technologies that can be exploited to enhance dialogue and interactivity in an online setting.

One such technology is podcasting, which offers a low-cost, low-barrier solution for the timely delivery of fresh, audio-based educational content. The Really Simple Syndication (RSS) format (see Chapter 2) enables users to subscribe to audio feeds in digital form with a few clicks. (It should be noted, however, that many authors use the term 'podcast' to refer to MP3 files that are made available for manual download via a web browser.) RSS-based podcasting has much to offer in the way of simplicity, convenience and time savings for the busy distance learner, since he or she does not have to plough through a plethora of sites for relevant content, nor is there a need for the even more tedious continual monitoring sites for updates. As new podcast files are published on subscribed feeds, they are automatically downloaded, with no user intervention. If the user has a computer continuously connected to the internet, the content can be 'dripped in' and made available when ready, so that the 'click and wait' situation common in streaming is effectively eliminated even in bandwidth-constrained environments.

Besides desktop computers, equipment capable of playing podcasts encompasses a range of portable devices, including dedicated MP3 players (for example iPods), laptop computers and tablet PCs, as well as various mobile phones and personal digital assistants (PDAs). This presents rich opportunities for mobile learning (m-learning), through which students can reconcile the scholarly tradition of sitting down to learn, from books or a computer, with the emergence of the mobile workforce to which many distance students now belong.

Case studies of podcasting in distance learning

Our universities are both located in regional centres of New South Wales, Australia (see Figure 9.1). Each is far away from a major metropolitan centre, with the closest capital city being Sydney. CSU, whose largest campus is in Wagga Wagga, is Australia's eighth largest university and the country's largest provider of distance education, with approximately 22 000 of its 34 000 students undertaking study via this mode. The remainder of the student population attends classes on campus at one of CSU's regional campuses or specialist centres, or at one of CSU's many partner institutions worldwide, which deliver the university's courses on their own premises.

UNE is at Armidale on the northern tablelands of New South Wales. Since its inception, UNE has taught most of its students off campus: today 15 000 of its 17 000 enrolled students study at a distance. UNE maintains several access centres within the region where students can meet their peers, use high-tech web-based video conferencing and access a variety of resources.

Figure 9.1   Locations of CSU's Wagga Wagga campus and UNE's Armidale campus

Note: Map courtesy of the New South Wales Department of State and Regional Development – reproduced with permission in modified form.

Case Study 1: Charles Sturt University

In June 2005, Chan and Lee of the School of Information Studies at CSU's Wagga Wagga campus started investigating the use of pre-class podcasts as a means to address preconceptions and anxiety that university students bring into the lecture hall (Chan and Lee 2005). Creating a productive and satisfying learning experience involves actively engaging students and having them take responsibility for their own learning (Schunk and Zimmerman 1998). Preconceptions about a subject or its content, along with anxiety in various forms, can act as immediate impediments to productive learning. It is also well known that pedagogical methods based on social constructivist theory, such as discovery-based learning, problem-based learning and collaborative learning, have a significantly higher probability of success if students come to class already inspired to learn and willing to participate (Ramsden 2003). Chan and Lee believed that, given the large uptake of portable music players among their students, the use of a series of short audio clips, delivered in a timely fashion through podcasting, could be an effective way of preparing students for formal learning activities. Podcasting leverages the psycho-acoustic and affective qualities of audio (Clark and Walsh 2004), promising to be more effective and flexible than traditional methods such as subject websites and printed handouts.

The investigation was initially limited to first-year students studying an information technology subject taught by Chan on campus at Wagga Wagga. It expanded to encompass a range of undergraduate and postgraduate students, studying subjects at other CSU campuses as well as off campus in Australia and overseas. The creation of podcasts for various subjects was driven by a group of volunteer students who were not enrolled in, or had previously completed, the respective subject (Lee et al. 2006). These student producers were responsible for the entire podcast production process including generating and selecting ideas for podcast scripts, script writing and editing, voice acting and/or presentation, digital audio recording and editing, quality assurance and publishing/distribution of the finished podcasts.

When the student producers' group was first established, the members were not provided with any formal training; rather, they were introduced to the podcast production process by means of examples. They gradually developed competence in various facets of the process through practice runs, with decreasing levels of guidance from the lecturer, as well as through their interactions with one another. Subsequently, newcomers to the group were coached and mentored by more experienced members. There was minimal lecturer intervention in tasks carried out by the group; the student producers exercised a high degree of autonomy and creativity.

The emphasis was on producing short, three-to-five-minute audio segments that the researchers believed students would listen to in their 'wasted' time or 'dead time' while waiting, travelling or doing household chores – what Metcalf (2002) calls the 'stolen moments for learning'. The

podcasts were structured as talkback radio-style 'shows', with student pre-
senters holding discussions on subject-related issues in a relaxed and
informal style. The lecturer and other subject experts were occasionally
brought in as 'guests' to offer insight into more difficult or complex issues
and topics. Material contained in the podcasts was supplementary in nature
and not directly examinable: it was designed to give students background
information, arouse their interest in the subject and expose them to subject-
specific terminology, as well as allay their concerns. This novel approach to
peer teaching or tutoring appears to be similar to what Gee (1992, 1996)
terms socializing into a 'Discourse' (with a 'big D'), and is reminiscent of
the 'legitimate peripheral participation' of newcomers to a community of
practice, portrayed by Lave and Wenger (1991).

Podcasts for each subject were made available to all students enrolled,
including those studying in on-campus and distance education modes. Students could either download the MP3 files manually or configure their
podcast-capable RSS aggregators ('podcatchers') to check periodically
for new files and download them automatically. Students received basic
instructions on how to perform these tasks.

Evaluation strategy and outcomes

Given the profile of the CSU's student population, Chan and Lee evaluated
the podcasts' impact and effectiveness from the perspective of a distance
education audience. Anecdotal feedback from students as well as data from
surveys and interviews suggested that the researchers' approach to podcasting was highly successful. Reported uptake of the podcasts was excellent,
with most survey respondents downloading and listening to most of the
podcasts in their entirety and many listening to the podcasts' multiple
times (Lee and Chan 2007b). Listening to the podcasts stimulated the
distance learners' interest in the subject matter and supported their
engagement, while addressing the motivational elements of effective learning (McLoughlin et al. 2007):

> Like pulling on your running shoes seems to mentally prepare you for
> exercise, so listening to podcasts helps . . . [me] . . . prep for . . . [my] . . .
> study session (Lee and Chan 2007a: 212)

> I was . . . pleasantly su[r]prised to hear [the textbook author in one of
> the podcasts] . . . [Hearing] comments from such an authoritative
> source was . . . uplifting (Lee and Chan 2007b: 98)

The podcasts also appear to have reduced isolation-induced anxiety and to
have promoted inclusivity for distance learners enrolled in mixed-mode
cohorts consisting of both on- and off-campus students (Lee and Chan
2007b). As two students commented:

> [Listening to the podcasts was] like [placing] a phone call to the

lecture[r] to see if I was progressing in the right direction (Lee and Chan 2007b: 96).

. . . as a DE [distance education] student, it's nice to hear a tutor touch on subject matters (Lee and Chan 2007b: 98).

Students also perceived the podcasts as highly beneficial to cognitive aspects of their learning, as shown by their:

- actions in clarifying and enhancing their understanding of the material;
- formative and summative feedback on the podcasts' benefits in providing backup to and reinforcement of what they had learned;
- retrospective reports of how the podcasts were useful in guiding them in planning, and in helping them self-evaluate, their independent study efforts.

Patterns and locations of use

The study at CSU also yielded surprising results about how distance learners used the podcasts (Lee and Chan 2007a). It was anticipated that students would take advantage of being able to transfer the podcasts to portable devices for listening 'on the move'. For example, they might want to listen to podcasts while performing household chores or travelling on public transport. Instead, students preferred to listen to and interact with the podcasts primarily through their computers, and Lee and Chan interviewed some of them to gain deeper insight into why they did so. Interviewees' responses largely indicated that they preferred to give the podcasts their undivided attention, and that they perceived listening as a learning task best performed within a designated study location, usually at home. Students who listened while performing other tasks said their decision was influenced by the fact that the podcasts did not comprise examinable material. At a deeper level, it emerged from the interviews that how students used the podcasts depended on their own individual learning styles, preferences and study strategies. For example, some students reported using the podcasts as pre-study listening material, to preview textbook content or to serve an affective function such as 'mentally preparing' them by setting the mood for their personal study time. Others listened to each podcast repeatedly, initially using a portable device for a 'quick scan' of the material, then moving to a computer for more in-depth concentrated listening in the absence of distractions. Many interviewees said they simply found it cumbersome to transfer the podcasts to portable players: it was not worth the time saved by being able to listen on the move. However, it was not entirely clear what influence the podcasts' design, including their format and length, had on this view. For example, would students find it worth while to transfer longer podcasts, such as full-length lectures, to portable devices?

The study did not show categorically whether the distance students' usage patterns of the podcasts were a result of difficulty they had in absorbing and processing information from multiple concurrent sources, or were simply caused by self-efficacy, which may have been a result of how they were conditioned to learn in their prior studies (for example being told to 'sit and concentrate'). Another plausible explanation for the unexpected results is that the students simply might not have wanted their study to infringe on their personal and professional time, and so consciously chose to demarcate boundaries to keep these aspects of their lives separate (Lee and Chan 2007a).

Case Study 2: University of New England

The School of Law at UNE attracts a diverse cohort of undergraduates. In this study, 1244 students enrolled in six law units during 2006 began using audio podcasts of lectures as a complementary learning strategy, alongside their printed study guides, texts and subject websites. The decision to add podcasts was related to teaching on-campus and distance students concurrently. At the start of the semester, law lecturers podcast their lectures, which varied in length but did not exceed 40 minutes. Podcasts comprising shorter commentaries were also produced. Some lecturers made use of assistance supplied by the Law School's technical support officer, while others familiarized themselves with the tools and technology. In producing the podcasts, minimal amounts of editing and splicing of the raw audio were carried out.

The study, which achieved a 31.2 per cent response rate, is reported on more fully elsewhere (Tynan and Colbran 2006). Most participants were undertaking law degrees, although some were business students. Some participants were enrolled in several target units. The sample reflected the typical diversity of students at UNE in terms of factors such as age, gender, ethnicity, employment status, year and mode of study. None of the participants had had access to lectures via audio delivery, from mobile or other technological devices. Few had had prior experience with podcasting.

Evaluation strategy and outcomes

Students claimed in anecdotes that podcasts helped them in their learning and reduced isolation they experienced due to studying at a distance. The Law School sought evidence to back these claims, and to this end established a research team in conjunction with UNE's Teaching and Learning Centre and the Institutional Research and Planning directorates. What were the benefits or otherwise of the podcasts? As Eash states:

> . . . the fact that the podcast is a new format isn't reason enough to use it . . . Instead, [there is a need to] ask questions. Is a portable audio format the best for this task? How does the podcast support . . . [the instructional] . . . goals? How does a podcast enhance student learning? (Eash 2006: 18).

Many distance students could not be present at lectures, while on-campus students were not required to attend them and often had competing demands on their time. Nearly half of the law students in this study wanted more flexibility in how they undertook their studies, which supported the researchers' belief that lectures at a fixed time and place were incongruent with their lives. The researchers set out to take a closer look at the experience of the large cohort of law students; this exercise also helped to substantiate their aforementioned claims, as well as allowing comparisons to be made with the assertions of other authors and the findings of studies involving smaller groups of students. Podcasting was thought to be a pragmatic way of ensuring that all students regardless of their mode of study could receive the lectures.

The evaluation procedure consisted of a number of stages. First, the research team collected data via a 39-question web-based survey, given the large number of students (Tynan and Colbran 2006). Second, the entire responding sample of students was invited to participate in follow-up, online focus groups. Silverman (n.d.) provides useful guidance for researchers wishing to pursue this approach. The team sorted participants randomly into groups, and conducted a single coordinated session for each group using a discussion board. Discussion in the focus groups was based on the quantitative results: this was to draw out examples of how students were using the podcasts in their own study, and to ascertain whether this use was effective in improving and/or enhancing their learning. A research assistant ran a total of 12 focus groups to minimize bias by the researchers and promote objectivity in the data obtained. The groups consisted of no less than three participants each and were held in real time to a predetermined schedule. They produced valuable qualitative results: detailed text analysis and coding of data is still being carried out.

While the research methods and instruments in this case were different to those used in the CSU case study, they too revealed that the podcasting activity yielded benefits for the learning process. UNE participants noted that the podcasts 'provide[d] external [distance] students with the same opportunities as internal [on-campus] students' and that they enabled community building in the sense of involvement with the subject, by supplying a source of 'focus and motivation, a feeling of being part of the class' (Tynan and Colbran 2006: 832). In the words of one student:

> They [the podcasts] bring subjects alive, allow a lecturer to bring in their own experiences and personality to make subjects more memorable, and bring more humanity to what can be fairly dry material. It can be soul destroying, reading rule upon rule, with no navigator to draw it all together and make it real (Tynan and Colbran 2006: 832).

Like the CSU study, the UNE study also revealed surprising results in some areas. Seventy-six per cent of the survey respondents listened to podcasts on their desktop computer at home. Again, this was unexpected given the rapid uptake of mobile devices among students. Students rated the podcasts very highly: they viewed listening to them as valuable to their learning and an effective use of study time. The ability to pause the podcasts to refer to other materials, and to replay sections of the audio, was cited as being highly beneficial. Being able to manage their own time also helped the distance students to avoid falling behind – this was consistent with anecdotal evidence that they wanted more control and flexibility in their study.

Students often transcribed the podcasts and reported this as an additional benefit in the learning process. Many used the podcasts similarly to face-to-face lectures and took notes while listening. Over 32 per cent of respondents indicated that they now spent more time on study than previously. The podcasts thus provided additional motivation for engaging with the learning material and with the law subjects at large.

Emerging themes from the case studies

Increasing learner motivation and engagement

Durbridge (1984: 100) emphasizes the distinct pedagogical advantages of audio, stating that '[a]s compared with a written text, the spoken word can influence both cognition (adding clarity and meaning) and motivation (by conveying directly a sense of the person creating those words)'. In both case studies, the distance students reported that being able to hear what tutors or peers were discussing was highly motivating. They saw increased engagement with the topic at hand through multiple modalities and perspectives as a key motivating aspect of listening to the podcasts. In addition, it is evident from the case studies that learner control (Dron 2007) is of paramount importance to motivating and engaging distance students.

Facilitating and enhancing learning outcomes

In both case studies, distance students' study habits altered through interaction with the podcasts, which they viewed as an effective tool or resource to complement their learning. For example, students used the podcasts to prepare mentally to study and to supplement other learning activities in their revision and preparation for formative and summative assessment tasks. At UNE, students used the lecture podcasts to revisit ideas and, through writing notes, to explore the subject matter in different ways. As one UNE student reported: 'I used to spend more time reading and wasting time figuring out the key areas of the subjects when I really just needed someone to give me an overview to put all my reading into context'. Similarly, a CSU student remarked that the podcasts '[b]ridge[d] the learning gap between [his] perceptions of what [he] read and what [was] actually required' (Lee and Chan 2007b: 96), while another said that they helped to clarify the '. . . exact details about the assignments, [so that she could] focus [her] work on . . .

[achieving] ... exactly what the lecture[r was] expecting' (Lee and Chan 2007b: 96).

Both case studies also suggest that improved student learning outcomes are possible through the appropriate use of podcasts. Students resoundingly acknowledged that being able to hear what their lecturers or peers were saying improved their comprehension of the subject material. It can be seen that podcasting can cater for a range of learning styles, and can empower students to choose and personalize how they undertake their study.

Mobility and lifestyle learning

Podcasts for mobile learning would seem to be a natural fit for distance education, particularly given the busy lifestyles of many distance learners, who must manage competing priorities. Although other digital media forms are becoming increasingly viable with portable video players, 3G mobile phones and smart phones, users' true mobility is restricted when they have to fix their gaze on a screen. Listening, by contrast, 'frees eyes and hands' (Clark and Walsh 2004: 8) to perform other tasks. Thus, 'iPod-learning' (Clark and Walsh 2004: 8) enables students to integrate learning with other activities, perhaps paving the way for truly pervasive, lifestyle-integrated mobile learning. It can cater for the unique work-style requirements of mobile workers, who form a large proportion of current and potential distance learners (Yuen and Wang 2004).

In both case studies, however, participants preferred to listen to the podcasts using a desktop/laptop computer at home, and dedicated time to doing so rather than listening in parallel with other activities. These unanticipated findings make us wary of extrapolations of how students' day-to-day uses of technology like mobile devices for work and leisure will carry over into formal learning settings.

Fostering a sense of community

There appears to be considerable scope to 'close the gap' and promote a sense of real community for distance learners. Podcasting may have potential for creating an inclusive learning environment that morphs the difference between an on-campus and distance education cohort. The researchers in both case studies believe that podcasting can form part of a practical solution to mitigate issues that result from distance learners' physical separation from their tutors, classmates and the university. Used appropriately, podcasting can play an assistive role in 're-integrating' (Keegan 1996: 116) the teacher–learner transaction in distance education, as well as facilitating peer-to-peer interaction and exchange to foster a sense of belonging to and involvement in an academic learning community. Doing so was a goal in both case studies and appears on some levels to have been achieved. Furthermore, there may be opportunities to reduce attrition, a major issue for distance cohorts and their institutions.

Conclusion

The two case studies presented in this chapter demonstrate that podcasting can provide a flexible option for the delivery of content to distance learners, and that it adds yet another modality of learning. The technology is enjoying a continually growing level of interest and uptake at many universities, but the literature advocating its educational uses is largely rhetorical. While there is no shortage of material on how to make podcasts and plenty of enthusiasm for using them, there is currently a paucity of hard empirical evidence of their actual benefits for learners and learning. The two case studies and the emerging themes drawn from them offer real insight into the characteristics, needs and preferences of distance learners when it comes to podcasting. It is hoped that they will serve as a valuable starting point for others wishing to pursue this line of research.

Longitudinal large-scale research is still needed that targets podcasting's unique capabilities and features while taking into account and building on previous research involving older or pre-existing audio technologies. Most studies to date are isolated and highly contextualized, rather than being generalizable to a variety of learning environments and audiences. Distance education cohorts have much to gain from the opportunities afforded, but it remains to be seen whether educational uses of podcasting will be grounded in theory and sound pedagogy.

10

Podcasts and resources

*Brian Cox, Raymond Macharia, Nick Short and
Kim Whittlestone*

Summary

Digital technologies offer a new way of bringing many older, but not outdated, resources into the 21st century, and a great opportunity for students
to integrate different parts of the curriculum into their learning. This
chapter describes the use of a novel technique to develop mobile podcasts
consisting of digital animated videos of old anatomical specimen pots with
an accompanying audio commentary. The purpose was to transform
museum specimens into 3D video podcasts to depict structures and tissues in
a particular area of the body. We coined the terms 'potcast' and 'potcasting'
to describe these reincarnated anatomy pots.

Context

The Royal Veterinary College (RVC) is the oldest veterinary school in the
English-speaking world with a history of educating veterinary surgeons for
well over 200 years. In recent years the College, like all the other UK veterinary schools, has seen a significant increase in student intake, causing problems in providing sufficient educational support for and access to anatomy
and pathology museums and dissection rooms. These facilities house a wide
range of important teaching resources including histological, anatomical
and pathological examples, and radiographic media.

Many of the older resources, such as anatomical dissections, histology
slides and specimen pots, while still of great value for teaching, are now
underused. This underuse is partly a result of reduced tutoring support for
large student cohorts, but it may also represent a view among staff that old
media, such as dissections carried out in the last century, are no longer of
relevance today. This reduced use of tried and tested methods can have a
negative impact on teaching, especially as veterinary education is so dependent on active and visual learning. For example, early in the course students

need to learn how to interpret histological slides and relate these to normal anatomical specimens. They then need to develop this knowledge to appreciate the abnormal, through viewing pathological gross specimens and microscopic slides. Finally, they go on to learn how to treat some of these problems by developing an understanding of surgical and medical procedures.

Veterinary and medical students often see learning anatomy as a mammoth task, requiring them to memorize large quantities of out-of-date material with no relevance to the real world, but a task that needs to be done to pass the exam. As highlighted by Cake (2006: 266), 'This perception is unfortunate, as a deeper evaluation reveals a beautifully ordered discipline rich in fundamental developmental concepts, underlying principles, and patterns that describe the basic "design" of the body'. Cake goes on to argue that traditional approaches to anatomy teaching (group classes based around dissected, prosected or museum specimens) are inherently educationally sound in that they provide the mechanism to facilitate active learning. What he identifies as a missing key factor in encouraging deep approaches (Ramsden 1992) to learning anatomy is student motivation, which depends in turn on students having a positive relationship with the course and their teachers.

E-learning at the RVC

Over the past five years the RVC has seen a rapid adoption of digital technologies to support teaching and learning. As in many other institutions, it began with PowerPoint presentations and computer-aided learning programmes in a Virtual Learning Environment (VLE) and evolved quickly into more sophisticated approaches, such as the use of communication and collaboration tools in online courses. Digital audio and video technologies increasingly have been used to enhance older forms of e-learning. Affordable digital dictaphones and video cameras are now available with a recording quality suitable for use in education, with easy access for staff to PCs and software with the processing power and storage capacity to rapidly edit, store and broadcast digital media. Improved networks, including broadband and campus local area networks and the use of a streaming server, mean that relatively large video files can now be viewed in an acceptable time. With lower prices and improved quality, portable audio and video players are now widely used by students to access both entertainment and educational content. Faster and more powerful hardware enable staff to record, edit and publish digital media simply and quickly. Most are familiar with digital video cameras at home and feel more comfortable in using new digital teaching resources. They are more prepared to get involved with technical staff in recording and creating material. Equally, most RVC students are now competent users of digital media: they are the new intake of 'digital natives', a term coined by Prensky (2001: 1), who claims that students think and process information in fundamentally different ways from their predecessors, because they have grown up using technology as an everyday part of their lives. Over 90 per cent of the RVC's 2007 intake had their own notebook computer and MP3 player, regularly downloaded music from the internet using packages such as Apple's iTunes and shared video files on sites such as YouTube. The College now provides video iPods on weekly loan from the library for students who cannot afford to purchase one.

At the RVC all academic staff and students are enrolled in the Blackboard Academic Suite. This VLE is currently hosted on a Blackboard server in the Netherlands and is shared with the five other institutions within the Bloomsbury Colleges' consortium. Until recently all the RVC teaching resources were uploaded onto Blackboard including lecture notes, assessments, computer-aided learning programs and video. But video and audio files have been increasingly moved over to a Windows streaming server with links to the relevant courses in Blackboard, providing significantly faster access to audio files and the ability to watch high-quality video without having to download large files to a local drive.

The VLE's functionality has been extended through adding a podcast publishing and a Really Simple Syndication (RSS) feed tool (Office LX), which allows podcasts and videocasts on the streaming server to be linked to specific modules or courses in the VLE. Students accessing a particular course can then opt to subscribe to the relevant iTunes or RSS feed, enabling them to synchronize their iPod, MP3 player or laptop with a module feed and automatically download recordings that have been loaded onto the streaming server. The great advantage with this approach is that various audio files (such as recorded lectures) and video feeds (for example surgical procedures) can be downloaded together as and when they are required within the taught curriculum.

These developments in e-learning have contributed to the rapid uptake of podcasting at the College: in 2004 few academics were aware of what could be done, but today they treat it as commonplace and it is increasingly in demand by students. The RVC has experimented with novel approaches to podcasting. Examples are summarized below:

Research podcasts consist of 30-minute interviews with research and teaching staff at the College, describing their specialist interests. The podcasts are recorded using digital microphones directly onto a dictaphone or PC and edited on either a Mac or PC using Audacity or Adobe Auditions. The files are converted into enhanced podcasts with Apple's GarageBand. Finally, the edited files are uploaded onto iTunes and also made available as M4A (enhanced podcast format) file downloads from the RVC website. To date 16 podcasts have been published and these are consistently the most popular veterinary downloads on iTunes.

Audio lectures are recordings, made by students, of standard lectures. They are recorded using an Olympus digital dictaphone which the students ask the lecturers to carry on a lanyard or in a shirt pocket. The students then do a basic edit of the recording on their personal PC or Mac using Audacity. The final MP3 files are uploaded onto a dedicated streaming server and linked in to the relevant PowerPoint files and RSS feeds in Blackboard. Student volunteers are now recording most lectures on all taught undergraduate courses at the College.

Videocasts include videos of key anatomical dissections, surgical procedures, seminars, animal handling and technical procedures. They vary in length from a full 30-minute video of a dog castration to a 5-minute sequence of taking a blood sample. Most are done in one take using a tripod-based mini DV camcorder, a remote Senhauser lapel microphone and extra light sources. In more complex sequences such as a dissection, several different camera angles may have to be used. These videos are also linked into courses in Blackboard in a similar way to the audio lectures.

Radiographic animations are created using a new technique developed at the College. A radiograph or X-ray is filmed with a digitally superimposed annotation or colouring of key structures. A voice-over from the subject expert explains the features being illustrated in the image. Each recording is up to five minutes long and can be viewed using a laptop or an iPod. These animations are a popular resource for students who often find it difficult to interpret a radiograph on first viewing and need to review the image in their own time.

Developing potcasts

'Potcasts' were a natural progression from the audio and video examples. Each is based on a four- or five-minute annotated video of anatomical specimen pots, with a voice-over commentary by an academic. The video is captured by filming the specimen while the academic uses a light pointer to indicate the key anatomical landmarks being described. The landmarks are highlighted by overlaying transient areas of colour onto the video image to make the anatomical structures stand out. In some cases, the videos are enhanced with arrows and text. The annotated video files are saved in .wmv and .mp4 formats and published on a streaming server with links to Blackboard courses and a dynamic web page. The files can then be viewed by clicking on the web links, or downloaded onto a hard disk, or synchronized with an iPod or laptop through Blackboard. The advantage of the last approach is that students are then able to visit the anatomical museum with their mobile device and view a description of the specimen pots, which they might be examining (see Figure 10.1).

The first topic area to be covered by the potcasts was chosen after a focus group with second-year veterinary students to determine which areas of anatomy they found most difficult to visualize. The module on the head was

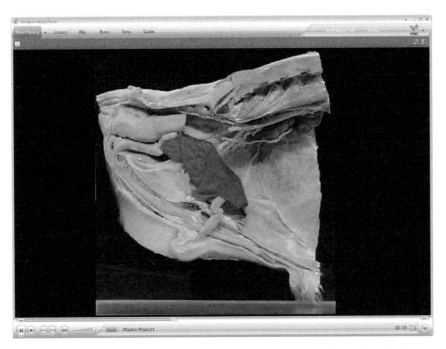

Figure 10.1 A potcast image demonstrating structures in the pelvis of a male dog specimen

selected, because it involves understanding multiple complex systems including the central nervous system, the visual system, the muscles of mastication, the respiratory system, the digestive system and the sound production system. It is taught in a four-week block, through a series of lectures, practical sessions, integrated structure and function (ISF) sessions and directed learning sessions. About 100 specimen pots in the anatomy museum are relevant to this module, but not extensively used by students.

The practical step-by-step approach to capturing a potcast is detailed below:

1. Set the perspex museum pot in good light with a video camera pointing at the relevant surface. Ensure the perspex is free from fingerprints and other dirt.
2. Run the video camera while the lecturer is talking and point to structures within the pot using a laser pointer.
3. Capture the first frame from the video – the 'clean' frame (that is, no laser pointer) – and open in Photoshop.
4. Watch the video and create a new layer on top of the clean frame in Adobe Photoshop for each area highlighted. Use the red paint tool at 50 per cent opacity to draw the shape of the structures being discussed.
5. Save the file in Adobe Photoshop's .psd format.
6. Import the video into Adobe Premiere and edit the audio as necessary.

7.   Import the .psd file from Photoshop with all the layers (each layer becomes a track in Adobe Premiere).
8.   Stretch the first frame of the pot to cover the full length of the audio (then turn that layer off).
9.   Watch the video and position each overlay track in the correct time position.
10. Apply a fade-in, fade-out to each overlay track.
11. Turn off the video layer and turn on the still image of the pot.
12. Export a full quality version of the video for archive purposes in .avi format.
13. Export a windows media format (.wmv) for website.
14. Convert the .wmv file into a .mp4 for use on an iPod (320×240, 300kb/sec, lowest quality) using Cleaner XL or similar tool and upload onto a streaming server.

Educational value and lessons learned

The Informal Mobile Podcasting And Learning Adaptation (IMPALA) team evaluated the RVC anatomy potcasting initiative. Six students who had used the potcasts met for about 40 minutes as a focus group, conducted using a semi-structured interview schedule to explore how student learning was supported by the potcasts. Staff experience of developing podcasts was gathered through an interview with the lecturer who developed them. Conversations with students and staff were recorded on a digital recorder and transcribed verbatim for analysis to identify key themes and issues.

Access to content

At the simplest level, this analysis indicated that potcasts provide students with easy access to content, enabling them to prepare for sessions, reinforce their learning and revise for assessments. Students' comments in the focus group highlighted these uses.

> Yeah that's the good thing is that you can watch it as many times as you like, we have like "Integrated Structure and Function" and things and they are really helpful at the time but I find that afterwards I come away and forget the whole thing. If you can just go back and play it again, you can look at it whenever really and write things down.

> It's like being in "Dissection" again, because obviously you're in "Dissection" and there's so much to look at and you forget some stuff, so if then you're watching a potcast, they're doing it all over again and you're like 'oh yes of course that's where it was'. But if you didn't have that you might just forget.

And I watched them after we'd done the dissection because they went back over it and I could say oh that was that bit. Because sometimes you can look at something for ages, not know what it is and then you've got the lecturers helping you like. So you can go and find it afterwards, its quite useful in that respect.

And it's also a bit simpler I think, hearing someone speak everyday language rather than textbook language. It's a lot more friendly and you remember it better.

Working in new ways

Potcasts were accessible anytime and anywhere, allowing students to work in new ways, for example when doing an anatomical dissection. Students commented that they watched the potcasts at home in the evening and the day before a dissection class. Being able to choose the time and place to watch empowered these students.

I always tend to look at things at home anyway because I'd be much more relaxed in my own environment and I feel you're not under any pressure to look at it in a particular time you just look at it at your leisure.

I sometimes take notes of stuff that I didn't know before, and then they talk about. Normally I pause it, write a bit down, play again, pause, write a bit down.

It's so much quicker as well, to read through a few pages takes a long time, but to actually see it and hear it at the same time is just a lot quicker.

I was going to say they tend to cover the sort of key points but compacted as opposed to spending two or three hours in dissection, you'd get the main bits of what you need to know in ten minutes or something.

Better quality of contact with lecturer

Interestingly, these students felt they were getting a better quality of contact with the lecturer through the potcasts than in the dissection class. They also described feeling positive towards the lecturers who had put in the effort to create the potcasts.

Well up until now, like in the dissections we haven't had much tuition; like we've been given a list of things to do and then we just have to get on with it ourselves, whereas now we actually have someone talking us through.

Yeah it was better, there's a lot less lecturers than there are groups so they can't spend the whole time with one group, so with the podcasts, it's like spending that one to one time with the lecturer rather than them just coming over for five minutes.

Yeah it's nice – the ones that do podcasts, you feel they sort of care a bit more because they're helping us with the podcasts. You feel like they actually want you to learn.

This positive student–lecturer relationship helps to foster students' intrinsic motivation, which has been identified by Cake (2006) as a key factor in encouraging deeper approaches to learning anatomy. The potcasts seem to be conveying the enthusiasm of the lecturer in a way that students feel is lacking in the traditional dissection class sessions. This ability to stimulate and convey a sense of their own interest in a subject was identified by Small-wood (2004) as one of the most important instructor traits for facilitating student confidence and independence.

Cognitive mechanisms

Learning anatomy is a cognitively intensive task, involving a new vocabulary for most students, dexterity to perform dissection, an appreciation of 3D space and an ability to store representations of these spaces that can be transferred into new situations. Anything that interferes with these processes interferes with students' learning. Moreno and Mayer (1999) demonstrated that students presented with narration and graphics were able to recall twice as much as students presented with text and graphics. Levinson et al. (2007) showed that students performed best in post-tests on brain anatomy when taught using key views rather than multiple views, especially students with low-spatial ability.

In dissection, students explore 3D space, but they have to work out what all the structures are, how they relate to each other and then create a mental map of this information. With some help to hand from anatomy demonstrators, their main guide has been a textbook or handout. Students doing the dissection have had to refer back, constantly, to these printed guides. With potcasts, which they carry with them on a mobile device, the anatomy is narrated and students can concentrate on annotated and animated graphics that help them remember a key view of the anatomy. They can then recall that key view in new contexts such as during dissections or surgical procedures in real time.

These issues are alluded to in a conversation between students involved in the evaluation:

In the dissections when you are watching someone, it's quite hard to see what's going on but [in the potcasts] the camera work is really good, it's really focused, really light and you can see right up close really clearly. That's another thing, in class he points to things with a pointer which is the only thing they can do but on the screen they actually highlight it with a like, I don't know a marker.

It's clearer.

So you can see exactly what they are talking about, it's really good.

It sticks in your head a lot quicker I think.

Same, for revision, I think that will be our main difference with revision this year because last year we didn't have them. It was really hard to revise anatomy because to see it 2D in a book is one thing but to see it when it's been filmed is a lot more helpful.

This last comment is revealing: this particular student perceives the videos to be better than '2D in a book', suggesting that they have a 3D quality that helps when learning anatomy.

Conclusions and future developments

Anticipating the potential impact of e-learning in veterinary education is difficult because of the rapid and unpredictable advances in technology, but it is clear that digital media are here to stay and will be delivered wirelessly at faster rates, through more sophisticated devices, and at ever more affordable costs. Digital audio downloads (and recently video) have become mainstream with the advent of widespread broadband access, easy-to-use software such as iTunes and affordable digital media players. In education, these technologies offer exciting opportunities to reach out to learners in new and sometimes surprising ways.

At the RVC more than 30 staff members now use digital technologies, although most did not own an MP3 player and were not previously familiar with podcasting. This relatively simple and accessible technology draws on existing teaching resources in new and effective ways. Factors behind its early success included the active support of learning technology staff and peer endorsement.

The students have been enthusiastic from the outset. They appreciated that digital recordings would enable them to prepare for lectures and practicals, revise after a teaching session and catch up if they were forced to miss part of the course (for example due to illness). Students also played an active role in capturing podcasts and videocasts including a first-year student who recorded, edited and published almost all the lectures on a degree course. This advocacy by the students had a significant effect in providing positive feedback to academics, further encouraging them to allow recording of their lectures and practicals. The RVC has demonstrated some of the potential of podcasting and videocasting.

New generations of digital natives now entering university have grown up using digital and social media as part of their lives and expect education to embrace these technological approaches. The RVC is extending to the wider curriculum some of the projects described here. A major and under-exploited attraction of podcasting and videocasting is that they can be shared with other institutions, with an opportunity to create central repositories of resources, particularly those demonstrating best practice, for use by students on multiple campuses. Universities may be able to identify new income streams through selling content to other institutions or through subscription services for lifelong learners, provided that the institutions can maintain the support and involvement of students and staff. Continued pedagogical research into the impact of these new approaches will be needed, to refine methodologies and to reassure fellow academics that the technology will enhance and support their teaching, not threaten it.

As a final comment from the lecturer involved shows, the potential of potcasts for teaching and self-study is still evolving:

So in other words, it becomes a teaching tool as well, a kind of inter-active tool. You are using it to teach at the same time as asking the students a certain question that might provoke their thinking into more critical thinking. I feel our teaching will be much better, it will be more creative for the students, it will be more interactive and I think that the investment in terms of time, is valid. In other words, the students will be able to interact with the material, they'll be able to learn more and will be able to think even more critically and not only that, you have kind of an integration, they'll be able to bring that structure they're looking at and link it with some other materials that they'll be doing in later years, or their clinical years.

11

Podcasts and students' storytelling

Martin Jenkins and Jo Lonsdale

Summary

This chapter reports on the use of digital storytelling as a means of encouraging student engagement and reflection. We piloted the use of digital stories, which are student-generated MP3 files combined with digital photographs, in several disciplines and contexts at the University of Gloucestershire in 2006 and 2007. Our evaluations show that staff and students have found this approach to be a positive experience in encouraging student creativity. The nature of the stories created raised issues about how to evaluate student reflection and progression when using this approach. We explore these issues through a case study of students' storytelling as part of undergraduates' induction into Higher Education (HE).

Storytelling using podcasting

Storytelling has many uses in education. In particular Moon (2006) notes how stories can be used as a means of facilitating learning, encouraging connections in the minds of students. Storytelling provides a potentially powerful approach for students to make their learning explicit and to give meaning to their experiences (Nygren and Blom 2001). The construction of a story is a cognitive process that requires the individual, or group, to make judgements and inferences: 'about discrete items of information and the adequacy of the unfolding story. Selecting, comparing, inferring, arranging and revising are activities which we regard as cognitive strategies' (Robinson and Hawpe 1986: 116). Creating a story can be seen as 'effective causal thinking' (Robinson and Hawpe 1986: 112).

Within storytelling there are different oral and written traditions. The oral tradition is more personal, presenting the personal voice and many stories within cultures are handed down allowing scope for development as the story is retold. Storytelling is a social process. Written stories need to stand alone as they are separated from the writer; this is seen to encourage 'a more reflected expression' (Nygren and Blom 2001: 373).

Digital storytelling provides a means of combining elements of both oral and written traditions and enabling 'the modern expression of the ancient art of storytelling (in which) stories derive their power by weaving images, music, narrative and voice together, giving deep dimension and vivid colour to characters, situations, experiences and insights' (Leslie Rule of the American Digital Storytelling Association, quoted in Crow 2006: 1). Digital storytelling is a tool that uses technology in an environment that is enjoyable and student-centred (McDrury and Alterio 2003; J.S. Brown 2005). It offers ways for students to contextualize and improve their learning and digital skills.

Digital stories are media artefacts combining still images and MP3 files. Using the Informal Mobile Podcasting And Learning Adaptation (IMPALA) model of podcasting (see Chapter 15), digital storytelling can be classified as a variant of podcasting with particular emphasis on students as developers, the medium as a video 'podcast' (using still images) and its purpose to develop active learning.

At the heart of digital storytelling is the development of the narrative. Our approach to developing digital stories involved the development of this narrative through student collaboration with technology to enable a fresh approach to student engagement and reflection. This way enables students to explore and develop communication and expressive skills using images, text, sounds and sequences and gives them a chance to develop a new literacy.

Students in the digital age

The use of digital storytelling acknowledges the claim that many younger students learn differently than previous generations of university students. They may seek to use technologies in which they are already conversant (Prensky 2001; Oblinger 2003). Many such students are now regular users of social networking sites, such as Facebook and MySpace, and contribute their own stories in digital form.

Older and non-traditional students are considered 'digital immigrants' and less used to new technologies (Prensky 2001). However, these students may be comfortable with the use of 'story' as a medium and a means of engagement (Moon 2006). They can be helped to use newer technology by collaborative working (Oblinger 2003).

Use of digital storytelling

Drawing on the educational benefits of storytelling as a technique, staff and students at the University of Gloucestershire tried digital storytelling in 2006 and 2007 in a variety of contexts. Table 11.1 illustrates some example uses, mapped against the variables from the IMPALA model (see Chapter 15).

Table 11.1 Example uses of digital storytelling at the University of Gloucestershire (2006 and 2007)

IMPALA VARIABLES	*Environment (Student induction (transitions into HE) activity (Jenkins and Lynch 2006))*	*Landscape design (Used to encourage reflection on developing design ideas and the use of models)*	*Accountancy (Used as a means of presentation for a first-year skills module)*	*Sports development (Second-year students reflecting on how their chosen sport has influenced their own personal development)*	*Leisure, tourism and hospitality (Final-year students using this technique to reflect on a critical incident from their industrial placement)*
Purpose	Develop active learning; reflection	Develop active learning; assessment; reflection	Assessment	Develop active learning; reflection	Develop critical reflection
Convergence	Stand alone	Stand alone	Stand alone	Stand alone	Stand alone
Developer	Students working in groups of 5–6	Individual student	Students working in groups of 5–6	Individual student	Individual student
Medium	Video	Video	Video	Video	Video
Reusability	Temporary	Temporary	Temporary	Temporary	Resource for future students
Structure	Focused on specific event	Developed across a whole module	Specific assessment activity	Specific assessment activity	Specific activity
Length	Short (2–3 minutes)	Short (2–3 minutes)	Short (5–15 minutes)	Short (5–10 minutes)	Short (3–5 minutes)
Style	Informal	Informal	Informal	Informal	Informal
Capacity	Over 100 students	Small group (6 students)	Personal tutor groups (15 students)	Module size – 40 students	Small group (6 students)
Frequency	Once	Once	Once	Once	Once

EXAMPLES

Evaluation by staff and students of digital storytelling

We evaluated the use of digital storytelling through staff focus groups and interviews to gather evidence of the quality of student work produced. We gathered student feedback for our induction case study through a questionnaire and focus group interviews. Here we report the qualitative feedback from focus groups.

Student feedback on the use of digital stories was mainly positive. Student comments show that stories were welcomed as offering a very different approach to what they had expected at the induction week.

> The production of the digital story and reflection of what we had done . . . I found it really enjoyable and a new take on an evaluation for the day (student A from induction activity).

The approach challenged students to consider how they presented their ideas, drawing out storytelling as a process that encouraged them to explain their learning, including the emotional aspect:

> . . . you look at emotions where to begin with you just kind of say what happened, but when you're telling it as a story to other people you kind of think about your feelings, rather than just what happened (leisure, hospitality and tourism student B).

The simple technologies involved helped make the digital storytelling readily accessible; students found them easy to use and that they encouraged discussion:

> Actually putting it together – we spent lots of time talking about it – but . . . producing the piece of work didn't take that long at all (leisure, hospitality and tourism student C).

Where students were under time pressure to complete the digital story, their answers revealed less satisfaction, as a comment from a student who experienced this time pressure illustrates:

> Digital story we were forced to do at end seemed rushed and pointless (student from induction activity D).

Staff views of the impact of digital storytelling on student learning focused on student engagement, suitability for task and the quality of the outputs. Staff considered that the storytelling technique presented successful opportunities for creativity:

> This is the only assessment we have run where students have written to thank us for the assessment . . . so I have some confidence that it has engaged the students (sport development tutor 1).

I think I'd say really it was the enjoyment. The joy of the process that they conveyed (accountancy tutor 2).

The approach shows evidence of allowing students to push their own individual boundaries:

We had one hugely challenging, interesting, enjoyable piece of work that was a story in the true sense – it was a fiction but it was based on the student's life and values (sport development tutor 2).

In common with students, staff found that, where there was very limited time to use this technique, it impacted upon output, with comments expressing a desire for more time, both in planning and implementation:

I think the digital story telling reflection would have worked better if the students had had more time to reflect . . . choose photos (induction tutor 1).

Time for staff to do preparation needed – far too little this year. Part of that, to build in time for digital storytelling (induction tutor 2).

Staff saw the use of digital stories as having a wider potential and other disciplines in our university are now considering using them in sociology, social work and theology. However, where stories have been used to encourage a focus on student reflection some staff expressed concern:

We tend not to have any marks allocated to this reflective element . . . because the module content is not about the learning process . . . it's about subject content (induction tutor 3).

The positive comments reflect the educational value in students producing digital stories that can also have value as resource for further reflection. The telling of the digital stories in a peer-learning forum gives students a chance to connect with the thought processes of others, and supports 'scaffolding'; a temporary support mechanism to develop learning (Garrison and Anderson 2003: 88). Formal critiquing, by staff and students, of stories can enhance reflective learning, and may assist the voicing of student's tacit understandings. The accountancy students critique their own work alongside their peers. The tutor for the accountancy module observed:

the students . . . almost watch it (the podcast) again with our eyes because they were commenting on it as well which is not something that normally happens in the traditional way – they just stand up and get it over with and don't really want to think about it again, but they were quite critical, more so than was appropriate actually. Like – if we did it again, we'd do this bit differently – and so on. Yes, it was very good from that point of view it forced them, well not forced them, it encouraged them all to reflect on what the purpose of such a thing might be and how it could be used so (accountancy tutor 2).

Evaluating the educational impact

Case Study: Using digital storytelling during induction

The University of Gloucestershire's approach to active learning is supported and promoted through the Centre for Active Learning (CeAL www.glos.ac.uk/ceal/index.cfm). CeAL focuses on inquiry in the field, studio, laboratory and classrooms, using authentic sites and community-related and employer-linked activities. Active learning is seen as more than learning by doing: 'learning is the process whereby knowledge is created through the transformation of experience' (Kolb 1984: 38). Students are enabled to construct theoretical understanding by reflection on their activities and experiences, in communities of active learners where staff and students inquire together. This approach has been developed from the Kolb experiential learning cycle (Kolb 1984) and the performances of understanding (Blythe and Associates 1998).

The University's Department of Natural and Social Sciences, in conjunction with the CeAL, introduced a specialized induction for students to assist in their transition to HE through social learning. A one-week event ran in each of the years 2004, 2005, 2006 and 2007. The event aimed to provide an enjoyable, relaxed learning experience that introduces students to active learning, offers the opportunity to meet staff and fellow students, helps students develop social networks, learn skills and develop their independence. The week's activities include group work and a scenario related to the discipline. The intent is to 'embed students in a rich . . . . . learning community built around a practice' (J.S. Brown 2005: 25) where students can share artefacts and enthusiasms enabling the early formation of communities and the beginnings of 'learning-to-be' alongside 'learning-about' (J.S. Brown 2005: 26). The induction week is linked to a compulsory semester 1 skills module that seeks to further develop and embed skills.

In 2006, the theme was sustainability. Digital storytelling was first introduced as a technique to encourage and embed student reflection on the activities in which they were engaged (McDrury and Alterio 2003). This field-based activity at the end of the week was the focus of their group reflections.

Students were prepared for the fieldwork through a series of briefings and preparation activities, including training sessions for digital storytelling. They were introduced to guiding protocols based on those used on *Capture Wales*, a digital storytelling project run by BBC Wales (www.bbc.co.uk/wales/capturewales). Students were first shown some existing digital stories and were provided with digital cameras and laptops. The stories were to be a maximum of 250 words and two minutes in duration. Students recorded their audio directly onto the laptops using Audacity software. For logistical reasons, and because it was our first attempt at using the technique, the students were asked to create only the components of their digital story: the story, as an MP3 file, and the pictures that would illustrate it. The completed stories were put together the next day by CeAL staff using Windows Movie

Maker and shown to students at a social event on the last day of induction week.

Impact on student reflection

The students generated 29 digital stories. To evaluate the extent to which the stories provided evidence of student reflection, we rated them against Moon's map of learning (Moon 1999), which was developed as a means of 'analysing the events of learning in order to locate reflection' (Moon 1999: 152). The five different levels provide a means of representing reflection in the students' learning processes. We also used the Model of Reflective Learning through Storytelling (McDrury and Alterio 2003) that represents how individuals identify, tell and build on their story. Important in the McCrury model's latter stages is how stories can be expanded and amended through collaborative processes (McKillop 2005).

Table 11.2 shows the different categories for these two models.

Table 11.2 Categories for Moon's Map of Learning (1999) and McDrury and Alterio's Model of Reflective Learning (2003)

Moon's Map of Learning	McDrury and Alterio's Model of Reflective Learning
Level 1: Noticing	Story Finding
Level 2: Making Sense	Story Telling
Level 3: Making Meaning	Story Expanding
Level 4: Working with Meaning	Story Processing
Level 5: Transformative Learning	Story Reconstructing

Moon's map of learning (1999) proved the more useful for our digital story process and our analysis ultimately focused on this model. Because of the way our stories were developed, we were not able to evaluate the collaboration represented by the McDrury and Alterio's (2003) but intend to do so in future. In evaluating the impact of each story, we took into account the narrative, the use of images including their relevance, the technical competence in producing the story, including reference to the protocols provided; and its emotional impact.

Table 11.3 shows that 13 stories demonstrated 'noticing', level 1 in Moon's model. McDrury and Alterio (2003: 45) see students operating at this level of Moon's model functioning as surface learners. Their learning is influenced by their prior knowledge, their emotional response to the learning event, what they perceive the purpose to be and how it is presented to them. Twelve of the stories were at level 2, 'making sense'. These students were not yet starting to make connections with prior knowledge and experience. The three stories at level 3, 'making meaning', demonstrate connections missing at level 2. One story reached level 4, 'working with meaning', where

Table 11.3 Number of stories from 2006 induction per category rated against Moon's Map of Learning (1999)

Level	Induction (group stories)
Level 1: Noticing	13
Level 2: Making Sense	12
Level 3: Making Meaning	3
Level 4: Working with Meaning	1
Level 5: Transformative Learning	0

reflection and problem-solving were evident, and students' judgements were based upon these.

We expected our evaluation to find concentrations at the lower levels, given that these students were only on their fourth day at university! However, we were heartened by evidence of 'making sense', and in some cases reflection.

The focus in our analysis was been on the induction week's output: the digital podcast. Yet, where digital stories are used for reflection, the learning may not always be immediately apparent as 'narrative models of knowing are models of process in process' (Josselson and Leiblich 1995: 35). Thus, although the stories evidenced some, but not high levels of reflection, they were useful as an engaging focus for collaborative reflection. Such a group process at induction is seen as a means of assisting individual students both in reflecting and in entering the HE student community, although its use does need to be carefully integrated and sufficient time allowed.

Conclusions

The use of digital storytelling in HE is still in its infancy but offers new ways for students to articulate their own experiences, present their work and to reflect upon it. Developing podcasting did not hamper even the 'digital immigrants' and students felt proud of the podcasts they produced.

The digital nature of these podcasts makes them ideal for storage and easy retrieval. Review is possible at regular intervals to make personal and group development explicit, and become part of an organized collection of evidence of reflection. This encourages the acquisition of 'learning-about' and 'learning-to-be' skills (J.S. Brown 2005) for lifelong learning and the development of skilled 21st century citizens.

12

Podcasts and collaborative learning

Libby Rothwell

Summary

This chapter describes a study that sought to integrate informal podcasts with formal face-to-face teaching to support campus-based students' collaborative learning. It was conducted with first-year undergraduates in humanities and social science programmes. I outline the rationale for introducing podcasts as a learning resource, as well as their design and development. I then analyse the impact of podcasts on students' learning experiences and present a model of how podcasts helped students' learning. Finally, I reflect on key issues that I encountered as a novice podcaster.

Aims and objectives

With my colleagues, I had two main pedagogic aims: to help our students get a better understanding of some of the key concepts and theories in intercultural communication and to facilitate collaborative learning and skills development through dialogue. The podcasts would not replace or substantially replicate material delivered in the taught sessions, but would act as optional pre- and post-lecture/seminar learning support. In this way, the podcasts might increase motivation to participate and decrease first-year first-semester anxiety (Chan and Lee 2005).

The format chosen for the podcasts was largely dialogic. Dialogue plays a significant role in teaching and learning processes (Webb et al. 2004; Allen 2005). Laurillard (2002: 87) emphasizes the importance of dialogue for university education and proposes a conversational framework, which considers the teaching learning process as 'an iterative conversation'. According to Webb et al. (2004), dialogue includes instructions, guidance and feedback from teachers, interactions with fellow students and other people, and the learner's own self-reflection. There is a preference among students to work within their own cultural groups. Cultural mixing does not happen spontaneously (Carroll and Ryan 2005). O'Dowd's (2003) intercultural learning project demonstrated the potential of exchanges to improve cross-cultural understanding. Podcasting's spoken exchanges could offer further opportunities for intercultural learning. The UK National Student Survey (NSS) results consistently show a demand for more feedback and more discussion with tutors; podcast dialogues offer another means of responding to this demand.

Podcast content

Since we wanted the podcasts to complement, not replace, the taught sessions, and to motivate students to listen to them, we kept them short and chose a format similar to a radio magazine. The series of audio files, each 8–10 minutes long and featuring more than one speaker, was delivered at fortnightly intervals throughout the semester via the Blackboard Virtual Learning Environment (VLE). The podcasts consisted of a variety of elements: staff summaries of a key concept, theory or explanation of terminology featured in the weekly set readings and lecture programme; dialogues with students in the form of interviews or shorter sound bites; for example 'how language is important to my sense of cultural identity'; discussions and conversations on assessment tasks between students, mentors and tutors; tutor feedback on questions or comments arising from the taught sessions; formative feedback on students' draft assessment tasks, 'top tips' on presentation and research skills given by mentors, and information about local resources, such as the Faculty's Academic Skills Centre, the English Language Support Scheme for International Students and the Student Union Volunteering Scheme.

The development process

Material for the podcasts was developed in a variety of ways. The staff introductory sections, links and rounding-off comments were scripted, and recorded in my office using the freely downloadable software, Audacity. A number of semi-structured small group discussions were recorded in the Faculty e-learning centre; these featured one or two of the module tutors or key Faculty staff, students taking the module and final-year students. Some of the development process was more opportunistic; when students dropped into the staff office to ask a question that related to the module, we asked their permission to record the exchange where we thought it might be interesting or useful to the cohort as a whole. Other content was developed from interactions captured 'live' during seminars, using a digital recorder. Some material was entirely student-generated, using their own MP3 device.

As a novice podcaster, I was extremely grateful to be fully supported by the Faculty in this initiative. One of the Faculty e-developers was assigned to provide help by showing me how to use Audacity, assisting in the group recordings, editing and uploading the audio files into the Blackboard VLE. Each podcast was given a title, and accompanied by a brief description of what it contained, so students could see at a glance where to find items when they needed them. At the beginning of the semester, we introduced the podcasts in the context of a wider discussion on approaches to learning and resources for learning. To encourage students to listen, some lecture time was devoted to a demonstration of how to access the podcasts, with accompanying written instructions. Students were notified when each podcast was released, and invited to contribute comments and responses to activities via the Discussion Board and in seminars.

Staff and students involved

All five tutors who delivered the lectures and seminars referred to the podcasts in their teaching as a way to stimulate seminar discussion. Two of the tutors were actively involved in the production process. In 2006, 65 students took the module as a compulsory part of their first-year programme. Most of them were taking English language and communication in combination with another discipline from within the Faculty of Arts and Social Sciences, such as journalism, literature, creative writing, French, drama, business and sociology. The majority of students were female and for about 15 per cent of the cohort, English was not the first language. The average age of the students who participated in the podcasting research project was 20, which reflected the age profile of the group as a whole.

A special feature of this module is that a team of trained final-year student mentors work alongside tutors in the seminars to support the new students. In the first year of the podcasting initiative, five trained student mentors were involved. These mentors proved invaluable in liaising between first-year students, feeding back their questions, comments and suggestions for podcast content to the module tutors. The assessment takes the form of a portfolio of work: a number of short tasks embedding academic skills development and an essay. Students are encouraged to make several attempts at the short tasks for formative feedback during the course of the semester. They select their best efforts for inclusion in the final portfolio submission. The mentors noted that one task in particular, involving critical analysis of an intercultural incident, was proving problematic for students in the seminar to which they were attached, which prompted the mentors to make a podcast of their own discussion of the incident.

Students' use of podcasts

Half the cohort of students listened to one or more of the six podcasts. Of these, 10 per cent reported listening to five or six and 26 per cent to three or four. Reasons for not listening were explored in the questionnaire. For many students, lack of time was the main reason given for not listening. Other reasons were: not being aware of their availability on the VLE, technical problems in accessing them, and not seeing the relevance for their learning on the module. Further reasons for not listening were uncovered in focus group interviews. The most cited reasons were lack of interest in the topics and the fact that listening to podcasts was not compulsory or not necessary.

The questionnaire included an item that asked what activities students carried out online. Their responses revealed that only 9 per cent of the group used it for listening to podcasts. This relative lack of familiarity with Web 2.0 technologies might partly explain their level of podcast use.

Location and patterns of listening to podcasts

An interesting finding was that a significant portion of students (44 per cent) listened to podcasts 'always or nearly always' off campus. This information shows how students preferred to access podcasts in an informal learning environment and emphasizes the process of learning as a mix between formal and informal contexts. The remaining majority of students listened to podcasts 'live' directly from the VLE. A minority of students (7 per cent) chose to use a dedicated MP3 player to listen to podcasts, while a further 21 per cent students saved podcasts to their laptops for later listening.

Students were asked the reasons for not downloading podcasts onto a dedicated MP3 player. The majority of students claimed that there was no need to download for later use because they could access the module anytime they wanted. A third preferred to use MP3 players only to listen to music. Maybe these students considered listening to academic materials on their MP3 players an intrusion into their personal lives or possibly, they did not want to use up space. A few had technical difficulties of downloading, and several thought there was no need to listen to the podcasts more than once.

Most of the students (53 per cent) followed no particular pattern in listening to podcasts. This result possibly shows a 'needs-driven' podcast usage: they listened to them when they felt the necessity. More than a quarter used podcasts at the end of the week, while a few listened 3–4 days after they were made available. Seven per cent listened just before the seminars. None listened to them just before the workshops or within 24 hours after they were made available.

The interviews showed that many students preferred listening to podcasts in the evenings when they were quiet and relaxed at home. These students possibly needed a calm place to listen to academic materials.

> I prefer to do it in the evenings when I'm relaxed at home and have nothing else to do instead of trying to do it in the university and rush out to work (student A).

Almost half of the respondents just listened to podcasts without doing any other activity. A third took notes. Such a situation much resembles students' response in a more formal classroom setting: listening to the lecturer while taking notes. Thirteen per cent visited various sections of the module that were being referred to in the podcast. In the lecture, students have to follow a route dictated by the tutor, whereas podcasts could promote learners' personal navigation at their own pace and rhythm. Only a handful of students did other activities. This shows that students see studying as separate from personal and social activities.

Contribution to student learning

The focus groups and personal interviews further explored students' views on the specific features of podcasts that were particularly successful in supporting their learning. Interviews revealed three broad categories: learner choice and flexibility, discussion format and conversational style, and a different way of learning. Each category is explored with illustrative comments from student interviews.

Learner choice and flexibility

Most students (61 per cent) listened off campus, indicating the potential of podcasts to deliver learning material beyond the formal educational setting. Many students highlighted the flexibility and convenience of podcasts because the learners could listen to them at a place, time and pace of their choice: anywhere, any time. The following comments illustrate podcasts' ability to reach learners on the move:

> Yeah, it just gives you an extra dimension of learning, you know, if you haven't got the time to sit down and read a book, . . ., I can just . . . on the iPod . . . just go out and I can listen to it, you know, if I'm walking to somewhere, I can listen to on the way (student B).

Another advantage of podcasts mentioned by many students as adding value was that they could revisit topics that they had studied. Some of them pointed out the benefit of being able to stop and play the podcast in case they missed a section or if they wanted to listen to it again:

> And the main difference in fact is you can stop the podcasts and go back to it if you want to listen to it again. With the lectures, it's not so easy (student C).

Students pointed out how learning from podcasts shifted control over the pacing of learning activities into their own hands from the teacher. Note-taking in a lecture was given as an example:

> In lectures you have to take notes down pretty quickly because they move to the next points in the time . . . and [in] podcasts, you can stop,

take notes down, continue whatever you like . . . and I think that allows the person who's listening to learn at their own pace instead of being set by the lecturer (student D).

Students further pointed out the advantages of being able to listen to podcast content a number of times: to catch up the points that were missed in a lecture, to understand concepts further, to clarify and to confirm understanding and to test their knowledge:

> If I download a review of the lesson, the last lecture, I can listen to that before the next one, just to give me a refresher of what I've done previously, so I got a refreshed in my mind when I'm going in, what kind of things we've been looking at, you know (student B).

Some students appreciated the fact of having access to the subjects that were discussed in class when they missed lectures. An example came from a student who enrolled in the module a few weeks later than the starting date and, therefore, missed a few lectures. Podcasts were helpful for her to catch up; they provided an additional resource that she was able to combine with lecture notes:

> . . . so having missed a few lectures, it made an awful lot easier to . . . download the podcasts, just to get that brief, a review of what I missed . . . not feel like that I missed a lot when you put together the lecture notes. Because the lecture notes are ok, but again it's very much like flat and plain, just read it and you've got, having that podcast is just an extra bit of information you might have missed, that might not be in that paper (student B).

Many students commented that listening to podcasts with reviews of key concepts was very useful because they provided students with an opportunity to go back to the lecture material.

Some students also found that the podcasts with reviews of key concepts helped them to take notes easily. One student described how being able to listen to key concepts again helped him to fill in the gaps in his notes.

> [It's] useful because when the things done in the lectures you don't always get everything written down, the lecturer is talking quite quickly, so you don't have an opportunity to go back and listen to the main points again. And with podcasts, it's great. It will make you feel probably more secure if I haven't got everything written down (student D).

As the above section shows, students identified podcasts as offering choices in how they can carry out their learning activities.

Accessing the tacit knowledge of peers

Students' comments on the format of the podcasts highlighted how the particular design features had contributed to their learning. The podcasts included not only the voices of tutors, but also contributions from other students that were incorporated in a conversational and discussion style:

Yes, it does make it interesting because it is a proper discussion. Even though you can't participate in the discussion, you listen to [it], and you're gaining a lot of information . . . on the subject (student E).

Tacit knowledge is defined as 'knowledge that is, metaphorically, acquired through osmosis'. It is a form of knowledge acquired 'on the job' (Sternberg and Caruso 1985: 146). Explicit knowledge, in contrast, is codified and expressed in symbolic form or language. Students on a Higher Education (HE) course generally use knowledge that is explicit, formalized and communicated to them through lecturers, seminars, textbooks and other formal learning resources. Although students have access to their peers' tacit knowledge and experience through informal conversations, the podcasts provided an additional resource that can capture such knowledge in a formal and reusable way.

Listening to podcasts had an added benefit, beyond just the preparation of the assessment. Many students described their feeling of listening to podcasts as motivational. Students commented that the informal conversational style makes the podcasts interesting and alive:

I really appreciate the discussion format, I mean the lecturer and the mentors, they discuss about how to do presentations, and giving tips and advice and everything. This I really like (student E).

Listening to podcasts, I think it must be alive. It shouldn't be like a person just reading because otherwise, I don't think students will be interested in listening to someone just reading. It has to be some kind of debate, conversation, active, alive, and inviting the person, draw the attention of the person, and try to really put that person in the mood to listen to you (student F).

Many students reported that the podcasts based on conversations and discussions on assessment tasks between students, mentors and tutors were helpful in clarifying the tutors' expectations and, therefore, boosting confidence:

And we had the mentors advising us because they are [third] year students, so they have been doing presentations, so they knew about it, they have already done it. So they have been advising us how to do presentations (student G).

Useful, it cleared up some points. It just helps me to guide myself along a bit, so be more confident (student H).

Others found the podcasts in which mentor students discussed how to do portfolio tasks helped students to learn by drawing together different viewpoints from different parties:

The third one was really useful because . . . mentor students, they were talking about the portfolio task, which one you have to write, the assignment, so it's very useful . . . and they show you their point of view, so you can have the different or you can have the same . . . so I find it very useful (student I).

The above comments and observations by students reveal an important point about the potential of podcasts as a means of tapping into the knowledge and experience of peers and senior students as a valuable learning resource. Podcasts have the potential of capturing this informal and tacit knowledge that can be reused and made available to a wider student cohort.

A different way of learning

Most of the students interviewed pointed out that learning with podcasts represented a new and attractive experience:

> That is a very new experience. In fact I've never heard of podcasts before I came to the university, I've had no idea of what that was. I just thought, 'wow! what a great idea'! . . . because it's just very easy to access . . . (student A).

> . . . first of all, it's not like, I mean papers, like books, you've just got to listen to it. It's another way of learning, and it's a new way of studying (student B).

Another student pointed out that he had listened to podcasts as a form of diversion from other academic tasks and as a form of relaxation. For this student, podcasts offered a mix between entertainment, relaxation and learning:

> I listen to [podcasts] in the evening, and try to practise, revise everything, what things you mustn't do and must do. . . . Sometimes, when I'm in the Learning Resources Centre, I usually listen to the podcasts for example if I'm feeling a bit tired of typing the assignment, . . . It's a kind of entertainment . . ., so you just go and listen to podcasts. You're relaxing yourself listening and learning (student E).

Students tried to characterize the nature of this informal way of learning through podcasts. One student considered learning from podcasts as 'not serious learning':

> It's not really serious learning. But you do learn from it (student E).

Listening to podcasts also offered a psychological benefit; many students perceived that listening is effortless and requires less concentration than reading:

> Listening . . . requires less concentration on your part. [Learning] just happens, you know (student H).

Some of the above comments hint at a preference for learning by listening, which cannot be generalized for all learners. Students receive and process information in different ways: 'Some students are comfortable with theories and abstractions; others feel much more at home with facts and observable phenomena; some prefer visual presentation of information and others prefer verbal explanations' (Felder and Brent 2005). What is important for the tutor is to try to offer different learning material to students in order to facilitate the different learning processes while keeping their interest and attention. Podcasts offer the teacher a new tool to provide access to information in audio format.

Students' comments on learning by listening to podcasts reveal that they experienced a way of learning that is contradictory to traditional conceptions of learning as an activity that is carried out by attending formally scheduled classrooms, reading books, and paying 'serious' attention to learning activities. For those who listened to the podcasts, the experience was characterized as carrying out formal learning through informal processes.

A model of how podcasts helped students' learning

An analysis of data on how podcasts helped student learning have enabled the development of a model illustrated in Figure 12.1, adapted from Edirisingha et al. (2007b: 100). In the middle of the figure is the key objective in developing the podcasts, that is helping students to develop skills required

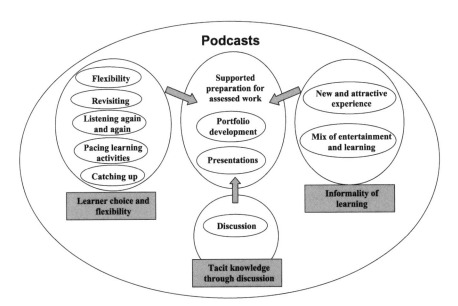

Figure 12.1   Features of podcasts that facilitate learning

Source: adapted from Edirisingha et al. (2007b: 100).

for two kinds of assessed work: portfolio development and presentation skills. The three surrounding circles depict the three main features of podcasts that supported student learning: learner choice and flexibility, accessing tacit knowledge of peers through discussions and an informal way of learning.

Reflections of a novice podcaster

This chapter has suggested that there are positive benefits in using jointly produced podcasts as a supplementary resource to foster a learning community at first-year taught undergraduate level. All pedagogical initiatives have limitations as well as advantages, however, and I want to discuss briefly what I see as issues yet to be resolved in our current model of provision.

The first issue is that of resources: staff time and staff expertise. As a first-time podcaster, the introduction of podcasts was an experience that was at times frustrating, ultimately rewarding, but also very time-consuming. Lack of broadcasting experience and technical expertise led me to underestimate the time needed to hone my own input, the key concepts. Student feedback suggested that these key concepts sections were helpful to their learning but they were in practice quite difficult to implement. Since the aim was to stimulate critical discussion of the concepts rather than reproduce a lecture in miniature, I abandoned the safety-net of the carefully written script adopted at the beginning in favour of more loosely structured discussions of the concepts with members of the module teaching team. However, the unscripted, dialogic nature of these sections and the range of other contributions demanded a considerable amount of editing to blend the various 'voices' into a 10-minute seamless whole. The need to create a bigger 'bank' of material in advance was one important lesson learned.

The second issue is one of ownership. Although Faculty technical support was provided for this initiative within the Faculty Blended Learning Strategy, the expectation was that it would be developmental. To take this initiative further, therefore, members of the English language and communication teaching team will be working with the Faculty learning technologist to review key modules in order to develop a range of sustainable podcast material and other e-learning resources to support students' learning. Experience has shown that a possible tension between institutional and pedagogic objectives may arise in the formal development of this initiative. Since our podcasts were made available via Blackboard and supported by the Faculty, the institutional view was that technical quality should be as high as possible, and that imperfections should be 'cleaned up'. This admirable aim was sometimes at odds with our aim to encourage learners to generate their own material for podcasting, however 'quick and dirty' the recording methods were.

The third issue is the evaluation of the impact on students' learning. The findings presented in this chapter suggest that the podcasts provided a valuable addition to the educational experience for those who participated, but how do we measure this? There is some subjective evidence in the form of seminar participation and informal student feedback: both Discussion Board activities and podcasts were non-compulsory, but the podcasts had a greater 'take-up' and were more successful in promoting lively seminar interaction. Furthermore, there was a noticeable reduction in failure rate through non-submission on this module compared with the previous year, although this cannot be reliably attributed to any single factor. Informal feedback from the five student mentors suggests that this group gained considerable benefit in terms of confidence, teamworking and leadership skills; three of them reported that prospective employers had cited the students' role in the podcasting project as influential in their decision to offer them the position.

Podcasting as a vehicle for delivering content in educational settings has attracted much recent interest and debate. However, relatively few studies have focused on the impact of podcasting on the social and communicative dimensions of student learning. For those who have an interest in spoken text as a social process and product, podcasting offers the possibility of building a database of authentic 'voices', rich in meaning potential, constructed and managed by students in collaboration with tutors. To convince both future students and institutional budget-holders of the efficacy of our model of provision, my colleagues and I will be working to gather further evidence.

13

Podcasts for reflective learning

Dick Ng'ambi

Summary

This chapter is about the role of podcasts in mediating reflective learning. I explain how podcasts were used in an on-campus postgraduate course and how they supported students' learning through reflection.

Introduction

Learning is an outcome of activities designed with explicit or implicit goals that may include reflection. Unlike live radio broadcasts, podcasts are seldom listened to in real time: the difference between an event that generated a podcast and when a podcast is listened to suggest that podcasts can have an impact on subsequent actions, and are useful for action learning. Drawing on a typical student's experience at the University of Cape Town, I show how he used podcasts, in a low-resource context, for reflective learning. With student-generated content and interview material, I use content and thematic analyses to uncover lessons for developing an implementation model. I conclude with practical suggestions for educators at universities who wish to integrate podcasts into their teaching.

Podcasts for mediating reflective learning

If students can download podcasts of lectures or presentations and can listen to them at their convenience, as often as they wish, they can reflect on what they learn. Teaching materials may thus be reused, teaching expertise may be shared and student note-taking during lectures may change. A lecturer may point students to podcasts of his or her previous lectures or those delivered by others. Podcasts therefore provide useful opportunities for reflective learning. Podcast-mediated reflective learning may even be a measure of student growth and competence (Dillon and Brown 2006; Flanigan and Amirian 2006).

The Chinese proverb, 'if you wish to know the mind of a person, listen to his words', says a lot about the relationship between podcasting and reflective learning. Listening to student-generated podcasts may give educators insight into what students know and can know. Educators may use such insights to design student learning activities that draw from previous student learning experiences and may require students to reflect on these experiences. If the experience has an accompanying audio trail, the reflection becomes even richer.

To this end, podcasts are catalytic to reflective learning. In order for students to stay focused in the process of reflection, some guidance is required. Questions are a useful tool to give structure to reflection. Podcasts are not intrinsically learning tools, so to use them as such requires that they are carefully integrated into the curriculum at the pedagogical level.

Access to podcasts for students in developing countries

Student access to the internet in developing countries is uneven. At the University of Cape Town, students mainly access the internet from computer laboratories on campus or through university computing services provided near student residences. While the university provides and maintains computing infrastructure, there are two devices that universities do not provide but which students regard as necessities: a mobile phone and a flash drive. Podcasting at my university depends on limited internet access plus these handheld devices. Mobile phones and MP3 players are less affected by the intermittent electricity supply. Once podcasts have been downloaded onto an MP3 player, low bandwidth is not a problem. Some universities in Africa do not have course websites and cannot support online courses that rely on broad bandwidth.

African societies have rich social cultures and traditions in which reading and writing is never used. Podcasts can create archives of cultural events that could be used to mediate reflection, or as an educational resource. In a study that measured Africa's e-readiness in the global networked economy, Ifinedo (2005) argues that Africa's rich cultural traditions could be used to improve the overall position of the global networked economy. It is the responsibility of African universities to exploit the potential in order to contribute to that economy. Colle (2005) contends that for universities to be relevant to the world around them, they need to become active rather than passive players. Perhaps one way universities could be proactive is by exploiting existing social practices and ubiquitous technologies in particular contexts, and by finding points of leverage.

Role of reflection in education

Reflection is not a new phenomenon in education. In fact, it could be argued that education is about reflective learning. Students take notes during lectures to aid their post-lecture reflections; lecturers assign tasks to help students reflect on the topics; tests and examinations are reflective activities. Riedinger (2006) contends that the purpose of reflection is to help sum up what has been learned, how it was learned and to determine what could have been done differently. Podcasts can aid the reflection process by allowing events to be relived audibly. Both reflections and podcasts are post-event activities happening at different times and even in different spaces from the objects of reflection or recording. Reflection is a process in which the mind thinks about an event or action that took place earlier. Reflection therefore happens when the mind is active even though the body might be immobile. Leont'ev (1978: 156) postulates that a person would not understand an explanation if it is heard at a time when the mind is passive 'because nothing enters the consciousness'. Since the human mind is not active all the time, it follows that, for reflection to be effective, a student needs to choose a time for reflection when the mind is either active or can be activated. The advantage of podcasting and convenient handheld devices is that it allows the opportunity for reflection, anywhere and at any time.

Reflection is fundamental to expansive learning. In expansive learning, activities are constantly transformed and activity systems continue to grow. However, expansive learning is not an outcome of unguided transformation of activity systems, and reflection without cues may not guarantee expansive learning. Effective guidance recognizes prior knowledge of the one to be guided and offers prompts or cues in which to expand understanding. One of the ways of achieving this is through asking questions.

Questions as drivers of reflective learning

Questions can trigger and guide reflective learning. Questions generate reflective inquiry and are the foundation of action learning (Marquardt 2005). Listening to podcasts in which insightful questions are asked could stimulate reflection. Marquardt (2005) suggests six components of question-driven action learning: a problem; an action learning group; a process that emphasizes insightful and reflective listening; a requirement for action; a commitment to learning; and an action learning coach. When used for reflection, the purpose of questions is not to get answers but to prompt reflection. The use of questions for reflective inquiry is dependent on both the context (purpose of activity) and power relations between the questioner and the questioned. The purpose of questions may be misunderstood depending on power relations. It is thus important that a learning group (questioners) be composed of peers who assume changing roles (that is the questioned becomes the questioner).

Teaching and learning issues addressed using podcasts

Reflective learning was used in a postgraduate module at my university, within the Sakai Virtual Learning Environment (VLE) (www.sakaiproject. org). The module's learning outcomes were:

- to acquire competence in conceptualizing educational challenges and possible roles of educational technologies in addressing them;
- to acquire critical thinking skills in the context of general use of information and communication technologies (ICTs) in education, and educational technologies in particular.

The teaching challenge was to design learning activities in which students could acquire skills in identifying key issues reported in educational technology literature, and in writing reflective academic essays. The learning challenge was to scaffold students' reflection and facilitate acquisition of critical thinking skills.

Students received pre-seminar reading materials, attended guest lectures, were assigned individual readings and made presentations to classmates. The lecturer guided students' learning through his design of their learning activities. The scaffolding process involved students engaging with assigned readings, integrating their arguments with guest lectures, making presentations, having peers ask questions, and writing reflective essays for submission. Podcasts were integrated with the learning activities designed to scaffold students' reflection.

Figure 13.1 represents students listening to podcasts of a discussion from a student seminar and individually reflecting on questions asked during their presentation. The podcasts' transformative effect is measured by the extent to which future actions differ from the students' initial positions. For example, do students change their answers to questions? Were their spontaneous answers in seminars changed after reflection?

Methodology

Using an interpretive research approach, I studied the experience of a single student in depth to bring richness to the findings and enhance the integrity of the evidence. Burrell and Morgan (1979: 28) point out:

> An interpretive paradigm is informed by a concern to understand the world as it is, to understand the fundamental nature of the social world at the level of subjective experience. In an interpretive paradigm the aim is to unravel how social reality is constructed from the realm of individual consciousness and subjectivity, as seen by the participants and not from the observer point of view.

Figure 13.1   Podcast-mediated reflection

Scaffolding reflective learning with podcasts

First, students attended two presentations by guest lecturers that were recorded for podcasting. The students were introduced to podcasts and where to find them, and were told how they could be used for reflection. Prior to the first student seminar, each student was assigned a unique reading, chosen to stimulate reflection, on which to base his or her presentation. Box 13.1 is an extract from an assigned reading.

Donald Ely's (1999) article was assigned to a student called Bwalya (not his real name). Bwalya was a foreign student who had not heard about podcasting

---

Box 13.1   An extract from an assigned reading

Instructional technology is not yet a discipline

The term 'discipline' is usually reserved for areas of inquiry and application that have been established over time and follow established paradigms. There is likely to be a consistency in their basic beliefs, rationales and common principles that define the scope and structure of the discipline . . . shifting emphases within the field that is known as instructional or educational technology seem to indicate that the field does not qualify for status as a discipline (Ely 1999: 306–7).

Box 13.2   Bwalya's task for the seminar

Activity

Brief: The objective of the seminar is to use the assigned readings to provide an argument re the foundations of ET and/or using ICTs for teaching and learning. You will be expected to anchor your discussion to critical issues or themes that arose in the last two guest seminars.

Time allocated: 15 mins presentation and 5 mins questions.

NB: Every student will be expected to ask at least one question per presentation.

---

before joining the course. Box 13.2 shows his task for the seminar, posted in the VLE.

The assignment required students to relate issues raised by article authors to the guest lectures. Although each student had a different article to read, students had shared understanding of issues from the guest lectures. The task was designed to ensure that peers drew from the guest presentation to ask potentially reflective questions. The gap between guest presentation and reflection was crucial. Box 13.3 shows the post-seminar task.

The cycle of activities was repeated four times: students being assigned a task, presenting to peers and encouraging peers to ask insightful questions, the lecturer as observer assigning a reflective task, and students submitting a reflective essay. In each cycle, guest lectures and the papers assigned to students changed but the activities and tasks remained unchanged.

As a module requirement, students did individual projects lasting five weeks on curriculum topics that they had proposed. Bwalya proposed to 'explore dimensions of podcasting with specific reference to education'. He

---

Box 13.3   The post-seminar task

Assignment 1

Task:
Summarize the assigned paper in your own words, making sure you identify key issues the paper raises with particular reference to seminars 1 and 2.

Carefully respond to comments and questions your peers asked you during the student seminar 1 (Thursday, 8 March).

Length: Not more than 2 pages (or 1000 words) of single-spaced 12 pt font.

---

wanted to reflect on how podcasting was integrated into a course in which he was a student. He was curious and fascinated: he had never listened to a podcast. He was like other students who experience disparities in technological access, particularly those students from poor socio-economic backgrounds where technology diffusion is slow and access issues are paramount. When on campus, Bwalya downloaded podcasts to a flash drive and at home, usually in the evening, he listened to the podcasts on a stand-alone computer.

Evaluation of student learning

I evaluated Bwalya's learning through content analysis of his project and I interviewed him about his handling of Assignment 1, his presentation, and the questions that were asked by his peers. I also used thematic analysis to analyse the interview transcript.

Content analysis

Bwalya was diligent but he could not attend all lectures. Like other students, he had access to reading materials and guest lecturers' PowerPoint presentations, and was expected to be an active participant during student seminars, which were run by students and where the lecturer was a coach and time manager. Each student had to ask at least one question during each student presentation. Asking questions involved two things: acknowledging a point made by the speaker, followed by a question. Box 13.4 shows questions

---

Box 13.4   Questions asked during Bwalya's presentation to facilitate reflection

Q1. There is one point that you made about instructional technology being caught up with distance learning. I was wondering if it was not vice versa. Is it not that distance learning is catching up with instructional technology?

Q2. You explained Donald Ely's opinion about Educational Technology being neither a discipline nor a field but you have not said what your own opinion is. I am interested to know your views on this.

Q3. With all the statements and philosophies on Educational Technology you have talked about, I am left wondering how it will ever be a discipline. It appears that the definition of a discipline itself is not grounded on generally upheld or agreed upon ideals to underpin it. What is your comment?

---

asked during Bwalya's presentation to enable him to reflect on his own arguments.

Although Bwalya tried to answer the questions spontaneously, he was not prepared for them. Getting peers to ask questions, in a safe atmosphere, gave him confidence to respond and defend his argument. He did not have to have correct answers, because questions were to foster reflection. The post-presentation assignment asked him and the others to submit well-reflected responses to the questions. It was here that podcasts were invaluable, because Bwalya's presentation, the questions that were asked, and his responses, were all recorded as a podcast and posted on the VLE. Bwalya could download it from there.

Assignment 1 required students to respond to comments and questions from peers, by reflecting on the presentation, the question and the responses. Bwalya had to engage with the assigned article again, listen to his presentation and to the discussion. Box 13.5 is an extract from Bwalya's essay.

Bwalya thought about the questions and responded affirmatively. Responding to Q2, he used the words '. . . I personally . . .' to express ownership of opinion regardless of any opposing view. His response referred to discussion questions, Ely's paper and other literature, while staying focused on the task. Similarly, after the guest lectures and student seminars ended, after Bwalya had time for reflection between when he listened to the podcast and when he wrote his essay. As he said:

> From February to May we interactively engaged with key issues and debates in ICTs in education . . . during our seminars, presentations, debates, discussions and interactions were recorded and posted online

---

Box 13.5   An extract from Bwalya's essay

Extract from Bwalya's reflective response

. . . I was asked to personally say whether Instructional Technology should be categorised as a discipline or a field, and, if it was still classified as a field, how the shift from field to discipline would materialise. Another classmate found that distance learning was being altered by Instructional Technology in contradiction to what I had presented. As far as the categorisation of Instructional Technology is concerned and the existing literature at my disposal, I personally and currently agree with Ely in terms of recognising that Instructional Technology is still emerging as a field related to teaching and learning. However, this fact should not diminish the importance of the field or the contributions that it makes to the improvement of learning. The future progress of Instructional Technologies and shift into a status of discipline is unknown but current evidence shows that the field is 'growing up' and there is increased sense of the field becoming more professional . . .

---

using podcasts . . . I was so fascinated by that experience. It happened that one day I missed a seminar, only to find out that I could listen, at my own convenience, to what every participant said online. It was so amazing that from their discussion I could learn and catch up with them. This essay is primarily meant to be a personal exercise. I see myself joining the podcasting community for a long time . . . I have come to understand the values and opportunities podcasting offers and the changes it brings in the educational process.

His reflection sums up how podcasts impacted on Bwalya's learning experience. Because he had not heard about podcasting before, the impact could only be attributed to his experience in the course. On the surface, Bwalya was just an ordinary student, but his essay shows a deeper understanding of the potential of podcasting beyond what he initially grasped. In the course evaluation afterwards, Bwalya wrote, '. . . this course helped me to expand my outlook, know more, think and understand . . .'

Thematic analysis

Two months after the course ended, I interviewed Bwalya. Here is my thematic analysis.

Reflection as a sense-making activity
The difference between listening and reflection is that the latter is a sense-making activity. Bwalya had to find a time when his mind was active, to make sense of previous actions.

> . . . what I found helpful is that afterward I could go home and listen to what had happened during the seminar and when I say listen it means to make sense of what was said at that moment and question myself that if I was given an opportunity to do this same thing again, would I have the same position now that I have been informed by past experiences . . .

Reflection is a process of learning from the past to improve the future. Podcasts facilitated possible change of future behaviour. Reflection enabled Bwalya to improve how he carried out subsequent tasks.

Reflection as a key to expansive learning
One component of action learning is having a challenge or a problem as a point of departure. Bwalya found the tasks challenging and enriching. The effect of having peers comment on his presentation expanded his learning.

> . . . we were given handouts to read and to summarise them, to present them, to listen to their questions and to tackle them. I would put this all into an account of learning process, it was a very challenging thing but

at the same time it was a very, I would say, enriching experience in the sense that while listening to my classmates I could learn something that I did not know . . .

Bwalya learned from his peers in two ways: their insightful questions enhanced his learning and he listened to podcasts to learn about how his peers answered questions.

Gap between reflective and spontaneous responses
The difference between the responses students gave during face-to-face sessions and their written responses suggested that podcasts may have mediated reflection.

> . . . I noticed that the kind of answers I gave when I was asked immediately were different from what I submitted in a paper when I took time to reflect and that is the usefulness of the recording . . .

Asked to explain why the responses differed, Bwalya said:

> . . . when I am asked to give a answer in a spontaneous way, give one answer but then after reflecting and consulting other sources and listening to other opinions, my learning experience will become more elaborated because I've been going through a process and that is what the process is all about, it means it takes you somewhere and in our process it was, it took me from what I said to what I wrote . . .

Bwalya's comment suggested a useful complementary relationship between podcasts and academic discourse.

Distance between event time and reflection time
Bwalya usually accessed podcasts from desktop PCs in computer laboratories. He used headphones to listen. Not having an internet connection at his house, he downloaded podcasts onto a flash drive and listened to podcasts on his PC at home.

> . . . what I would do . . . is to . . . listen to them (podcast), get out of the computer lab and few days prior to our next seminar . . . . . when I was planning to type what I was supposed to submit electronically as a piece of reflection . . . I would go back and now type it but it was mostly happening there in the computer lab.

To access new podcasts, Bwalya went back to the laboratory to download, listen to podcasts from the desktop and then type the reflective essay.

How podcasts can support struggling students
Podcasts are useful to students who struggle with the English language. They help students to express themselves orally, get feedback and take time to

carefully construct text for submission. This is particularly critical in environments where students have variable levels of preparedness for tertiary education.

> . . . having English as not my first language, I found myself sometimes struggling, even now I might be struggling but I was not disturbed, some of them (peers) were far ahead, that was the impression I had about myself but we could still socialize and help one another and listen to one another . . .

English was Bwalya's third language. His perception was that other students had an advantage because they were proficient in English.

Podcasts change social interaction
Although podcasts levelled the social playing field for Bwalya, he was worried about saying something that he might later regret. His concern was that once it had been recorded, it would become 'permanent'.

> . . . I know it has got its drawbacks in the sense that a person may regret in the future what he or she said at a certain stage but my point here is just to say that it does more good to use podcasting in an educational setup in a sense that it helps me relive that experience than it does harm, so I would recommend it, especially to people who come from the same background that I do, having English as a third or a fourth language, I need more time to re-listen the same story in order to be in a better position to understand it, to criticise it, to agree with it, to deserve it, that is what my experience with podcasting has been and I would like to take it one stage further . . .

The potential to regret one's words later could be seen as a drawback of podcasts, but podcasts cannot mediate the reliving of experience without an audio account of an event. This highlights the importance of the scaffolding roles of podcasting for students whose mother tongue is not English. For Bwalya, face-to-face sessions probably did not provide him with time to understand what was being presented, or time to think critically about it, or even to agree with it.

So what is podcasting?
In Bwalya's words:

> . . . Podcasting is a way of helping a person to participate in a learning process even if a person is not physically where the learning process took place. It is also a way of keeping in a safe way knowledge that has been built in a different set up; it is a way of contributing to the production of knowledge and that could be used as well; it is a way of saying that we appreciate communication that took place and we value it and we want to make it accessible to other people. It is all those together . . .

Podcast-mediated action learning

Podcasts mediated action learning in the following ways: First, the learning activity was designed to let students reflect on an assigned task. Since the lectures were in the past, students had to become active listeners to podcasts of guest lectures. Second, presentations were students' attempts to expand their own understanding and podcasts also mediated post-presentation reflection. Both the pre-presentation preparations and post-presentation submissions were handled by individual students. This was particularly important given that students were being assessed. Third, although the role of the group was not assessed, the value to the group was the richness of diverse reflections on the previous guest seminars, prompted by the assigned readings, and discussions during the student seminars. This was complemented by group podcasts as it was difficult to pay attention during the student seminars, ask insightful questions and learn from the overall discussions.

Podcast implementation model

One lesson from this project is that effective implementation of podcast-mediated reflective learning requires careful planning at the level of activity and also at the pedagogical level (see Figure 13.2).

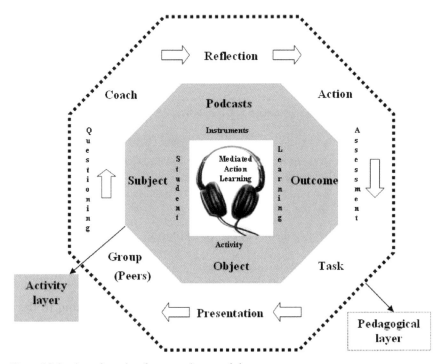

Figure 13.2 A podcast implementation model

The activity layer integrates the student engagement with learning activities in which podcasts are used to facilitate the accomplishment of intended outcomes. However, the activity layer is too high a level to guide implementation. Tasks are assigned at the pedagogical layer. Included in the task is the requirement that students draw from the lectures they attended. The purpose of this is to allow students to start the exercise with reflection. At the end of the task, students make presentations to peers. The role of peers is to assist a presenter to reflect on the task and how it was performed. This is accomplished through asking insightful questions. The coach observes the student presentations without interfering except as timekeeper. After the presentations the coach asks students to reflect on their presentations and write and submit a reflective text. To support the post-presentation reflection, podcasts of presentations are made available on the VLE. Students take necessary actions to ensure delivery of the new task. The reflective text is assessed, students are given feedback and a new task is assigned. At the core of the model is mediated action learning.

Checklists for effective implementation

My analysis leads me to propose an activity checklist and a pedagogical checklist.

At the activity layer:

Subject: The student

• A member of a class registered for a module

Object: Presentation and short essay on discussion session

• To reflect on a presentation and to write a reflective essay on the discussion session of the presentation

Instruments:

• An academic article, PowerPoint presentation and post-presentation podcast
• Engage with reading material and prepare a presentation
• Respond to questions from peers triggered by the presentation
• Listen to the presentation again and write a short piece of text

Outcome: Reflective learning
• Presentation
• Podcast
• Short essay

At the pedagogical layer:

1. Integrate a learning activity with the course learning objectives.
2. Decide how students will perform the task.
3. Let students perform task (recorded).
4. Let peers give cues to help one another focus on the task (recorded).
5. Create a brief distance between performance of a task and reflection.
6. Give students guidelines on the aspects of the task they need to reflect on.
7. Give students access to the podcasts produced from items 3 and 4 above.
8. Assess deliverable (outcome of reflection).

Conclusion

The requirement for reflective thinking to occur is an active mind. Reflections are therefore not confined to particular places or times. One advantage of podcasts is the potential for 'anywhere anytime' support for reflective thinking. This affordance is possible because users can listen to podcasts with mobile devices. I have shown that podcasts can also be used in low-resource contexts where learners may not have mobile devices to play, such as MP3 players or iPods. Podcasts' pedagogical advantage is that with relevant cues they can promote reflective thinking and expand learning activities. The use of questions in non-threatening contexts can generate reflective inquiry. Questions can serve as foundations of action learning. For reflective thinking to be meaningful for students, it should have an outcome that students can submit and be assessed on.

Listening to podcasts does not necessarily translate into learning. Like other technologies, the challenge lies in how podcasts are integrated into the curriculum. My single subject case study helped to unravel intricacies of the podcasting intervention. My analysis led to a synthesis of a podcast-mediated action learning framework, and to a podcast implementation model in which podcasts are inserted at the intersection of learning activity and pedagogy.

Acknowledgements

I wish to acknowledge the financial contribution of a Stimulation Fund grant from the University of Cape Town to undertake the research that formed this chapter. I am grateful to Bwalya (not his real name) for granting permission to use extracts from his written submissions and for consenting to being interviewed.

14

Students' podcasts as learning tools

Chris Cane and Annette Cashmore

Summary

This chapter reports on a pilot study. The aim of the activity in the study was threefold. First, to engage the students on a genetics module with the subject material through the development of podcasts. Second, the activity would give students who had not chosen the module the opportunity to consider some of the issues of modern medical genetics by later listening to the pod-casted material. Finally, since the podcasts are available to first-year students who will be choosing modules for their second year, they are a useful archived window on the content and approaches used in the module. This study demonstrated that student-developed podcasts can be a useful learning tool both for developing subject-specific understanding and in developing a wide variety of transferable skills.

Context

Modern medical genetics presents many challenges, both scientific and ethical. This podcasting activity was developed for use with a group of second-year medical students who had elected to take an optional semester-long special study module focusing on developments in genetics and their ethical implications. The students have a wide choice of these special study modules and about 30 students per year take the genetics module. In the past the module has used a mixture of lectures, and seminar-style sessions and is assessed by essays and group poster presentations. While these activities do develop the students' understanding of issues of modern genetics, the module team wanted more variety in the types of activities used. Additionally, since many students choose special study modules on other topics, it was felt that it would be useful to get the 'genetics students' to engage in some sort of outreach activity to raise the awareness of their peers of genetics issues.

The use of Web 2.0 technologies in medicine and healthcare education is currently in discussion (Anderson 2007; Giustini 2007; Kamel Boulos and Wheeler 2007). However, most focus is on the use of podcasting and other tools using staff-produced materials with the student being a passive learner. Other examples of medical uses of podcasting have also been described, for example, with surgical procedures (Whitehead et al. 2007). Clearly, podcasting by staff has a role in producing training materials for medical professionals, but here we describe a pilot study where the students are active producers of content rather than consumers.

The pilot study

The cohort of 30 second-year students who chose to study the module in 2007 were divided into five groups. Each group was responsible for researching their own topic relevant to ethical issues surrounding genetics, and developing their own podcast. The podcasting activity sessions took place over three consecutive weeks. During the first session a short introduction to the technologies involved was given, since many of the students had not encountered podcasting before. The use of Audacity as an editing program was also introduced. Different content formats were covered and these included round table discussions, debate or interviews providing for each member of the group to make an equal contribution. The students decided on the topic and format for their podcast themselves, and then spent the rest of the session researching and discussing their topics. The next week was spent with further research and starting to record material. The third session involved more recording and editing. The topics students chose were designer babies, genetic screening/testing, diabetes, DNA fingerprinting and haemophilia. Each podcast was 5–10 minutes in length. When completed, the podcasts were made available on the Virtual Learning Environment (VLE) for other students to use.

Evaluation methods

The impact of podcasting on the students' learning was evaluated through a variety of methods. The aim of the evaluation was to determine what effects the podcasting activity had on the students who produced them, both in terms of improving their understanding of the topic material, and also in developing their presentational skills. The effectiveness of the activity in stimulating student discussions was assessed in two focus groups with 13 students during the middle of the semester. Student interviews, which lasted about an hour, were also conducted using a semi-structured interview schedule developed to explore how student learning is supported by podcasts.

All interviews were recorded on a digital recorder and transcribed verbatim for analysis to identify key themes and issues. Additionally, the download statistics were monitored, and their responses to a short online questionnaire on the usefulness of the podcasts for other students were analysed.

Findings

During the introductory sessions students were asked if they had any prior experience of podcasts; approximately one-third of the students had listened to podcasts and over three-quarters had a portable device capable of playing MP3 files. This is rather higher than the findings of Sandars and Schroter (2007) who surveyed the use of Web 2.0 technologies in medical education.

From focus group and less formal feedback sessions, it was clear that the podcasting sessions did have a very positive effect on student learning. After analysis of the responses, a number of themes emerged:

Broadening knowledge and disseminating information

This project had the dual aims of getting students to engage with ethical issues in genetics, and disseminating this knowledge to their peers who chose other modules. In the focus groups students commented that the process of researching material and thinking about how to present it to a non-specialist audience had broadened their knowledge and understanding of the topics. It was also clear that students had also engaged with the second aim of the project, as some students commented that podcasts could be used as a tool to disseminate information relevant to genetics to other students who were not taking the module.

> The purpose I think was to relay information of what this module's all about to students who aren't on the module itself so they can find out what we do in the module, and the ethical side . . . issues that we were talking about. It's kind of like an insight into the module and into what we do (student A).

Students also identified the podcasts as a simple, portable and informal way of getting information.

> I think it's a simple way of getting information in a portable format as well, so you can have it on the move . . . simply put in student language . . . a student look at the topic and a person who doesn't do this course they can get the information in a simple and quick way and a portable way (student B).

Some students also identified the wider uses of this technology to distribute lecture and other course material. The responses from students concerning the value of podcasts for their learning were very positive.

It is interesting that this student-developed content generated this comment as this approach has been used quite successfully to produce student-written revision guides (Jones and Morris 1998) and in student contributions to specialized journals such as the *Student BMJ*. With appropriate staff input to ensure accuracy, this could well develop into a valuable student resource over time. In some ways this could be considered an extension of the informal study groups that the students are encouraged to organize.

Enhancement of team work and organizational skills
Some students highlighted the importance of working in groups to medical students. They believed that developing podcasts is another way to enhance team-working skills.

> I think it's a key concept in working as a doctor especially, you have to work in a team all your career I think, so that's what the medical school are trying to get to and get us into the habit of being able to work in a team, and identify key strengths and weakness in a team and develop yourself in different roles within the team (student C).

Students reflected on their experiences, some of them felt that one lesson they learned from the development process is planning your activities well in advance.

> . . . we planned it, got the script together, organised it, and said this is what's going to happen and at the end this is going to be the outcome, that made it a whole lot easier, rather than starting with nothing and then trying building up from there (student D).

Most groups shared responsibilities to ensure each member of the group made equal contributions to the development process. They divided tasks so that each member of the group was responsible for researching a particular aspect of the topic, preparing the script, and recording an individual session on that. Some groups recorded a 'round table discussion' as it happened and did not edit, whereas others used a more sophisticated approach involving recording separate contributions and then editing them together.

> . . . it is just a group effort the way we designed our podcast is we split it up. . . . Some of us were doing cell biology, pathology, introduction, conclusion, and we recorded separately and then just put it together. Rather than all doing it at the same time this was an easier way of doing it (student E).

One group of students preferred to develop their podcast by adding music and fun elements into it. They believed that the informal style would appeal to students.

> . . . we wanted to make it fun we didn't want to make a serious laborious, monotonous recording. So we added in some jingles, we just wanted to make it fun because the objective of the podcast that we were given was that it's a podcast for people who are in the first year, now to choose what they want to do the special study module. If they want to do genetics they can learn from listening online to some of the things we've

done. . . . we thought you know it would be nice if they've got a bit of music, you know some laughter and then some serious bits in between (student F).

Another group of students chose to do their podcast in a debate style. They also believed that the informal conversational style is appropriate for first-year students.

Technical issues and new technologies
Students also reflected on another lesson they had learned. The recording stage took longer than students anticipated. It wasn't as simple as they thought, although many students felt quite confident with the technologies.

. . . when we started recording I thought it would last half an hour, but it took something like two and a half hours just to record it simply because we were making ridiculous mistakes, so it was a lot harder than I thought (student G).

Another positive aspect of the sessions was to familiarize students with new technologies.

. . . it just made me appreciate how we can use different types of media to learn. . . . using different media to learn just makes it a bit easier. It breaks a bit of monotony just reading lecture slides. I suppose in future if we had podcasts of lectures available it would be quite nice to be able to listen to them while you're revising for exams. It made me appreciate that you know there are other forms of media available and it can help us (student H).

Motivating students
Although medical students are often highly motivated and focused on their studies, several students described their experiences of developing podcasts as motivational and interesting. They said that they enjoyed the process because they were doing something new and something different. Students also commented that they took on a more active and creative role during the development process.

. . . we're always at the receiving end of listening to lectures . . . so in doing this we actually got to appreciate how much organising goes into something like this (student I).

It is too early to determine whether the podcasts will motivate following cohorts to study genetics; however, evidence from the download statistics and questionnaire (see below) suggests that more than just the participants have listened to the podcasts and found them useful.

Download statistics and questionnaire data
Download statistics were collected; however, due to limitations of the VLE through which the podcasts were distributed, it was not possible to break

down the data into different groups of students. Overall there were 565 downloads of the podcasts (Table 14.1). Unfortunately, it is not possible to say whether any one individual downloaded a podcast more than once. Students who downloaded the podcasts were invited to complete a short online anonymous questionnaire. Thirty-six students responded and the data were collated (Table 14.2). The majority of students who downloaded the podcasts (53 per cent) were students who had taken the module.

Table 14.1 Podcast download statistics

Podcast topic	Number of times downloaded
Designer babies	128
Diabetes	104
Genetic screening	114
Genetic testing	98
Haemophilia	121
Total downloads	565

Note: Podcasts were distributed through the Leicester Medical School's Learning Environment. Each time a podcast file was downloaded, the system logs this. However, due to system constraints no further data was available. Downloads were recorded over a period of 8 months.

The responses to the podcasts were overwhelmingly positive, both concerning the content and the use of podcasting in this context.

Table 14.2 Questionnaire responses

Question	Response
Which year of your course are you in?	Year 1 – 11
	Year 2 – 25
	Other years – 0
If you are a second-year did you take the genetics special study module?	Yes – 19
	No – 6
	Not applicable – 11
I found the content of the podcast(s) interesting	4.1
I found the style of presentation engaging	3.7
I would like to listen to more student-produced podcasts	3.9
I think podcasts of other course material would be useful	4.2

Note: Questions 1 and 2 asked which year of the course the students were in and if they were second year had they taken the genetics module. The remaining questions used a Likert scale from 1 (strongly disagree) to 5 (strongly agree).

Conclusions and recommendations

The approach used in this preliminary study proved very successful in engaging students and broadening their understanding of the topics covered. Data from focus-group sessions highlighted many other benefits, particularly in developing teamworking, organization and other transferable skills. The aim of the approach used was to benefit both the students who made the podcasts and also those who listen to them. While it is clear that the participants benefited on a number of levels, and we do have some data on the impact of the podcasts on other students, a further larger study will be necessary.

We shall be repeating the podcasting sessions with this year's cohort of students. One problem with the work described here was lack of sufficient portable digital recording equipment restricting the choice of material that could be recorded. We now have a class set of MP3 recorders that will allow students more flexibility in recording, including the possibility of interviews both of other students and of researchers, in a classroom setting and 'in the field'. One new development planned in addition to the current project is for students to interview leading local researchers on their work and to prepare short overviews to engage students' interest and enthusiasm for genetics. We have already trialled this on a very limited scale in the integrated science programme at the University of Leicester. It is intended that this resource of interview material can become part of the Virtual Genetics Education Centre being developed by the GENIE Centre of Excellence of Teaching and Learning to allow a much wider dissemination of the content.

Due to the success of the approach with the medical students, we are extending this to science undergraduates taking genetics courses. In particular, we are keen to engage first-year genetics specialists to consider ethical issues surrounding modern molecular genetics. Again, we hope to be able to make the podcasts available to a wide group of students as a useful learning resource. Following the positive feedback from the questionnaire, we also intend to introduce short podcasts produced by members of staff highlighting key topics in the course. One further area for inclusion in a larger scale study will be to investigate how and where the podcasts were listened to. Other developments might also include a student-produced, staff-moderated wiki as a valuable educational exercise for the contributors and as a study aid for users. Medical wikis have been proposed as a rapidly evolving method of dissemination of current practice (Giustini 2007), and these would be easily adaptable into a teaching environment.

15

Developing pedagogical podcasts

Palitha Edirisingha, Gilly Salmon and Ming Nie

Summary

Here the Informal Mobile Podcasting And Learning Adaptation (IMPALA) research team presents a 10-factor design model as a guide for practice for developing podcasting for learning in Higher Education (HE). The model guides you through the process of developing your own educational podcasts and offers you options for your own teaching and learning challenges and contexts. Each factor in the model underlies and leads to a design step. The design model is grounded in our research and emerged from in-depth data analysis in the IMPALA case studies, with additional data from the four independent studies in this book. We hope you will explore it and embrace it as an easy-to-use, research-to-practice model.

Introduction

We support Beetham and Sharpe's approach to 'rethinking' pedagogy and learning design for the digital age as a way of bridging theory and practice and an approach to presenting evidence that can be contextualized and applied (Beetham and Sharpe 2007). Hence, we have 'pulled together' the outcomes from the IMPALA and friends' experiences in a way that we hope you can explore, use and build on them in the service of podcasting for learning.

The 10-factor design model

Our analysis of podcasting experiences enabled us to identify the following 10 factors to be taken into consideration when developing podcasts to support teaching and learning in universities. Each factor leads to an important design step:

1. the purpose or pedagogical rationale;
2. the medium used (audio only or audio and visual);
3. the convergence (how much the podcasts are integrated with other e-learning);
4. the authors and contributors of content;
5. the structure of podcasting (frequency and timing);
6. the reusability of content;
7. the length;
8. the style (presentation, interview, dialogue);
9. the framework of content organization;
10. the access system (via VLE or internet-based feeder service such as Really Simple Syndication (RSS)).

Each design step offers one or more options (see Table 15.1).

You can use the model in several ways. If academic podcasting is new to you, we advise you to follow the model step by step, considering each factor in detail, as we do below. In practice, podcast designers sometimes have to vary the sequence or backtrack in using step-by-step models. For example, you may decide to change the medium that you chose for the podcast (Step 2) after you have looked into the access system (Step 10). If you have some experience of developing and using podcasts in your own teaching and/or you have supported colleagues in developing podcasts, you can review the model to compare it with your own approach. We hope that the model will in any case provide you with new perspectives on academic podcasting, with the focus on student learning.

Step 1: Decide the pedagogical rationale and the driver

We think that it is truly essential to make the decision to use podcasts in your teaching based on a teaching and learning problem, challenge or issue that you have identified. All the chapters in the book show examples of what we mean by this. We know that some of you may be interested from the technical point of view, and some by the novelty factor, but our research clearly showed that students were not similarly impressed without a clear rationale that links podcasts to your current or further developments of your teaching and learning activities. Podcasts with a rationale behind them are also more likely to appeal to your academic colleagues and course team.

We develop pedagogical rationales for podcasts through examining the teaching and learning issues that they can address. In this book are a range of such issues, each identified by university teachers. Among these issues we hope at least one may prove to be a spark for you, helping you to think about podcasting for your own teaching and learning, but we are confident you will have many more.

Table 15.2 provides a summary of the pedagogical rationales we identified,

Table 15.1 A 10-factor podcast development model

Factor	Options
1. Pedagogical rationale	Limitations of lectures in teaching complex and difficult topics
	Limitations of conventional approaches in teaching use of software tools
	Limitations of conventional feedback approaches
	Issues faced by first-time online learners
	Issues faced by distance learners
	Developing competency in:
	• collaborative skills; • active learning skills; • presentation skills; • essay writing skills; • reflective skills; • research skills; • articulation and communication skills.
	Improving the usefulness and attractiveness of teaching and learning resources
2. Medium	Audio podcasts Audio + vision podcasts
3. Convergence	Integrated with other media such as a VLE Stand-alone
4. Authors and contributors to podcasts	Subject or module lecturer
	University teachers
	Other university staff
	Fellow students
	Senior students
	Other stakeholders (experts or local community)
5. Structure of podcasting	Single-session podcasts
	Multiple sessions (weekly, fortnightly or monthly podcasts)
	Targeted podcasts for specific sessions, such as assessments or exams
6. Reusability	Temporary or reusable podcasts
7. Length	Short or long (less or more than 10 minutes) podcasts
8. Style	Formal, informal; and style of presentation: monologue, dialogue, interview or other
9. Framework	Signposting, navigating, planning
10. Access system	Via VLE A feeder service (RSS)

Table 15.2 Teaching and learning issues and podcasting

Chapter	Teaching and learning issue	Approach to using podcasts	Integration of podcasts
4	Complex concepts in undergraduate physics	Pre-lecture listening to podcasts containing difficult concepts	Supporting learning from lectures
5	Learning to use software tools	Instructional video podcasts	Supporting learning in practical classes
6	Location-based learning	Instructional video and audio podcasts	Supporting learning in the field
7	Limitations of conventional feedback on students' assessments	Podcasts with individual and group feedback on assessments	Supporting learning through feedback on assessed work
8	Use of online learning by first-time, campus-based online learners	Podcasts advising on time management, and study schedules	Supporting online learning by learners based on campus
9	Anxieties of learners regarding distance learning	Pre-class podcasts addressing anxieties of distance learners	Supporting learning by distance learners
10	Independent learning from existing resources	Video podcasts based on anatomical specimens	Supporting learning from existing resources
11	Acquiring active learning skills	Podcasts of 'digital stories' created by students	Supporting the development of learning and study skills
12	Acquiring collaborative learning and study skills	Podcasts by lecturers and students advising on presentations and assessed work	Supporting the development of learning and study skills
13	Acquiring reflective skills	Podcasts recording student presentations and peer comments	Supporting the development of learning and study skills
14	Acquiring skills in research, articulation, presentation and communication with general public	Student-created podcasts on contemporary genetic and medical-related topics	Supporting the development of learning and study skills

the approach adopted by the university teachers in each case to using podcasts and how this particular approach to podcasting is linked to curriculum choices and students' learning.

If you would like some ideas, a summary of how others have identified issues and how their approach to using podcasts is linked to other teaching and learning activities follows. If you are working in a team, you may find it helpful to collaborate in writing a 'learning mission statement' that will help you to work out and state your rationale, and to make sure that your plans for developing the podcast are clearly linked to how your module is taught and learned.

Understanding complex concepts in undergraduate physics (Chapter 4)

For the Edinburgh physicists you can read about in Chapter 4, their challenge was that lectures are of limited value in helping their undergraduates, who may hold fundamental misconceptions about physics, to understand conceptually complex topics. The pedagogical rationale for using podcasts was that if first-year undergraduates, before coming to formal lectures, listened to podcasts addressing these difficult topics they would understand more in the lectures. They were also interested in investigating whether podcasts could facilitate and promote students' own reflections on their understanding of the challenging topics – something we know, of course, is critically important in learning developments in HE (see Chapter 13). A further objective for using podcasts was to explore whether students could grasp concepts of physics that are traditionally taught using visual representations, through the medium of audio.

Learning to use software tools (Chapter 5)

The teaching and learning issue identified by Nick Mount and Claire Chambers reported in Chapter 5 was the demand placed upon undergraduate students to be competent in using a range of software tools, which is essential for taking part in successfully learning their disciplinary knowledge. They knew that learning to use these tools was still dominated by paper-based manuals and tutorials that make heavy demands on staff time, given increasing student numbers on certain courses. An additional issue was that their specialized software, such as Geographical Information Systems (GIS), was new to most students. Students general information and communications technology (ICT) skills were not of much help. Nick Mount and Claire Chambers reasoned that the students needed demonstration video podcasts that would provide a step-by-step guide to carrying out various operations with the software. They planned that their video podcasts would be closely linked to students' learning activities with computers in practical classes.

Supporting learning in the field (Chapter 6)

The main teaching and learning objective identified by geographers at three UK universities was supporting learning from fieldwork. As you can read in Chapter 6, they illuminate the opportunities that podcasting brings in enhancing the student learning experience and in linking learning spaces.

Improving the quality of feedback on students' assessed work (Chapter 7)

Derek France and Chris Ribchester knew that providing feedback on students' assessed work was important in teaching and learning, but they identified limitations on how much students could benefit from the usual text-based feedback. To improve the quality of feedback, and to support their students' learning from feedback, they developed podcasts that would help their students to interpret and act on the feedback the university teachers provided.

Learning to be first-time online learners (Chapter 8)

Although John Fothergill knew that students enrolled in campus-based institutions generally learned through face-to-face methods of teaching such as lectures and seminars, the university's Virtual Learning Environment (VLE) gave him an opportunity to deliver some content online, thus offering his students some flexibility of learning, with pace, time and locations suited to their individual circumstances. His students were mostly first-time online learners and many of them were overseas students learning in the UK. He found that they needed a little extra support to benefit from online delivery of content. He also wanted to bring the course to life and add 'lustre'. His rationale for using podcasts was to provide scaffolding and guidance to students and to enliven the course. As John Fothergill points out in Chapter 8, his use of podcasts was directly linked to how the module was taught online.

Distance for learners (Chapter 9)

The teaching and learning issue identified by Mark Lee and Belinda Tynan was the preconceptions about a subject or its content, along with anxiety in a variety of forms that their students brought to their learning. They observed that these acted as immediate impediments for students' productive engagement in collaborations and a variety of activities that promote learning. They also tried to address the limitations of the usual conventional printed study guides that are important resources for distance learners.

Their rationale was that podcasts had the potential to address such issues and they set out to explore the beneficial effects of providing supplementary material as podcasts.

Improving the usefulness of existing teaching and learning resources (Chapter 10)

The animal vets' rationale for using podcasts, in Chapter 10, is to make more effective and wider use of well-established (and a rather amazing collection) of teaching and learning resources available at the university. The college's anatomical museum has a vast collection of anatomical and histological specimens collected over its 200-year-old history. These preserved specimens normally require tutor support for exposition to ever increasing numbers of students. Through the use of video podcasts, the vets were aiming to address the issue of providing personalized access to specimens.

Developing collaborative and active learning skills (Chapter 11)

The main teaching and learning objective identified by Martin Jenkins and Jo Lonsdale in Chapter 11 was to facilitate the induction of new entrants into HE. They also wished to further encourage student collaboration, and develop learners' active and reflective learning skills. They decided to introduce the technology of creating and distributing podcasts during the university's induction week. They reasoned that 'digital storytelling' by the new students could help their induction and foster desired skills.

Developing students' presentation and portfolio skills (Chapter 12)

Libby Rothwell's Chapter 12 illustrates an approach to using podcasts to help undergraduates in their presentation and portfolio work, both of which are assessed. Her key challenge was teaching a core module taken by students from different fields of study, who had limited peer-to-peer contact time to establish a cohort identity. They were required to develop a portfolio that was assessed at the end of the semester. She explored podcasts to offer additional support to her students in developing their module-specific learning and study skills.

Developing students' reflective skills (Chapter 13)

Dick Ng'ambi's teaching and learning rationale was to develop his postgraduate students' reflective skills. You can read more about it in Chapter 13. His students are required to write a reflective academic essay as part of their assessment. He identified the potential of podcasts to facilitate reflection: students are able to listen to them many times, even after the creation of essay content. This delay fosters reflection.

Developing research, articulation and communication skills (Chapter 14)

Chris Cane and Annette Cashmore in Chapter 14 identify many teaching and learning challenges: they teach students in a discipline where mastery of subject matter involves learning the science as well as learning the ethical issues surrounding the subject matter. Students must also engage with the broader discipline, and learn about new discoveries in it as preparation for becoming bioscientists and medical practitioners. In medicine, they must be able to articulate and communicate scientific knowledge to laypeople. They planned that podcasting would provide a way of developing such skills in their students.

Step 2: Select the medium

The purpose of developing podcasts and how students are going to use them will help you to decide which medium you need for your podcasts. Your choice is from audio only or whether to incorporate audio with visual material such as video, still images and graphical illustrations. You might like to take a quick review of the types in Chapter 3 (pp. 22–5). Eight out of eleven of the approaches presented in this book used audio only podcasts. Our analysis of development of the IMPALA podcasts over two academic years shows that audio podcasts were considered adequate for the teaching and learning issues that they were designed to address. Almost all the IMPALA practitioners were beginner podcasters and at the time of developing our approaches to using podcasts, audio-only podcasts were favoured due to the simplicity of the technology. Our Appendix should work for you if you have limited local help.

The teaching and learning issues identified for the three podcasts with vision (learning to use software tools in Chapter 5; 'potcasts' in Chapter 10; and 'digital stories' in Chapter 11) all demanded the use of video and other imagery. The video podcasts on GIS software were developed by an academic with strong technical skills for recording and manipulating video imagery with the help of a learning technologist. The development of museum 'potcasts' involved, in addition to lecturers who teach the subject, an experienced learning technologist to develop the final product. The vets report that each two-minute video podcast needed around four hours of an academic's time and around four hours for a technical member of staff. So they say around £230 per durable, reusable 'potcast'. The digital story podcasts were created by students. Students were 'digital natives' who were able to learn the basic skills with minimum training, although the final editing was done by faculty learning technologists to meet a tight deadline.

Most of the audio-only podcasts were developed by the practitioner lecturers themselves, or by students. They acquired the basic skills needed for recording and editing digital sound files using a laptop and freely available software (see Appendix).

If you are new to developing podcasting and/or working with limited resources with no time for developing sophisticated podcasts, or if you are working alone without much help, our advice would be to start with audio-only podcasts. As we have shown throughout the book, it is easy to identify teaching and learning issues that can be addressed through the use of audio-only podcasts. And there are special characteristics of voice that might interest you and benefit your students (we wrote about these in Chapter 1, pp. 4–6). We suggest that you only develop video podcasts if the teaching objective really requires visuals and the shelf life of the video podcasts are very long. The GIS podcasts and 'potcasts' are clear examples of podcasts with longer shelf lives.

Step 3: Choose convergence

Of course you would expect us to remind you that it is a good practice to integrate your podcasts with the rest of your teaching and learning provision and especially with e-learning activities (Salmon 2002). Our research into students' use and how they perceive the usefulness of podcasts showed that the more they see podcasts as part of the overall teaching and learning provision, the better motivated they will be to access and use them. If your students merely perceive your podcasts as added extras, most will be less interested in them.

The best example we can offer of integrating podcasts with the rest of the e-learning activities is the 'profcast' approach presented in Chapter 8, where podcasts served as the starting point for a student's typical weekly learning activities. These podcasts were released on a Sunday evening as the students started their study week on a Monday. They provided feedback on students' work in the previous week and a feedforward for the following week with advice on which sections of the module were to be studied and how. These proved to be highly motivational as you can read.

In Chapter 5, the software instructional videos replaced traditional paper and tutorial-based instruction. Almost all the students used almost all the podcasts that were available, and some used these podcasts many times because they perceived the benefits of using them. In Chapter 12, the podcasters integrated their podcasts into the Faculty's student learning skills programme. There was high use of these podcasts too.

Step 4: Choose authors and contributors to podcasts

By now you would expect us to point out that who contributes depends on the purpose of the podcasts, and the challenge being addressed. The IMPALA cases and others reported in this book use three broad approaches:

- solely university teacher-generated;
- solely student-generated;
- a mixture of student- and instructor-generated.

A university teacher or instructor was the sole contributor for the physics podcasts (Chapter 4), the 'profcasts' (Chapter 8), the software instructional podcasts (Chapter 5), feedback podcasts (Chapter 7) and 'potcasts' (Chapter 10). They dealt with key disciplinary knowledge and advice on learning and studying. At the other extreme were the student-generated podcasts: digital stories (Chapter 11), reflective podcasts (Chapter 13) and 'genetics' podcasts (Chapter 14). The objectives for these podcasts were to address specific teaching and learning issues via the voices of students and to develop students' own learning and study skills. In the third category, combining student- and teacher-generated content were podcasts for distance learners (Chapter 9) and study skills podcasts (Chapter 12).

Our best advice is to think creatively and consider ways of incorporating voices and perspectives from your students and other stakeholders as often as you can. An approach reported in Chapter 12 was to record students' talking about learning issues and former or senior students providing advice, in addition to academic staff. Chapter 9 takes a similar approach: current and former students discussed their anxieties as distance learners and shared ideas on ways of resolving them. Our evaluations showed that students like to listen to the voices, opinions and contributions of other students as well as their teaching staff. In this way you can make your podcasts much more interesting and rather different from other formal teaching and learning material.

Step 5: Decide on structure of podcasting

Again, depending on your objectives, you need to choose the best way of structuring your podcasts and how frequently to deliver them. First, are they going to be offered singly or as a series? If as a series, will the series be weekly, fortnightly or monthly? Will they be targeted on specific events, such as induction week, or aligned with assessment times such as examinations?

Our research shows that students are more likely to access and use podcasts if they are made available on a regular basis, say weekly, on a particular time of the day and the week. We also know that regular podcasts enable students to get used to using them and working out their own pattern, so it is a good idea to give students time to get used to them but make them gradually more challenging. If the podcasts are going to be offered as episodes, their frequency (weekly, fortnightly or monthly) depends on how you link them to the rest of the teaching and learning activities. You can help students develop a regular habit of using podcasts by letting them know in advance the frequency and the day of the week that they are going to be made available. And you must deliver according to the plan!

A good example is in Chapter 8, where the professor made available his podcasts (the 'profcasts') on a Sunday evening, without fail, for more than two academic semesters. Students got used to accessing his podcasts on the same day or the following day, almost like tuning into their favourite radio programme. New entrants to the university knew about his podcasts even before they decided to enrol on the module. These students also thought their professor was a great teacher and highly accessible to them. We conclude that the structuring and regular issue of podcasts can have a profound effect on how students relate positively to their lecturer and regularity helps them to pace and keep on track with their learning.

Step 6: Decide on reusability

Now we are begging. Please consider the reusability of your podcasts, in their entirety or in part, from the very beginning. Developing podcasts, although enjoyable and useful for supporting student learning, has resource implications, and in the long run, podcasts have the potential to move from a 'peripheral' to a 'core' technology (Salmon 2005). This book provides examples of both reusable podcasts and one-off podcasts that cannot be used in later years. Physics podcasts (Chapter 4), GIS instructional podcasts (Chapter 5) and 'potcasts' (Chapter 10) are examples of reusable ones. The disciplinary knowledge covered in these podcasts is fairly stable therefore the authors have been able to reuse them. In the planning stage, the resources that were allocated to developing these podcasts were considered to be a worthwhile investment, partly in the light of their reusability.

The distance learner podcasts (Chapter 9) and study skills podcasts (Chapter 12) are one-offs because they were produced to address particular teaching and learning issues identified at the time of production. However our analysis of content of these podcasts shows that the content covered in these podcasts can be useful for new cohorts of students. Indeed, the author who produced the study skills podcasts was planning to reuse them, because the issues they addressed are equally relevant to new cohorts of students.

Other podcasts, such as those offering 'feedback' (Chapter 7), 'digital stories' (Chapter 11) and 'reflective skills' (Chapter 13) are context and student-cohort-specific. Feedback podcasts usually need to be remade for each new cohort. The other three kinds will usually be produced afresh by students each year but in some instances these podcasts can be offered to new student cohorts with clear guidance on how they can be used. For example, new cohorts may be able to benefit by listening to feedback given to former students on assessed work, such as common mistakes in essays.

Chapter 8 provides useful guidance on how John Fothergill reused some material produced in his previous 'profcasts'. He was able to reuse, for example, a news item on the anniversary of the invention of fibre optics, but he recorded new content for the feedback on student progress. He was able to reuse the same jokes, recorded the previous year!

So you can see how important it is to consider reusability at the time of planning your podcasts if you possibly can. As with all learning resources, you will need to get organized. The recording and editing technology is easy to use if you want to include old material in new podcasts (see Appendix, pp. 194–6).

Step 7: Choose length

You may be tempted, as the owner of the voice in your podcasts, to think that your students would listen to your podcasts regardless of how long they are! Our research, with students who listened to IMPALA podcasts over a period of two academic years, showed an inverse relationship between the length of a podcast and the propensity to listen to it. In fact, 10 minutes seems to be the right maximum length that students are willing to listen to. Based on the findings from the pilot study, IMPALA podcasts were made not to exceed 10 minutes. By limiting the length of podcasts, we also found that students were more likely to listen to them on the move, while they commuted to university, while doing their part-time job, such as stocking the grocery counter at the supermarket, or when using the treadmill in the gym. In short, the shorter podcasts help students to engage more often and less formally – just how they listen to their music on an iPod. According to our students, an hour-long podcast, such as a lecture recording, requires sitting down with a notebook and listening attentively, and such use has its place, for example, when revising for an exam.

For the podcaster-developer, packing what you need into 10 minutes demands greater focus on the learning objectives and deeper thinking about content to achieve them. And you might need to make more short podcasts rather than fewer long ones.

Step 8: Select style

By style, we mean the degree of formality adopted and the genre (for example interviews, discussions) selected for your podcasts. The style of a podcast is important for several reasons. As we have pointed out, at the moment most educational podcasts are audio for simplicity and usability. Therefore, they need to be interesting to listen to as well as being informative, if they are to hold students' attention.

As a novice academic podcast producer, you may feel it is difficult to produce such engaging podcasts, like good quality radio programmes. However, our IMPALA partners found it was not difficult to adopt an informal style rather than a formal one. We suggest you make notes on what you are going to say, and just talk through your notes as if you were speaking to a group of students or running a small group tutorial, rather than write down and read every word. Specific techniques adopted by IMPALA partners were to start by talking about the weather (quite usual in England!) or a particular football match they had just watched (also normal conversation!) before recording the actual podcast, leaving in small mistakes made while recording, such as saying 'I'm sorry I just dropped the mike – it is OK now'. A friendly tone invites students to learn and helps to build intimacy with the speaker, as illustrated by some students who listened to feedback podcasts reported in Chapter 7. Other approaches to making your podcasts more interesting to listen to is to incorporate informal learning content such as people's experiences, opinions, and perspectives through interviews, discussions and other forms of dialogue, as shown in Chapters 9, 12 and 14.

Step 9: Decide on framework

Your plan, agenda or framework for each podcast is important for engaging your students and helping them to learn successfully. Unlike a text file, an audio file is limited in that we cannot glance at the whole document, or quickly scan it to get a sense of its content, to see how we wish to use it. With a sound file, the student needs to listen to the whole thing (or take random samples) in order to understand what it is about. At the very least, it is important to tell your students at the beginning of the podcast what is going to be covered. This is normal practice in radio programmes, such as documentaries and current affairs, as well as in delivering lectures, so it will not be new to you.

If your podcasts are going to be in a series, it is most useful to think about the overall framework for each one and use it, then stick to it for all of them.

The 'profcast' framework is an easy and successful structure to adopt (Chapter 8), but no doubt you will think of others. The 10-minute profcasts were divided into three sections:

- An introductory news item related to the subject matter (to engage the student).
- The middle part where the content- and study-related items are discussed and presented.
- The end part where the author does a joke or a rap (to make sure that students listen to the end!).

The podcaster maintained this framework for both iterations of his series of podcasts, and evaluation showed that students liked it and they became familiar with the framework by the second or third episode.

We also suggest that you indicate what students are expected to do when they are listening to your podcasts, or afterwards. If you want students to take notes, talk to others, carry out activities and return or visit certain sections of the VLE, you need to say so at the beginning. Perhaps you do not want them to do anything particular, other than listen, and you may want to let them know at the start that they can listen to your podcasts while carrying out other routine activities such as walking.

If you have suitable equipment or technical help, you might like to review our section on 'enhanced podcasts' in Chapter 3 (pp. 24–5), where a somewhat more sophisticated approach can be taken to navigation for listeners.

Step 10: Select access system

Some of you might be puzzled as to why we left to last the delivery and access issues. We know that those of you most interested in podcasting as a technology will find this strange! There is more about these in Chapter 3 (pp. 25–7).

While we agree that podcasts are different from other digital media files in their ability to be delivered on the internet using a feeder technology, such as RSS and can be syndicated and aggregated automatically, our focus is on pedagogical aspects of podcasting. Our close observation of more than two dozen practitioner lecturers developing podcasts to support teaching is that academics tend to choose a technology that is readily available at their universities and with which their students are familiar. Therefore, the university supported VLE was the preferred platform for delivery to and access by students for almost all the work presented here. Most of the HE institutions have invested heavily in their preferred VLE and teams of academics, staff developers and technologists are putting commendable efforts into integrating VLE for teaching, learning and assessment. The students all have access, and the podcasts are protected behind firewalls and passwords. Our IMPALA research shows that about 95 per cent of HE students use their VLE on a regular basis.

Therefore, we say why not use your VLE to deliver your podcasts? The technology involved is simple; it is the same as uploading a text or Power-Point file to the content area of a VLE. Once you let your students know where you archive your podcasts, they need little guidance to download them to their preferred MP3 player, whether to a personal dedicated player or to a laptop. More institutional VLEs will be developing a podcast publishing tool, which enables you to publish your podcasts onto an external aggregator service such as iTunes (see Appendix, pp. 201–3). Currently, proprietary VLEs such as Blackboard offer 'add-ins' that support RSS feeds, so you might like to check up on what your own institution can offer. We are still waiting for ways in which students can add their own podcasts to a VLE though.

However, if you want to publish on the internet, we look forward to being able to access your words. Chapter 3, the Appendix and the website for the book (podcastingforlearning.com) have more details. Of course you can also 'broadcast' podcasts in your lecture theatre (see Chapter 4).

Intellectual property

Whether your podcasts are teacher- or student-developed, or a combination, you need to consider any intellectual property (IP) issues, including potential future reuses, reworking or re-versioning of the podcasts. You will find more advice and links on the website but please note:

- Performing rights in recorded materials generally belong to the original performer.
- Copyright in any graphic, photographic or video image or music is owned by the creator.
- Integrating within a single podcast different types of material, or material from different contributors and collaborators, may mean that many IP rights will be attached.

We suggest that you should:

- be clear to original contributors about how the podcasts will be used, and seek their permission;
- consider potential future uses for a podcast recording at the beginning of the process;
- consult your university copyright officer (often in the Library).

The Legal Department of JISC (www.jisclegal.ac.uk) produces a range of helpful publications. Some projects provide help with 'legal deposits' ('The Spoken Word', for example, spokenword.ac.uk).

Enabling and assisting learning

On the whole, using audio makes learning materials appealing and useful for a wide range of learners, including those who have most disabilities, such as dyslexia and sight loss. In many countries there is legislation to ensure that disabled students are not disadvantaged. In the UK, for example, The Disability Discrimination Act and the Special Educational Needs Disability Act 2001, require universities to anticipate and make reasonable adjustments to meet the needs of disabled learners. The main disadvantaged group is made up of those with hearing loss, but it is fairly easy to provide a transcript, which helps. Your university accessibility officer will provide you with more information and our book website has some useful links.

Design coda

We hope the pedagogical podcasting model for higher education is flexible enough to accommodate the inevitable technical changes and improvements that will occur and be available to all of us. We hope this chapter will be the start of testing and improving on the model in different contexts and in new ways. We think we have made clear that the model's success in practice depends on a close match between the podcasting and the learning and teaching challenge and the approach to pedagogical design (not the technology!).

We would be delighted if you would let us know how you get on with designing and delivering your own podcasts based on this 10-step design model. We are easy to find through the book's website, www.podcastingforlearning.com.

16

The future for podcasting

Gilly Salmon

Summary

This chapter offers pointers for discussion, ideas for the further research and development of podcasting, and a quick speculation about the future of podcasting for learning in universities.
   But first, a 'digital immigrant' gets her Pod-visa:

Introduction

When I'm an old woman, I shall carry,
Six different iPods – and none of them will marry,
Standards for compatibility or service integration,
Communication with me will depend on your imagination.

I shall spend my pension on silly downloads and updates,
That will render my technology completely incoherate,
I'll exceed my monthly data transfer rates and message limit,
Abandoning responsibility for my 'free voice' spirit.

I shall sit on the pavement and obstruct normal business,
Until I get a mobile connection that has been built for easiness,
I will take any free media from shops and from papers,
Installing them all with no identity shapers.

If I don't know what day it is – why should I not
Forget my password and bank sorting code?
And disperse my personal data amongst six youthful avatars,
Shared in Second Life – as contingency against disasters:
Where dress codes permit the wearing of silk sandals,
And summer gloves with reckless abandon,
Where no one worries about wearing slippers in the rain,
And there's instant transport from terrain to terrain.

I shall put false but convincing entries into Wikipedia,
For who else should profess to the new media?
I will make up for the sobriety of my text based youth,
With podding indulgence that may border on uncouth.

I shall copy software under the authority of my blue hat,
Which clashes with my dress and the licence dictat,
So maybe I ought to practise some of this now,
So that those that know me can easily show.
That whilst I carry six iPods for internet use,
My behaviour is not that of recently learned abuse,
That I have always had proneness for the disruptable
Not suddenly that I'm old and starting to wear purple.

With acknowledgement to Jenny Joseph's original poem 'Warning' 1997

Pod capture: our moment in time

Nearly everyone involved in Higher Education (HE) is constantly attempting to find new ways of learning and teaching, facing up to new challenges, meeting changing learner demands, achieving more with fewer resources – and in our special era – working out how technologies can be harnessed productively and successfully. The contexts and conditions for learning technologies are changing very fast. We cannot take control of the external environment but the new technologies pouring across our boundaries do offer us all very special opportunities.

Enter the sparkling new podcast, stage left. The audience in this theatre is made up of students who have grown up with the internet as part of their lives – and their learning. Their adoption of technologies in their everyday communication and entertainment has already outstripped our understanding of appropriate pedagogical responses in universities. Hence, mobile learning and its cousin podcasting are variously viewed as a passing wave, a threat to formal education, or the answer to the question of how to engage and enthrall learners of the future.

Podcasting for learning is part of the vast and confusing changes occurring throughout HE, throughout the world. We have just got used to using the internet as part of our core offerings – we create or aggregate content for our students to consume. But new directions on the web invite contribution and choice (often known as Web 2.0) and gives us a new landscape. Learning, knowledge and technology is converging; everything and everyone is increasingly mobile and many people have multiple 'presence' online. So the future is complex, uncertain and a little difficult to predict! In the complex marriage of technology and pedagogy, our new challenge is to consider where podcasting for learning could go next.

Podcasting is part of a wider movement towards internet-mediated collections of people linked by their common interests and by producing, sharing, collecting and remixing diverse 'stuff'. In addition, the interest in voice messaging may result in a new genre for collaborative and remote groups – already I have started work on the younger sibling of e-tivities (Salmon 2002): pod-tivities! Podcasts and podcasting do not have learning explicitly built into them: we design in the pedagogy. We should start from a learning challenge, allow ourselves to 'evolve' and examine ways of supporting and extending learning. I believe strongly in finding, evaluating, creating, contributing and working together for knowledge-sharing, and that these must be the best places to start.

In Chapter 3 we pointed out that podcasts and podcasting are brand new as learning technologies. Will podcasting go on to transform the world of learning in the second decade of the 21st century? Maybe, but maybe not. Can a podcast enhance existing practices? Will audio files become 'blended' and as common as .pdf files in Virtual Learning Environments (VLEs)? Perhaps those ideas are a little more likely? What is definitely true is that what happens depends on the response of the educators – each of us – and not something intrinsic within the technology.

Most groups of people who try to exploit a novel product or service for their hopes and intents tend to overestimate the short-term effects and underestimate the long-term wider impact. There is a word for this common phenomenon: macromyopia (Dodge 2007). Macromyopia happens because new ideas and technologies feel 'normal' and 'obvious' to trailblazers. Innovators look at the early success of something for a smallish and specific purpose and tend to assume it will 'scale up' in the same way (if only others would see the 'light' . . .). They cast few glances backwards or sideways. They are focused on what they are building and contributing and rarely see the often much bigger and longer-term ramifications. In universities, the early pedagogical podcasters cannot understand why the many advantages of podcasting for learning are not 100 per cent obvious to their lecturing colleagues. However, I recently overheard this remark in the senior common room: 'I'm not sending my child to university to lie on the grass with an iPod!'.

The developers and providers of a technology add their own 'hype' and promote their products because of the investment they have made, adding to the confusion. Digital entertainment, for example, has been adopted differently than anticipated and is impacting on a wide range of unanticipated arenas – such as advertising (Berman et al. 2007). I have found that use of learning technology in universities, with their short-term research projects and annual plans and budgets, often suffers from macromyopia.

In most cases the pioneer of a product or technology achieves some early success in a narrow way. The big win may come later by incorporating the new technology into an existing product or service and creating a 'best-of-both-worlds' solution that appeals to a much broader range of people and applications. Of course, the success or failure of innovations always depends on a combination of factors at work. But in most cases the problem is not inferior technology: it is people understanding the potential benefits and needs of mainstreaming, which require policy and business decisions, and, in universities, unpicking and 're-engineering' the complex relationships with existing and often very successful practices that have stood the test of time.

I hope this book has shown you that there are good teachers across many disciplines creating the 'first wave' and showing us the way. No one involved in the Informal Mobile Podcasting And Learning Adaptation (IMPALA) research studies, nor IMPALA's friends, were ardent techies – there was no blind faith in the power of technology for us; a podcast is a distributed downloadable audio file. Nothing more, nothing less. The critical issue is that podcasting is a technology with potential for learning. The learning challenge needs to be perceived and the design for learning acted upon by university teachers. So where it goes is up to us – researching, trying things out and listening long and hard to our students, and evaluating the results in an objective manner. What is truly new is that learner experience and contribution is in the middle of the innovation, for the first time. And it is only just beginning.

Towards the end of the first decade of the 21st century, educators are in a hugely privileged and influential position. The opportunity to participate in changing the learning world is really a very rare one, and so I hope you are able to cherish it. You will face challenges. Every disruptive technology has always been dynamic, sometimes even a see-saw of successes and failures, sometimes a 'tipping' point in which the early adopters begin to be moved aside as the innovation is mainstreamed. Tensions are likely as the pod frontier is civilized, between people who like university teaching just the way it is and those who have hopes of what it might become.

I think that it is time we followed our learners. Not to be dazzled by the technology, but to take a look at what loads of people are actually doing with podcasting and their level of engagement. And then to examine the business and teaching models to see if it makes sense, in what circumstances and whether they can be scaled up to a meaningful size.

We know that roadways towards productive learning through new technologies are littered with expensive wrecks. Clearly, we must learn from past mistakes if podcasting for learning is to have a future (Watt 2007). I think many of the lessons of avoiding technologies as drivers have been learned, but sustainable planning for flexible and uncertain futures is also not yet in evidence. Scaling up plans will need to include a mature systems-based approach to addressing technical barriers, building institutional capacity for pedagogical changes and technology–university partnerships.

In the future, we will face up to the term 'web feed' as a normal part of our vocabulary with its associated cultural words; rip, mix and burn. There is an inherent promise to speed up creativity, repurposing, collaboration and contribution from all – and distribution to multiple channels. You will have a simple technology with the power to create new and more engaging, happier, mobile, flexible learning in the future. The opportunity to create easily something new and worth while does not come often, so I hope you will take it. The barriers to entry for staff and students are very low. Get ready by trying it out now!

Whether or not podcasting will add real long-term value to student learning or merely prove disruptive and diversionary depends on how the educators imagine, design and integrate its potential. There is no one overriding vision or value – these can be entirely your own. In 2005, I wrote about how all of us in universities needed to strategize to exploit learning technologies for 'taking off in powered flight', rather than merely flapping around (Salmon 2005). Podcasting offers us a nice flat runway. I believe that its time has come. Get in the cockpit, colleagues – don't miss this opportunity!

Our future needs to include research on whether podcasting for learning in HE will result in more creative, engaging and feasible plans to address the needs (demands?) of 21st-century learners. Here are some ideas to get you started (Table 16.1).

Table 16.1 Ideas for future implementation and research in podcasting for learning

Purpose	Opportunities and challenges	Future of podcasting could support...	Research and development questions
Assessment and feedback	Aligning methods of assessment with approaches to learning and teaching Saving staff time while increasing student satisfaction with feedback	More efficient, effective feedback More self-assessment and reflection	What principles and approaches for assessment are successful with podcasting? Is feedback easier and quicker for staff and more acceptable to students through podcasting? What new kinds of assessment can be deployed with podcasting?
Personalized learning environments	Create a unique and personalized 'ecology' of software and services for each student to use to support their formal learning and work in collaboration with university-provided online environments and services	The attractiveness, efficiency and mobility of 'voice' The ease of use of podcasts – any time, any where Learner contribution and choice Personalization and update notification	What are the activity patterns for learners in personalized environments? Can these be structured and paced to support learning? How are media objects used for learning in social networks? How can we truly exploit mobility for learning? Could podcasts provide bridges across platforms?
Learning locations, mobility, ubiquitous access	Integration of off-campus learning with campus-based learning Exploitation of student-owned mobile devices	Seamless access to learning resources	What learning theories and approaches map onto mobility for learning? What specific applications offer the most value?

Transitions and boundary crossing	Collaboration across educational levels and for lifelong learning	Reusable, accessible podcasts for information and reach Voice- or video-based archives and portfolio building	What approaches are meaningful across levels and cohorts? Do media objects add value? Do podcasts help or hinder working across cultures and disciplines? Would podcasts help with expressions for cultures less inclined to text? Do podcasts facilitate progress towards lifelong learning? Do podcasts help people learning in their second or third language?
Non-text/radio	Engage the 'radio generation'?	Learning and knowledge community information feeds	Is there special value in podcasts for work-based and/or 'silver' learners? Will voice help with 'emotional intelligence' in teaching and learning? (Mortiboys 2005)
Tacit knowledge, informality	Productively incorporating informality into formal education	'Story telling is the killer app of evolution' (Sobol 2006)	What support and development do students need to benefit from effective use of informal tools for learning such as podcasting?
Dynamic, flexible, reusable resources	An old mantra but an enticing one: Any time, Any place: learners' choice	Harvesting, remixing Creating and shaping	How can we tackle the reusing and sharing of podcasts across educational communities?

Continued overleaf

Table 16.1 Ideas for future implementation and research in podcasting for learning

Purpose	Opportunities and challenges	Future of podcasting could support. . .	Research and development questions
Learner-centred, contributing student 'millenial' learning styles and media use habits	How Web 2.0 can we get (and want to . . .). What about Web 3.0?	Self-directing, producing, contributing	Can the academy tolerate 'half-baked' podcasts? What is the impact of amateurs and semi-professionals developing podcasts and bypassing the usual gatekeepers and guardians of learning material? Can we strike a balance between quality assurance and creativity?
Role of the lecturer – from the sage on stage, to the guide on side – and then the bod on the Ipod	Reclaim the emotional and 'human voice' aspects of learning Dispel the idea that you must be in the same physical space to teach	All lecturers think 'podcast' as well as or instead of 'lecture'	What are the training and development needs of staff? What skills and competencies can be developed? Will universities settle on being podcast producers and distributors and for what purpose? What are the change and 'scaling-up' models for mainstreaming podcasting in universities? What intellectual property issues are involved?
Personal ownership and second use – from entertainment to education	A device in search of a purpose? Billions of dollars are being put into the development of MP3 players of all kinds Education must not miss out!	While the technical people are always looking for greater media richness, there is also great value in the simplicity, immediacy and portability of the audio file.	What kind of podcast works best for each learning and teaching challenge, purpose, each discipline, subject or level of education?

Theme	Description	Detail	Questions
Small chunks	Web 2.0 and other emerging technologies invite small pieces loosely joined	Easily enhanced navigation in podcasting / Redesign for portability of learning materials	How can small pieces of learning be focused and paced to maintain attention? / Can 'small chunks' of media be reconciled with 'enterprise solutions'? / How can a wide range of collaborators including users work successfully together?
The greening of learning	Could we contribute to the sustainability of the environment?	Reduction in use of physical resources / Reuse and reversioning of digital resources	How green is your podcast? / What might the indicators of the greening of learning be?
Learner support and experience	Widening participation and appeal of HE	Podcasting could improve the accessibility and image of HE and studying at universities? / Future quality	Will podcasting contribute to raising standard across a wide front? / Will podcasting make learning in HE more appealing to wider audiences and/or increase social coherence? / Will podcasts help to raise the voice and engagement of the students to prepare for future changes?
Dynamic support of traditional teaching and learning	What about 'bluecasting' in lectures	Can we exploit cheap Bluetooth technologies in the classroom?	What approaches to mobility work well with campus-based learners? / What approaches work best for distance learners? / How can students use their personal devices in class?

17

The university in your pocket

David Bell

Summary

Another viewpoint and critique of podcasting for learning in universities: 'podagogy'

Introduction

Yesterday I told a student off for texting during my lecture. I felt lousy afterwards – not just guilty for having humiliated him in front of his peers in a rather schoolteacherish way, but also gloomy about yet another moment of digital dinosaurism, another instance where I felt out of touch with my students. I remembered Nick Mount at an Informal Mobile Podcasting And Learning Adaptation (IMPALA) workshop saying that he is the only lecturer he knows who starts his classes by asking students to turn their mobile phones *on* – they can text him questions as the lecture proceeds. In that moment I wished I was him, wished I too had kept pace with the changes in the learning landscape around me, wished I had stocks of techno-capital that are the props of digital nativism. And as I had spent the previous weeks thinking long and hard about e-, m- and u-learning, about always-on learners and teachers, I felt ashamed to have reacted so grumpily to a clear example of multitasking. And it never occurred to me that the texting activity I spied could be in any way connected to the lecture in progress, but maybe the student was using his phone to Google some key concept I moved too quickly past.

Clearly, I have yet to connect certain digital devices with learning practices, despite my recent immersion in the podcasting literatures. One thing I want to explore in this chapter, in fact, is the issue of this connectivity; I have been struck repeatedly during my forays into e-, m- and u-learning debates that there is a need to think carefully about the promises and the problems of assuming that learning can be seamlessly imported into digital devices. I will do this by looking at assorted strands of research into the forms, meanings and uses of digital devices, as well as reflecting critically on the amazing experiments that the contributors to this book describe and discuss. The core of my argument is the need to understand more fully how our relationships with these devices, and the practices that we have developed together, are more or less amenable to co-option for learning. I think that an approach to 'podagogy' (my shorthand for podcasts-in-learning), which fails to consider the broader socio-technical landscapes of which learning is a part, is doomed to failure.

Following Woolgar's (1991) discussion of the need to understand how users of technologies are configured along the road from production to consumption, I think we need to understand better how devices, users and practices are co-configured, and to unravel the messiness of this co-configuration. And, drawing on work in some of the more arcane byways of science and technology studies (STS), I think it is useful to think of devices, users and practices as material-semiotic entities – as at once things that *do* and things that *mean*. Michael (2003) has an excellent term for this: he talks of the 'function-expressions' of technological objects. Here he keeps fused together uses (functions) and meanings (expressions), reminding us that they can never be separated in our analyses. So a mobile phone has particular uses (both intended and unintended) – such as sending and receiving voice call; but it also has particular meanings – a phone can express our identity, be used to convey status, and so on. Approaching digital devices this way is, to my mind, the only way we will ever be able to get a handle on 'podagogy' and the various worlds it interfaces with. By drawing on selected research from across various disciplines concerned with 'socio-technical stuff' (and some 'learning stuff'), I want here to make some steps towards a few paths this line of flight might take us down.

Thinking techno-mobilities

My initial response to 'podagogy' has been to think it through the lenses of technology and mobility, or perhaps more accurately the lens of techno-logically mediated mobility, which I will call techno-mobility. Sociologists (and others) talk of a 'new mobilities paradigm' in their worlds, a need to rethink the patterning of societies and socialities in the context of mobility (Sheller and Urry 2006). All kinds of people and stuff are on the move, they tell us. There are many different ways that technologies afford (and inhibit) mobilities, but for an understanding of 'podagogy' we can begin with mobile communications technologies: wireless computing, mobile phones, hand-held digital devices, pervasive and location-aware devices, and all their pro-liferating close kin. For one of the chief benefits imagined for 'podagogy' (though not always borne out in evidence) is mobile learning – the new learning possibilities that techno-mobility offers. Here we need our first pause for thought, in order to understand how mobility is configured as a valuable attribute of certain types of people and of things.

This issue, of how some forms of mobility are given positive value, is addressed from the 'supply side' in a discussion by Moisander and Eriksson (2006) on how Nokia constructs ideas about the Mobile Information Society through its corporate communiqués, marketing and products, and in so doing also constructs 'mobile subjects'. Their interest lies in 'studying how global corporate actors of the ICT sector may be involved in making up the subjects of consumption by shaping the interpretive repertoires and cultural practices that are available for consumers as end-users of mobile devices' (Moisander and Eriksson 2006: 258). By framing mobility in particular ways, Nokia constructs 'mobile professionals' as the 'serious' end-user of its products, fitting its phones to the imagined needs of this class. This subject is also mobile in the sense of seeking upward socio-economic mobility through technology-enabled self-improvement practices such as m-learning: picking up new skills and knowledge on the go, upskilling while in motion. Young people are framed as future mobile professionals, Moisander and Eriksson add, with Nokia constructing their lifestyles as 'busy, controlledly drifting, nomadic' (2006: 269).

In this analysis, corporations such as Nokia are powerful actors, shaping the dominant discourses of techno-mobility, and thereby configuring the user. Such an approach is at odds, however, with STS discussions that stress instead a series of mutual shapings or co-configurings. This strand is arguably most evident in debates about the domestication of technology. As Lehtonen (2003: 364) productively conceptualizes it, the domestication of new technologies 'refers to a learning process whereby things and people reciprocally influence each other'. His account of the gradual settling-in of new technologies into user biographies reveals considerable give and take: potential end-users are not passively shaped by corporate hands, but also shape the uptake of new technologies and partake of a set of 'trials' whereby they try but are simultaneously tried by new technologies. People and things come together and build particular kinds of cohabitations. Lehtonen describes 'slowly emerging cultures of use' (p. 381) around new technologies, which are the product of negotiation between the uses preset into the device, and the uses that develop precisely *by use*. So use is not simply configured into products: as Bakardjieva (2005) writes, 'use genres' reflect a particular form of domestication, whereby the affordances of devices are fitted to purposes both intended and unintended. Domestication is, for Lehtonen, full of *surprises*. Getting to the rich biographies of people and things is for him the only way to unlock the surprising stories of domestication.

Research about how people live with technology has begun to untangle some of these stories, whether through detailed investigation of the times and spaces of interaction, as in Bakardjieva's (2005) or Lally's (2002) ethnographic work on domestic computing, or through empirical and theoretical discussion of the various relationships between devices and people. Recent work has taken ideas from phenomenology and from actor network theory (ANT) in order to get at the messiness of living with machines. An amazing instance of this approach can be seen in Richardson's (2007) discussion of 'mobile media' and what she calls the '*technosoma*': her argument is that interacting (with surprising intimacy) with devices such as camera phones,

MP3 players and Personal Digital Assistants (PDAs), brings forth 'a medium specific mode of embodiment, a way of "having a body" that demands a complex socio-somatic adaptation' (p. 206).

Richardson is keen to replace the body into thinking about technology, rather than to see it effaced or erased, as in earlier dreams of 'leaving the meat behind' by entering cyberspace (Bell 2001). In particular, her discussion of developments in mobile gaming offers insights for understanding mobile learning. She talks of the rewiring of gameplay in mobile contexts, a rewiring that jettisons ideas of immersion prominent in earlier models of computer gaming; instead, mobile gaming is 'characterized by interruption, and sporadic or split attention in the midst of other activities' (Richardson 2007: 210). Richardson highlights the value of a phenomenological approach to technologies-and-bodies, arguing that this opens up new possibilities to 'consider the ways in which tele-technologies modify the body, and the kinds of embodiments afforded by telepresent and mobile media' (2007: 214). This kind of theoretically rich attention to detail would, I think, yield immensely valuable results for understanding mobile learning in the context precisely of these modifications and affordances.

iPod therefore I learn?

The focus on living with technologies asks vital questions about e-, m- and u-learning, of course. It asks that we attend to both the already stable and the still emerging use genres into which learning is being shepherded. It asks that we do not assume a seamless transplant: just because a device has learning affordances does not mean that learning can (or *should*) be made part of the repertoires of its use. A recurring theme in the empirical studies in this book concerns those devices that are and are not used to access podcasts, and the times and places when podcasts are used by learners. Why is it that so many learners reported using their personal computer to access podcasts? Why did their learning take place when and where it did, and why did it not take place at other times and spaces – including those predicted to be 'fillable' with learning activity?

These questions require a many-headed approach. We need to understand, as Moisander and Eriksson (2006) showed above, how devices do come configured with uses (and users) in mind. But we also need to attend to the experiences of use, to those slowly emerging cultures of use that Lehtonen brought to our attention. The *potential* uses of digital devices are multiplying, to the extent that we do not quite know what to call them anymore. When does a mobile phone become something else? When does its 'phoneness' recede as it becomes also a camera, an internet connection, a TV, a GPS device, a games console, and so on? How do users develop use genres, some collective and some individual, some preset and some surprising?

To understand the relation between the affordances of technologies and the dispositions of users, we need to explore the discursive construction of particular technologies, and connect this to stories of experience, of use, of cohabitation. By this I mean we need to get a handle on the ways that devices are talked about, written about, thought about: how do certain discourses take hold, and help to shape technologies and uses? Selwyn (2002) insightful discussion of the discursive construction of the personal computer as an educational device in the UK in the 1980s is useful to us here. He shows, through a detailed reading of government policy and information and technology (IT) business strategy, how the idea of 'educational computing' was discursively constructed and perpetuated, becoming unquestioned common sense. While personal computers have arguably lost some of this primary attachment to learning, Selwyn shows how this particular history has shaped and continues to shape understandings and uses of computers. Learning has been naturalized as something that computers mediate. We could track parallel tales of the configuring of other technologies; this would certainly help us understand why learning 'sticks' to some devices better than others. That the personal computer has this history of educational configuring has doubtless contributed to the use genres reported in the case studies here: it is a 'proper' learning technology, therefore appropriate for educational podcast consumption. It appears, on the evidence laid out in this book, to be more amenable to 'podagogy' than other digital devices – even if the primary purpose of those devices is more closely bound up with podcasting.

As the computer becomes mobile, or pervasive, or ubiquitous, we need to look very closely at how computing practices and experiences change. Selwyn reminds us, however, that it is a mistake to think that 'the scope of the computer's educational potential is . . . limited only by technical considerations' (2002: 428). Conversely, it is a mistake to think that technical breakthroughs will automatically lead to new uses. Piling on additional functionality does not always lead to cultures of use emerging, as the recent history of 3G phones shows (Goggin 2006). Just because a device *can* be used for something does not mean it *will* be used for that purpose – this is a complex socio-technical issue. The function-expressions that Michael (2003) highlighted must always be borne in mind when we approach a technology, and particularly when attempting to configure new uses. Cultures of use reflect function-expressions vividly: why is it, for example, that many teenagers like to play music from MP3 files through their mobile phones, rather than using an MP3 player? What function-expressions are the technology and the music performing in this use genre?

Clearly, the histories of technologies are littered with stories of their unintended uses, their 'double life' (Bell 2006). Those histories tell us about the stabilization of some use genres, but caution us not to assume a straightforward, linear path. STS studies show us that relatings between people and things are emergent and contingent. This can be read as an optimistic note, because it emphasizes potential and possibility: it does not rule out, in our case, the idea of educational uses of digital devices. It is in the negotiation of function-expressions that change occurs. And this reminds us of the need to consider *expressions* as well as functions when we try to understand the 'unexpected results' reported here and in other studies of m-learning (Lee and Chan 2007a). Such results become much less unexpected if we take a closer look at the biographies of people and things, the cohabitations and emerging cultures of use – and crucially the function-expressions – rather than 'black-boxing' these considerations and emptying devices (and users) of this material-semiotic content. Bull's (2005) work on the iPod will certainly assist in unpacking the function-expressions of that type of device, and the emerging practices, experiences, understandings and imaginings that are bundled up with it. To approach the issue of 'podagogy', we need to cast our nets wide, far beyond 'technical considerations'.

Learning times and spaces

Bull's research points up the emerging use genres of iPod listeners, showing how they use their devices to create 'intimate, manageable and aestheticised spaces' (2005: 347) and how particular listening practices are stitched into the everyday routines of users in intricate ways. Work on listening is useful for us, therefore, in terms of understanding the repertoires of listening, the patternings and the experiences, in order to help us grasp what it might mean to *listen to learn.* I am particularly interested in the relationship between listening and boredom often mentioned in 'podagogy' work, and the idea of 'dead time' – time that needs filling with something. In Lee and Chan's (2007a) discussion of the gap between assumed and actual practices of 'podagogy', assumptions about dead time are factored into the design of learning aimed at turning dead time into 'short, informal learning events' (p. 205). This notion is underscored by ideas about time poverty, and the need to fill up time with purposeful activity. Dead time is wasted in a socio-technical context where speed and movement are positively valued and where time is scarce (Erikson 2001). Dead time also equates to the 'dead air' that one of Bull's respondents was so glad to be freed from: the dead air of silence. In a project exploring domestic music listening practices, Anderson (2004) connects listening to the issue of boredom; as he puts it, 'life is now conducted in the shadow of an assumption of boredom' (p. 739) – boredom must be kept at bay, dead air and dead time filled. And like Bull's iPod listeners, Anderson's respondents explain how they use music to affect their mood, to hold off boredom during repetitive and habitual tasks such as cooking or driving.

The problem that Lee and Chan (2007a) implicitly identify in their podcasting paper is that listening is an intensely variegated activity. We use listening in different times and places to do different things. Bull's and Anderson's respondents discuss the particularities of their listening practices, such as the songs they use to stave off boredom in certain contexts. Dead time is rarely arbitrarily filled; rather, listeners deploy music in context-specific ways. So the transplanting of educational listening into those moments of dead time is unlikely to succeed if it assumes that all that is needed is *something* to fill the silence. Likewise, participants in the case studies in this book all have their own understandings of when and where learning should take place, and how it should be conducted: attentively, purposively, with a certain air of seriousness and intent. Note, too, reports that students' listening practices were complexly interwoven with their other learning practices – listening was often accompanied by note-taking, for example, as if listening alone is not sufficiently 'learny'. Learning to listen to learn is not merely a technical issue, but a socio-technical one.

One of the key promises of mobile or pervasive learning is the 'anywhere, anytime' mantra. The migration of computational devices off the desktop offers up the possibility to create what Beer (2007) calls 'thoughtful territories' – information-rich environments that we move through and connect to. For researchers interested in learning futures, pervasive or ubiquitous learning environments are dripping with potential. Yet again, however, important questions remain: questions about how pervasiveness will be experienced, how ubiquitous potential will rub up against established and emerging cultures of use. Current experiments in ubiquitous computing ('ubicomp') offer us a glimpse of these thoughtful territories, but as yet can only guess at the applications that will stick and those that will not (Galloway 2004). Vital questions thus hang over the places and times of learning, and these will not be addressed simply by ubiquity. As with previously promised futures – telecottaging, for instance – the realization of new ways of living with machines turns out to be a complex, surprising process. Dourish and Bell (2007: 415) note that 'when computation moves off the desktop, we are forced to understand something of the spaces into which it moves, and the practical and cultural logics by which those spaces are organized'. Mobility does not necessarily mean we experience pockets of 'dead space', as anyone who has watched commuters on the move can testify. Spaces are full of affordances and function-expressions, too. What we might call 'mobility practices' therefore need to be explored closely if we are going to design 'podagogy' practices that work.

Life-log learning

Research into mobile or pervasive learning is in its infancy – as too are the technologies and applications themselves. Yet there exists what Lehtonen (2003: 369) calls a 'collective horizon of anticipation' about the utopian possibilities of a world just ahead. Readying ourselves for this coming world, as researchers, means learning to listen and listening to learn, too. It means devising research that can get at some of the complexities of the function-expressions and use genres of the devices that are filling up our lives. This is a huge research agenda. But it is a vital one.

It will come as no surprise that I want to advocate detailed empirical and theoretical work in order for us to understand better what lies ahead. For example, researchers interested in consumption have for some time now been developing a 'commodity biography' approach that is helpful here, in its focus on following things and people, tracking their histories and their current movements (for example Cook and Harrison 2007; Lash and Lury 2007). In-depth, up-close and long-term research is needed to get inside the cultures of use and cultures of learning that are being brought into contact by the mobile and pervasive learning agendas. The kinds of ethnographies of living with machines offered by Lally (2002), or Miller and Slater (2000) among others, have much to offer us in their patient and thoughtful observing of the intricacies of cohabitation.

Biographical, autobiographical and 'technobiographical' writing will be especially helpful for understanding how function-expressions are worked through at the level of experience and storytelling (Henwood et al. 2001). Ng'ambi's focus in Chapter 13 on the experiences of a single student shows how rich this type of data can be. Indeed, attention to micropractices is crucial to see what goes on in the 'dailiness' of interaction. At the same time, bigger histories need tracing, since technologies do not land in our lives unencumbered by their own pasts, and nor do we come together with devices without our pasts. Oral histories and forms of 'technostalgia' provide important resources for understanding how we have lived (and live) with machines (Kirkpatrick 2007).

We should also look for possibilities in the affordances of new technologies for new ways of doing research. As with earlier discussions of 'virtual ethnography' (Hine 2000), new devices present new opportunities, notwithstanding my earlier caution about the troubled relationship between potential and actual practice. Beer (2007) discusses how RFID tags might be used to track mobile subjects, for example, to pinpoint their engagements with informational environments – but he is also mindful of the potential ethical problems of this kind of data-mining. Dodge and Kitchin (2007) highlight the research possibilities inherent in emerging cultures of use such as life-logging and life-casting – the building and displaying of personal digital archives, from blogs, vlogs or moblogs and MySpace pages, to experimental multimedia personal digital repositories (see also Van Dijk 2005). New ways of life-recording are emerging as users experiment with the affordances of their devices and with ideas about archiving, memory, biography, and so on. Hence my idea of 'life-log learning' – of thinking about how new ways of logging everyday life might enhance our own learning as academics.

Learning as labour

I want to end this chapter with some worries – worries that I think we must address, not least because their presence impedes the potential of 'podagogy'. I have experienced a recurring feeling of disquiet while writing this chapter. Looking at Lee and Chan's (2007a) paper next to research by Moisander and Eriksson (2006), for example, I detected some unproblematized assumptions in the formers' discussion of the ways in which mobile learning can be made to 'fit in with the unique work-style requirements of the mobile workforce', and how 'more can be done to help them make more efficient use of their time, by harnessing . . . idle moments' (Lee and Chan 2007a: 202). Moisander and Eriksson's reading of Nokia, meanwhile, unpicks how the 'mobile professional' is constructed through corporate discourse, and how this worker is imagined as the 'serious' end-user of the company's premium products. One worry that I have is about what kinds of instrumental ends mobile learning is here imagined as serving, both in terms of filling up the idle moments of mobile workers but also by training learners to become mobile workers. Big, somewhat old-fashioned questions are deafeningly silenced here – about labour and exploitation, about political economy, about what we teach and what we think (or hope) that teaching will lead our learners to think and do.

I have further concerns about the invisible labour of the production of mobile learning – much like the 'free labour' exploited in other sectors of the digital economy, where interns and newbies are willing to work for free because the jobs are so 'cool' (Terranova 2000). Accounts of the production of podcasts must show the labour and skills involved – skills unevenly distributed among academics. And then, of course, comes the question of intellectual property. The digital artefacts we produce for mobile learning have a double life, whether they circulate 'everyware' in cyberspace or languish unloved on some dusty server. Gregg (2006: 153) sees many positive possibilities in opening up academia's practices to wider publics through what she calls 'conversational scholarship' and 'recreational intellectual practice', as seen in blogging. Yet there remain anxieties about deskilling, casualization, commodification, and so on. Again, old-fashioned questions, but ones we need to take seriously if we are also going to think about the take-up (or not) of m-learning by teachers. While France and Ribchester's (Chapter 7) and Cox et al.'s (Chaper 10) respondents commented that a lecturer producing podcasts accrued considerable 'cool' and was also viewed favourably by students for putting extra effort into teaching, there is a danger of this making a new digital divide – the m-friendly and tech-savvy on one side, and those assumed to be has-beens and Luddites on the other. We need to understand how the coming horizon of 'podagogy' makes teachers feel, not just learners – and this means the laggards and the refuseniks as much as the early adopters.

The creative labour and skill that goes into making podcasting work must be made visible by 'messier' accounts, not least to address academics' anxieties about media performance. Today's digital natives are media-rich and 'media-tropic' (Richardson 2007), and they know what makes good content. They know how to *make* good content, moreover – student-generated content, such as Jenkins and Lonsdale's (Chapter 11) digital stories, shows this. But for those less endowed with presenting skills, the onus to produce slick content is overshadowed by fears of making an unauthorized appearance on YouTube. So, as we toe the line between education and edutainment, we may need considerable reskilling, and that takes time and investment. The performance anxieties of the would-be podcaster must be assuaged through appropriate training and confidence-building. We need to learn to talk in ways amenable to podcasting, though this does not mean simply adopting 'yoofspeak', nor underestimating the discernment of our audiences. While e-, m- and u-learning have been trumpeted for making delivery efficiencies, we must weigh those against the multiple costs. And the much-touted 'always-on-ness' of mobile or pervasive learning further exacerbates work cultures where instant responsiveness is valued, as Middleton (2007) notes in her useful study of BlackBerry users. Do learners and teachers want to be always on?

From the learners' angle, it might be possible to read those 'unexpected results' from Lee and Chan's (2007a) research as attempts to maintain control over time to prevent exactly the problems that Middleton's BlackBerry users recounted: work intensification and work extension, the blurring of boundaries between work and non-work spaces and times, 'telepresentism', and so on. Was the refusal to multitask that Lee and Chan uncovered also a way of slowing things down, keeping things apart? While it might be stretching their findings to see this as active resistance, there is something to be said for thinking through the reasons behind these results. Keeping things in their place might seem like yet another old-fashioned idea in this speeding-up, multitasking world but, as Dourish and Bell argue, this ordering is in fact part of what makes us who we are:

> It is not simply that people behave differently in different spaces; rather, it is that being able to act different in different spaces, and to be able to demonstrably recognize and respond to the difference between one setting and another, is part and parcel of what it means to be a competent member of society. The problem with technologies that erase these boundaries then is not simply that they fail, themselves, to recognize socially relevant distinctions, but that they undermine the mechanisms by which members of society can demonstrate, to each other, their sensitivity to these nuances (Dourish and Bell 2007: 426).

The task of designing and using podcasts in learning, of locating 'podagogy' in its socio-technical contexts, must accommodate this point, and must proceed from understanding both the limitations and the possibilities that lie ahead. There will certainly be more 'unexpected results' for us all to ponder.

Notes

My chapter title rips off Kopomaa's (2000) book on mobile phones, *The City in Your Pocket*. The subheading 'iPod therefore I learn' bends Jones's *iPod Therefore I Am* (2005). In this chapter I use the term u-learning to mean ubiquitous (aka pervasive) learning. Thanks to the IMPALA group and all the contributors. Their ideas have given me so much to think about.

Appendix: How to create podcasts – practitioner's guide

Matthew Mobbs, Gilly Salmon and Palitha Edirisingha

Summary

This appendix provides a practical guide for producing podcasts. It covers technical aspects, such as equipment required, when to record podcasts, and editing and publishing your podcasts. It includes a section on copyright guidelines, if you are using material created by others.

You have completed the pedagogical planning of your podcasts, perhaps using the Informal Mobile Podcasting And Learning Adaptation (IMPALA) 10-factor model in Chapter 15. Now you are ready to get podcasting!

Section 1: Equipment for podcasting

You will need a computer with a sound card, a microphone and speakers. Or instead of the microphone and speakers you can use a separately purchased 'headset' that includes both. You wear the headset.

The quality of the microphone determines the quality of the recording. There are many types and prices available. You will not need the highest quality for podcasting but it is worth spending a little more than the lowest price.

There are two main types of microphone connection to the computer: the 3.5 mm Phono Jack and those able to connect through the USB port.

The USB connector is less affected by connection problems and results in a much cleaner sound quality. A USB connection is easier to plug in and use.

Section 2: Preparing to record

Undertaking some simple checks before you record will avoid technical problems.

Figure A.1   Windows microphone volume control

The recording volume of the microphone can be adjusted using the audio controls on your computer. Figure A.1 shows the microphone volume control for a Windows operating system. This can be accessed by selecting the **Control Panel** on the **Start Menu** of your computer. Select **Switch to Category View** in the left hand menu pane, then select **Sound, Speech and Audio Devices**, followed by **Sound and Audio Devices**. From the **Volume** tab select **Advanced**. From **Options** menu, select **Properties** and chose to **Adjust Volume** for **Recording**. Then click **OK**. The **Record Control** window will appear where you can adjust microphone volume control (Figure A.1).

If the volume setting is too low (demonstrated by a small sound wave on the audio recording software, labelled as 'Too Quiet' in Figure A.2), the recording will be inaudible. If the setting is too high (represented by the sound wave going beyond the boundaries set in the audio software, similar to 'Too Loud' section in Figure A.2), there will be some distortion of sound in the final recording.

For a good sound recording, the peaks of the sound wave should be within the tramlines as shown in Figure A.2. We added these tramlines for your guidance; they are not a feature of the software. Keeping your recording within them will ensure that all sound is detected and be of audible levels. To achieve this, the microphone volume for your computer needs to be set correctly using either the **Volume Control** shown in Figure A.1 or the **Audio Set-up Wizard**.

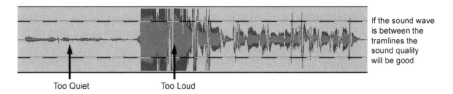

Figure A.2   Recommended volume level in Audacity

Experiment with the distance between your mouth and the microphone: increasing the distance will decrease the level of the recording volume; decreasing the distance will increase the volume.

Using your Voice

Tone of voice: A podcast made by a speaker with animated vocal expressions is more effective than a monotonous tone.

Umms and ahhs: A few are OK; no need to remove these during editing as long as the recording sounds natural.

Breathing noise: If your microphone is too close to your mouth, it may detect the sound of your breathing. A microphone attached to headphones is more likely to have this effect. The solution is to speak a little further away from the microphone.

Ambient sound

Ambient sound is picked up by the microphone. Prepare your environment: close windows, turn off your phone and put a notice on the door.

Section 3: Recording

Software

Several software packages, at a range of prices, are available for editing audio files. The IMPALA project found that free open source software is adequate: there was no need to buy expensive commercial software. IMPALA used Audacity downloaded from sourceforge.net. Audacity offered us the capabilities we needed to produce high-quality podcasts. We have used Audacity in the Appendix as an example. You can get Audacity from the link on the book's website: www.podcastingforlearning.com.

Audacity allows you to record multiple audio tracks that can be put together to create a seamless recording. Special effects editing tools, such as fade-in and fade-out, are also provided and are easy to learn to use.

Audacity supports advanced audio editing features including change-able sample rate frequency and export bit-rate (see Chapter 3, pp. 22–23) to vary the sound quality. Labels can be used to mark the sound track and to cut longer recordings into shorter individual tracks.

But Audacity does not have the in-built ability to create MP3 files. To achieve this, a free add-on to Audacity is needed. You need to download a small program, called lame_enc.dll, from the internet and install it on your computer. You can get 'lame_enc.dll' file from the link on the book's website: www.podcastingforlearning.com. Follow the installation directions. Make sure you do this before you start using Audacity.

Recording

After you have installed Audacity successfully on your computer, follow these steps.

1. Become familiar with the Audacity interface

When you first try Audacity, you need only use a few of the features. See Figure A.3 below.

The icons on the **Control Toolbar** work in the same way as those on a video or audio cassette recorder (Table A.1 opposite).

The **Meter Toolbar** is a measure of the decibel (volume) level of the microphone and output volume. The **Mixer Toolbar** adjusts the microphone input level and playback volume.

Four **Input Devices** can be used in Audacity: Microphone, CD Audio, Mono Mixer and Stereo Mixer. The microphone is required to record a podcast.

The **Time Rule** is a scale of time that represents the length of the recording. The **Timer Position** represents time within the recording where the cursor is positioned. This is mainly used in the editing process.

The **Sample Rate** figure represents how many samples of your voice the software records per second. This can be changed using the drop-down menu in Audacity. The higher the figure, the greater the quality of the recording and the higher the file size. The lower the figure, the poorer the quality of the recording but the saved file will be smaller.

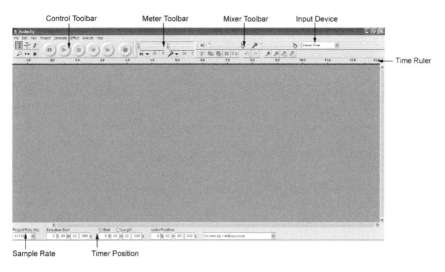

Figure A.3 Becoming familiar with Audacity interface

Record – initiates the recording of an audio file.

Figure A.3a Icon of Record button on Audacity Control Toolbar

Pause – temporarily stops the recording or playback. This is useful if you record one part of your podcast and then want to prepare yourself for the next section. To restart recording press the **Pause** button again.

Figure A.3b Icon of Pause button on Audacity Control Toolbar

Stop – ends the recording or playback. This must be done before any further editing is carried out.

Figure A.3c Icon of Stop button on Audacity Control Toolbar

Play – plays back a recording.

Figure A.3d Icon of Play button on Audacity Control Toolbar

Back Skip – skips to the beginning of the recording.

Figure A.3e Icon of Back button on Audacity Control Toolbar

Forward Skip – skips to the end of the recording or to a position where the cursor is placed.

Figure A.3f Icon of Forward button on Audacity Control Toolbar

The Cursor – This is a very useful tool that can be used either to select a certain position in a recording or to select a sample of the recording to be edited. We will look at this in more detail later in this chapter.

Figure A.3g Icon of Cursor button on Audacity Control Toolbar

2. Start recording

Set the **Input Device** as **Microphone**. Press **Record** and start speaking. As you talk, Audacity will produce a sound wave trace of your voice on the screen. The **Meter Toolbar** will fluctuate according to the rise and fall of your voice level. The **Timer Positions**, at the bottom of the screen, will count the length of your recording. Some of these features can be seen in Figure A.4.

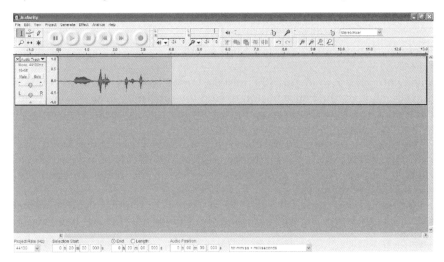

Figure A.4   Testing the volume of an Audacity recording

When you press **Stop** an Audio Track summary with technical information will appear at the left-hand side of the sound wave. This is a function of the software that is useful for sophisticated editing; for example, in the music industry. You can ignore this feature when you are creating academic podcasts.

3. Listen

It is a good idea to play back and listen to your recording. It may feel a little strange to listen to your own voice if it is for the first time, but at this stage you are interested in the sound quality! If you think the recording is too loud you can adjust the record volume level by moving the tab on the **Microphone** section of the **Mixer Toolbar** (Figure A.5). Experiment with different settings by adjusting this slider until it is at a level you consider acceptable.

Figure A.5   Audacity mixer toolbar

4. Correcting mistakes

If you make a mistake you do not need to start again (see Figure A.6). Be silent for about three seconds. This produces a flat line in the sound wave,

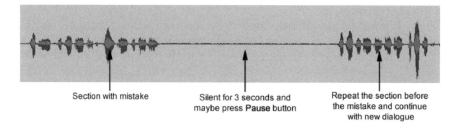

Figure A.6   How to correct a mistake when recording

which you can use to identify the mistake later. If you need time to compose yourself, click on the **Pause** button to stop the recording until you are ready. Then click the **Pause** button again to continue recording by repeating the section leading up to the mistake and carry on.

You can then remove the mistake. Once you have clicked **Stop**, listen again to the section in which you made the mistake and decide exactly which part ought to be removed, by using measurements on the **Timer Position**. This may take a few attempts.

Once you have chosen the part to be removed, highlight the unwanted section, as shown in Figure A.7, using the **Cursor** and the left-hand mouse button.

Figure A.7   How to delete a mistake in a recording

To remove this section press the **Delete** key on your keyboard: the sound wave will realign itself and shorten the length of the recording by the amount of time removed.

5. Adding extra dialogue and sound tracks
If you miss something out, you can record the missing dialogue and insert it in the required location. See overleaf.

Position the cursor at the end of the current sound track and click the **Record** button. This will open a second **Audio Track**, as seen in Figure A.8. Record your new piece and press the **Stop** button when you have finished it.

You can insert your newly recorded **Audio Track** into the original recording. First, position the **Cursor** line at the point in the recording where the second recording is to be inserted, as shown in Figure A.9.

Go to the **Edit menu** on the **Menu Bar** and select the **Split** option. This creates a small gap in the recording, as shown in Figure A.10.

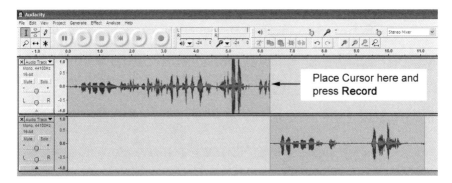

Figure A.8   How to record extra dialogues and sound-tracks

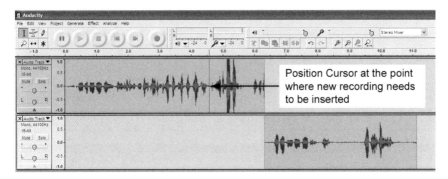

Figure A.9   Position of the cursor at insert point

Figure A.10   Creating a split in the audio track

Click on the **Time Shift** tool, as shown in Figure A.11 and to be found on the **Control** toolbar. The cursor will change to a horizontal double arrow.

Hold the **Cursor** over the new audio track recording, click and hold down the left mouse button and move the recording to a position where the start of it is aligned with the split created above, as shown in Figure A.12.

Figure A.11   Time shift tool

Using the **Time Shift** tool, hold the **Cursor** over the sound wave to the right of the split in the original **Audio Track**, click and hold down the left mouse button and move **Audio Track**, position it at the end of the new recording in the second audio track, as shown in Figure A.13.

The recording will now play back seamlessly with the newly recorded section inserted.

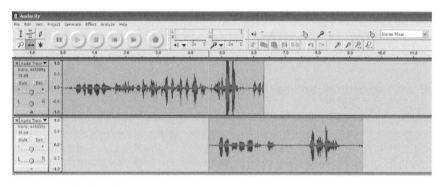

Figure A.12   Positioning a new recording

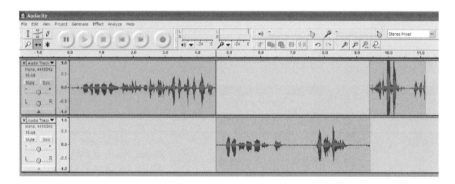

Figure A.13   Positioning a previous recording

6. Save your podcast

To save your podcast, select **Save Project As . . .** from the **File Menu**. This option saves the recording as an **Audacity Project**, which is a format with the file extension **.aup**. The format can then be played back and re-edited but only using the Audacity software.

Now you need to convert the .aup file to MP3 format. To do this, from the **File Menu** select **Export As MP3**. This leads to a **Save** window, which prompts you to name your recording and select where you would like to store it on your computer. Complete these settings and click **OK**.

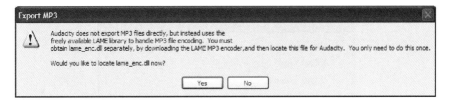

Figure A.14   Warning message when lame_enc.dll is not located

Note, however, that the first time you try to do this conversion a warning message, as shown in Figure A.14, will appear. This is because, as described in the Software section (p. 190) Audacity requires the **lame_enc.dll** plug-in to convert recordings to MP3 files. The warning message asks you to locate the **lame_enc.dll** file on your computer. The Software section provides information on how to download and install the **lame_enc.dll** file from the link on the book's web site: www.podcastingforlearning.com.

Now select **Yes**, and then use the browser to find the **lame_enc.dll** file you downloaded. This step of the process only has to be done the first time because Audacity will remember the location of the **lame_enc.dll** file every time you undertake this procedure after that. Audacity will now convert your recordings to an MP3 format.

Section 4: Publishing your podcasts

Personalizing your recording with ID3 Tags

ID3 Tags are the labels used to identify a podcast within the audio 'library' (or the collection of audio files) in your media player. ID3 Tags contain key information about podcasts such as the Track Number, Title, Artist and Album. The tags enable you to search your audio library and display the information when an audio track is playing.

The tags are important for keeping an audio library well organized, especially for students wishing to distinguish between their academic podcasts and music.

In Audacity once a recording has been saved as an MP3 file, the dialogue box shown in Figure A.15 will appear. This is used to add ID3 Tags and assign them to your recording.

Initially, the **Edit ID3 Tags** option requires a **Format** to be chosen. There are two options: ID3v1 and ID3v2. We suggest you choose ID3v2.

Table A.2 is a brief description of the tags that you can enter in the dialogue box, as shown in Figure A.15.

It is not essential to use all the ID3 Tags. We recommend you use Title and Artist as these are the pieces of information that are critical for your students to identify their podcasts.

Figure A.15   Audacity ID3 Tag editor

Table A.2 Edit ID3 Tag labels

Title	The title of the episode of the podcast. If the podcast is one of a series it is good practice to put the number in the title (for example Show #12).
Artist(s)	The person(s) performing (talking on) the podcast.
Album	Here you put your overall theme.
Track Number	This is used to keep a series of podcasts in order, like the tracks on a CD. So label your podcast, 1, 2, 3, etc. in the series.
Year	The year the recording was produced.
Genre	We suggest 'Vocal' for educational podcasts.
Comments	This option can be left empty but you can use it to add any relevant information about the podcast; for example, any resources you referred to.

Figure A.16 shows a completed example of the **Edit ID3 Tags** dialogue box for an IMPALA podcast. This one is for a recording in 2007 of student feedback. It also references the website.

If you want to change ID3 Tags later on, you can access the **Edit ID3 Tags** option at any time in Audacity from the **Edit Menu** by selecting **Edit ID3 Tags** and edit your Tags.

Figure A.16   Example of a completed ID3 Tag editor

Enabling your podcast to be heard

Once a podcast has been produced you need to distribute it to your students. In order for your students to access your podcast, it needs to be stored online on a suitable server. You can place it on your Virtual Learning Environment (VLE) or institutional web server, or one of many websites that will host podcasts for you.

Podcasts and VLEs
If your VLE has a Content Management System (CMS), store your podcasts there as you will be able to refer to them from several places within your online course material.

If your VLE does not have a CMS, the file can be uploaded to the required place within the course module as you would any other file, giving it an appropriate name and a description. You may choose a separate area just for podcasts or store them alongside any other learning material.

When you are ready for your students to access your podcast, let them know by email that it is ready and where to find it. You can also make an announcement on the course message board. The message should encourage students to visit the course and download the podcast.

Soon VLEs such as Moodle and Blackboard will have Really Simple Syndication (RSS) tools that will allow students to subscribe to feeds, offering a full podcasting service, so keep track of the latest developments about your VLE!

Web-based podcasts
You may choose to put your podcast on a website so it can be freely accessed. There are several websites on the internet that offer a small amount of free storage space and then require a subscription for additional space. Those that offer free unlimited space sometimes include advertisements in your podcasts or they may limit the size of each upload.

Some free hosting websites available in January 2008 include:

- Big Contact – www.v2.bigcontact.com
- BT PodShow – www.btpodshow.com
- GCast – www.gcast.com
- iPod Networks – www.ipodnetworks.com
- My Podcast – www.mypodcast.com
- Odeo – www.odeo.com
- Podbean – www.podbean.com
- Podcast Spot – www.podcastspot.com
- Podomatic – www.podomatic.com
- Talkshoe – www.talkshoe.com
- Wildvoice – www.wildvoice.com

Other websites are listed at: www.okaytoplay.com/wiki/Podcast_Hosting.

Traditionally, an RSS feed is used to make subscribers aware of the availability of a new podcast. RSS is used to publish updates to web content that is regularly changed, such as blogs, news or podcasts. RSS is a 'web feed' with additional information about the content, and can be used to alert 'subscribers' to the feed, informing them of alterations or the availability of new content. There is more about distributing podcasting in Chapter 3 (p. 26).

The symbols shown in Figure A.17 are those used to show that an RSS feed is available for that content.

There are RSS capabilities on all the host sites listed above.

If you want to subscribe to them, copy the URL of the host site into an RSS aggregator. An aggregator is a 'feed reader' that picks up feeds from various websites and informs the subscriber of any updates to the content.

Figure A.17 RSS symbols

The following RSS readers will inform you that a new podcast is available to download.

- NetVibes – www.netvibes.com
- Bloglines – www.bloglines.com
- Google Reader – www.google.com/reader
- My Yahoo – cm.my.yahoo.com
- News Is Free – www.newsisfree.com

These RSS aggregators actually download the newest podcasts for you. Two examples are:

- Juice – www.juicereceiver.sourceforge.net
- Doppler – www.dopplerradio.net

Once podcasts are downloaded, the students can open them or transfer them to suitable MP3 players as usual.

Publishing podcasts on iTunes
You can publish your own podcasts through iTunes. However, since iTunes does not physically store your podcasts, first you need to upload your podcasts to a hosting website with an RSS feed, such as those mentioned opposite. Now you need to tell iTunes where your podcasts are kept, by visiting the **iTunes Music Store** within iTunes software and selecting **Submit a Podcast** from the **Podcast** page shown in Figure A.18, opposite.

Then enter the URL of your podcast hosting website into the submission screen shown in Figure A.19 opposite.

Once submitted, the podcast will be available in the **iTunes Music Store** and the ID3 Tag information, along with a picture, will be displayed. An example of this is shown in Figure A.20, on page 203.

Downloading podcasts from iTunes takes little effort. You can search the extensive library, and subscribe to a podcast that interests you. You can search the iTunes catalogue by keyword, title, theme or producer.

Figure A.18　iTunes music store

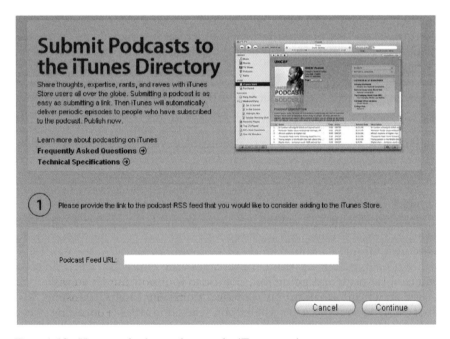

Figure A.19　How to submit a podcast to the iTunes music store

Figure A.20   Example of a podcast in iTunes music store

Once subscribed to, the iTunes aggregator automatically downloads the podcast and any subsequent episodes that are released later. Once downloaded, the podcasts are kept in the students' iTunes Library. Then the next time their iPod is connected iTunes will transfer them over to the portable device.

Section 5: Podcasts and copyright

We believe that the advice contained in this section to be accurate, but it does not constitute legal advice. If you are in any doubt as to whether or not you can use material, we recommend that you seek legal advice. Your institution's or organization's Copyright or Intellectual Property Rights officer will help you.

You may wish to include content that is not your own copyright, such as readings from literature or a script, or you may wish to make your podcast more creative by including music or sound effects. So you need to know a bit about copyright law and how it applies to podcasting. It is not difficult and if you know about it, it should not get in your way!

Copyright
Copyright law states that when a piece of work is created it is automatically copyrighted, even if a licence has not been applied for. Anyone who would like to use the work must seek permission from its creator before using it.

Some people are now making use of 'Creative Commons' on the internet, which has been introduced to allow the producer of a piece of work to inform others wanting to use it what rights they have. Creative Commons is a non-profit agency in the USA (www.creativecommons.org), that work internationally to make copyright more flexible.

Pieces of work covered by Creative Commons use a coding system to signify the rights assigned to the piece of work, which they call a 'licence'. You could consider assigning rights of use to your podcasts if you wish.

For more information on Creative Commons and podcasting, visit www.creativecommons.org, where you can find the 'Podcasting Legal Guide: Rule For The Revolution': (www.wiki.creativecommons.org/ Podcasting_Legal_Guide).

Podsafe music

Podsafe music consists of pieces that have been released into the public domain, and can be reused and edited to fit the needs of anyone downloading it. You can use podsafe music freely in your podcast, perhaps as introductory music or to represent a section break in the recording.

In January 2008, these websites claimed to be offering podsafe music.

- Stockmusic.net – www.stockmusic.net
- Podsafe music network – www.music.podshow.com
- Podshow – www.btpodshow.com
- Podcast NYC – www.podcastnyc.net/psm/podcast.html
- Garage Band – www.garageband.com
- PodSafe Audio – www.podsafeaudio.com
- UK Podcasts – www.ukpodcasts.info
- People Sound – www.peoplesound.com
- Soundflavour – www.soundflavor.com

Published literature

In the academic world, we are used to referencing other people's work. However, with a podcast you should be especially careful because of the 'broadcast' element. Always ask permission of the copyright owner, who is not necessarily the same person as the author, if you want to use the work of others, whether from books, journal articles, websites or blogs.

Acknowledgement

Thanks to Dominic Mazzoni, project manager at Audacityteam.org, for his permission in our reproducing the screendumps of Audacity for this chapter.

References

Allen, K. (2005) Online learning: constructivism and conversation as an approach to learning, *Innovations in Education and Teaching International*, 42(3): 247–56.

Anderson, B. (2004) Time-stilled and space-slowed: how boredom matters, *Geoforum*, 35(5): 739–54.

Anderson, P. (2007) What is Web2.0? Ideas, technologies and implications for education, *JISC Technology and Standards Watch*, February, Bristol. www.jisc.ac.uk/media/documents/techwatch/tsw0701b.pdf (accessed 7 January 2008).

Arnedillo-Sánchez, I., Sharples, M. and Vavoula, G. (eds) (2007) *Beyond Mobile Learning Workshop*. Dublin: Trinity College Dublin Press.

Atkinson, L., Buntine, A. and McCrohan, R. (2007) Podcasting at RMIT University: evaluating a faculty-based trial. Research proceedings of ALT-C, Nottingham, 4–6 September 2007, 75–90.

Attewell, J. and Savill-Smith, C. (2004) *Learning with Mobile Devices: Research and Development*. London: Learning and Skills Development Agency.

Bakardjieva, M. (2005) *Internet Society: The Internet in Everyday Life*. London: Sage.

Barnes, J.M. (1995) Embodiment, hermeneutic, alterity, and background relations on the Internet. Paper presented at the American Educational Research Association Annual Meeting, San Francisco, 18–22 April.

Barresi, M.J. (2007) Enlarging contexts: enhancing learning in developmental biology using web conferencing in the classroom, *Developmental Biology*, 306(1): 321–2.

Barton, H., Penny, P. and Riordan, M. (2007) Podcasting and mobile learning: can they aid social inclusion for students with dyslexia? Proceedings of EDEN Annual Conference 2007, Naples, 13–16 June. www.ericsson.com/ericsson/corpinfo/programs/resource_documents/iadt_eden_2007.pdf (accessed 20 January 2008).

Bates, S.P., Bruce, A.D. and McKain, D. (2005) Integrating e-learning and on-campus teaching I: an overview, in J. Cook and D. Whitelock (eds) *Exploring the Frontiers of e-Learning: Borders, Outposts and Migration*. Research Proceedings of the 12th Association of Learning Technology Conference, Manchester, UK, 6–8 September.

Bates, S.P., Howie, K. and Murphy, A. St.J. (2006) Electronic voting systems: from one-way transmission to two-way conversation, *Journal of the Higher Education Academy Physical Sciences Centre*, 2: 1–8.

BBC NEWS (2006) Download fans boost music sales, 24 August. www.news.bbc.co.uk/2/hi/technology/5281272.stm (accessed 15 January 2008).

BBC (2006) Podcast lectures for uni students. www.news.bbc.co.uk/1/hi/england/west_yorkshire/5013194.stm (accessed 14 January 2008).

Beer, D. (2007) Thoughtful territories: imagining the thinking power of things and spaces, *City*, 11(3): 229–38.

Beetham, H. and Sharpe, R. (eds) (2007) *Design for Learning: Rethinking Pedagogy for the Digital Age*. London: RoutledgeFalmer.

Belanger, Y. (2005) *Duke University iPod First Year Experience Final Evaluation Report*. www.cit.duke.edu/pdf/ipod_initiative_04_05.pdf (accessed 15 January 2008).

Bell, D. (2001) *An Introduction to Cybercultures*. London: Routledge.

Bell, D. (2006) *Science, Technology and Culture*. Maidenhead: Open University Press.

Bell, M., Bush, D., Nicholson, P., O'Brien, D. and Tran, T. (2002) *Universities Online: A Survey of Online Education and Services in Australia*, occasional paper series 02-A. Canberra: DEST.

Berman, S.J., Battino, B., Shipnuck, L. and Neus, A. (2007) *The End of Advertising as we Know it*. www-03.ibm.com/industries/media/doc/content/resource/business/2898468111.html (accessed 25 January 2008).

Biggs, J. (2003) *Teaching for Quality Learning at University*. Buckingham: SRHE and Open University Press.

Black, P. and William, D. (1998) Assessment and classroom learning, *Assessment in Education*, 5: 7–74.

Bloxham, S. and West, A. (2004) Understanding the rules of the game: marking peer assessment as a medium for developing students' conceptions of assessment, *Assessment and Evaluation in Higher Education*, 29: 721–33.

Bloxham, S. and West, A. (2007) Learning to write in higher education: students' perceptions of an intervention in developing understanding of assessment criteria, *Teaching in Higher Education*, 12: 77–89.

Blythe, T. and Associates (1998) *The Teaching for Understanding Guide*, San Francisco: Jossey-Bass.

BMRB (British Market Research Bureau) (March 2007) www.bmrb.co.uk (accessed 15 January 2008).

Boud, D. (2000) Sustainable assessment: rethinking assessment for the learning society, *Studies in Continuing Education*, 22: 151–67.

Bradbury, J. (2006) Podcasts, *The Lancet Oncology*, 7(4): 297–8.

Brittain, S., Glowacki, P., Ittersum, J.V. and Johnson, L. (2006) Podcasting lectures, *Educause Quarterly*, 3: 24–31.

Brown, J.S. (2005) *New Learning Environments for the 21st Century*. www.johnseelybrown.com/newlearning.pdf (accessed 23 January 2008).

Brown, S. (2005) Assessment for learning, *Learning and Teaching in Higher Education*, 1: 81–9.

Brown, S. and Glasner, A. (eds) (1999) *Assessment Matters in Higher Education: Choosing and Using Diverse Approaches*. Buckingham: SRHE and Open University Press.

Brown, T.H. (2005) Beyond constructivism: exploring future learning paradigms. *Education Today*, 2, Aries Publishing Company, Thames, New Zealand.

Bryans Bongey, S., Cizadlo, G. and Kalnbach, L. (2006) Explorations in course-casting: podcasts in higher education, *Campus-Wide Information Systems*, 23(5): 350–67.

Bull, M. (2005) No dead air! The iPod and the culture of mobile listening, *Leisure Studies*, 24(4): 343–55.

Burrell, G. and Morgan, G. (1979) *Sociological Paradigms and Organizational Analysis.* London: Heinemann.

Cake, M.A. (2006) Deep dissection: motivating students beyond rote learning in veterinary anatomy, *Journal of Veterinary Medical Education,* 33(2): 266–71.

Carless, D. (2006) Differing perceptions in the feedback process, *Studies in Higher Education,* 31: 219–33.

Carroll, J. and Ryan, J. (eds) (2005) *Teaching International Students: Improving Learning for All.* London: Routledge.

Cebeci, Z. and Tekdal, M. (2006) Using podcasts as audio learning objects, *Interdisciplinary Journal of Knowledge and Learning Objects,* 2: 47–57. www.ijklo.org/Volume2/v2p047-057Cebeci.pdf (accessed 21 January 2008).

Chan, A. and Lee, M.J.W. (2005) An MP3 a day keeps the worries away: exploring the use of podcasting to address preconceptions and alleviate pre-class anxiety amongst undergraduate information technology students, in D.H.R. Spennemann and L. Burr (eds) *Good Practice in Practice: Proceedings of the Student Experience Conference.* Wagga Wagga, NSW, 5–7 September.

Chan, A., Lee, M. and McLoughlin, C. (2006) Everyone's listening with podcasting: a Charles Sturt University experience. Proceedings of the 23rd Annual Ascilite Conference: Who's Learning? Whose Technology? University of Sydney, 111–20. www.ascilite.org.au/conferences/sydney06/proceeding/pdf_papers/p171.pdf (accessed 24 January 2008).

Chanock, K. (2000) Comments on essays: do students understand what writers write? *Teaching in Higher Education,* 5: 95–105.

Chinnery, G.M. (2006) Emerging technologies – going to the MALL: Mobile Assisted Language Learning, *Language Learning and Technology,* 10(1): 9–16.

Churchill, D. and Hedberg, J. (in press) Learning object design considerations for small-screen handheld devices, *Computers and Education.*

Clark, D. and Walsh, S. (2004) *iPod-learning.* Brighton, UK: Epic Group.

Clark, R.E. (eds) (2001a) *Learning From Media: Arguments, Analysis and Evidence.* Charlotte, NC: Information Age Publishing.

Clark, R.E. (2001b). What is next in the media and methods debate?, in R.E. Clark (ed.) *Learning From Media: Arguments, Analysis and Evidence.* Charlotte, NC: Information Age Publishing.

Cobb, T. (1997). Cognitive efficiency: toward a revised theory of media, *Educational Technology Research and Development,* 45(4): 21–35.

Cobcroft, R. (2006) *Literature review into mobile learning in a university context,* Queensland University of Technology. www.eprints.qut.edu.au/archive/00004805 (accessed 20 January 2008).

Colle, R.D. (2005) Building ICT4D capacity in and by African universities, *International Journal of Education and Development using Information and Communication Technology,* 1(1): 101–7.

Collis, B. and Moonen, J. (2002) Flexible learning in a digital world, *Open Learning,* 17(3): 217–30.

Cook, I. and Harrison, M. (2007) Follow the thing: West Indian hot pepper sauce, *Space and Culture,* 10(2): 40–63.

Crockett, N. and Pettersons, M. (1990) A comparative study of the effect of tutorial audio-tapes in teaching elementary statistics, *Open Learning,* 5(1): 53–6.

Crow, C. (2006) *Digital storytelling connects youth across cultural divides.* www.microsoft.com/windowsxp/using/digitalphotography/prophoto/bridges.mspx (accessed 23 January 2008).

Cullen, M. and Foster, C. (2007) A student perspective on learning futures. Paper presented at the Learning Futures Conference, University of Leicester, 9 January. www2.le.ac.uk/departments/beyond-distance-research-alliance/event/previous_ events/conferences/conferences2007/uol-learning-futures-conference/ uol-learning-futures-keynote-sessions/lf_keynote_students (accessed 3 January 2008).

De Waard, I., Kiyan, C., Lynen, L. Madder, M., Renggli, V. and Zolfo, M. (2007) Vodcasting in Education 2.0. Proceedings of 13th Online Educa Berlin Conference: 314–15, 28–30 November.

Dennett, C. and Traxler, J. (2007) Large-scale content and support for the mobile generation via Bluetooth. Proceedings of 13th Online Educa Conference: 255–6, Berlin, 28–30 November.

Department of Education, Science and Training (2007) *Publications – higher education statistics collections: students.* www.abs.gov.au/.../abs (accessed 23 January 2008).

Dillon, S. and Brown, A. (2006) The art of eportfolios: insights from the creative arts experience, in A. Jafari and C. Kaufman (eds) *Handbook of Research on ePortfolios.* Hershey: Idea Group Reference.

Dodge, D. (2007) *The next big thing.* www.dondodge.typepad.com/the_next_ big_thing/2006/06/macromyopia_and.html (accessed 22 January 2008).

Dodge, M. and Kitchin, R. (2007) Outlines of a world coming into existence: pervasive computing and the ethics of forgetting, *Environment and Planning B: Planning and Design,* 34(5): 431–45.

Dolphin, I. and Miller, P. (2002). Learning objects and the information environment, *Ariadne,* 32. www.ariadne.ac.uk/issue32/iconex/intro.html (accessed 20 January 2008).

Dourish, P. and Bell, G. (2007) The infrastructure of experience and the experience of infrastructure: meaning and structure in everyday encounters with space, *Environment and Planning B: Planning and Design,* 34(5): 414–30.

Downward, S., Livingstone, D., Lynch, K. and Taylor, R. (2007) Podcasting to enhance geography field-based teaching and learning. Paper presented at the Association of American Geographers Annual Meeting, San Francisco, USA, 17–21 April. www2.le.ac.uk/projects/impala2/presentation/impala2_ workshop/presentations/stuart/view (accessed 21 January 2008).

Draper, S. and Maguire, J. (2007) Exploring podcasting as part of campus-based teaching, *Practice and Evidence of Scholarship of Teaching and Learning in Higher Education,* 2(1): 42–63.

Dron, J. (2007) *Control and Constraint in E-Learning: Choosing When to Choose.* Hershey, PA: Information Science Publishing.

Du Gay, P., Hall, S., Janes, L., Mackay, H. and Negus, K. (1997) *Doing Cultural Studies: The Story of the Sony Walkman.* London: Sage.

Dufour, J.C., Cuggia, M., Soula, G., Spector, M. and Kohler, F. (2007) An integrated approach to distance learning with digital video in the French-speaking Virtual Medical University, *International Journal of Medical Informatics,* 76(5–6): 369–76.

Durbridge, N. (1984) Media in course design, No. 9, Audio cassettes, in A.W. Bates (ed.) *The Role of Technology in Distance Education.* Kent, UK: Croom Helm.

Dutton, J., Dutton, M. and Perry, J. (2001). Do online students perform as well as lecture students? *Journal of Engineering Education,* 90(1): 131.

Eash, E.K. (2006) Podcasting 101 for K-12 librarians, *Computers in Libraries,* 26(4): 16.

Edirisingha, P., Salmon, G. and Fothergill, J. (2006) Profcasting: a pilot study and a model for integrating podcasts into online learning. www2.le.ac.uk/projects/impala/presentations/Berlin (accessed 22 January 2008).

Edirisingha, P., Salmon, G. and Fothergill, J. (2007a) Profcasting – a pilot study and guidelines for integrating podcasts in a blended learning environment, in U. Bernath and A. Sangra (eds) *Research on competence development in online distance education and e-learning*. Selected Papers from the 4th EDEN Research Workshop in Castelldefels/Spain, BIS-Verlag der Carl von Osseitzky Universitat, Oldenburg, 25–28 October.

Edirisingha, P., Rizzi, C., Nie, M. and Rothwell, L. (2007b) Podcasting to provide teaching and learning support for an undergraduate module on English Lanugage and Communication, *Turkish Online Journal of Distance Education*, 8(3): 87–107.

Elkins, J.T. and Elkins, N.M.L. (2006) Improving student learning during travel time on field trips using an innovative, portable audio/video system, *Journal of Geoscience Education*, 54(2): 147–52.

Ely, D. (1999) Toward a philosophy of instructional technology: thirty years on, *British Journal of Educational Technology*, 30(4): 305–10.

Erikson, T. (2001) *The Tyranny of the Moment: Fast and Slow in the Information Age*. London: Pluto.

Felder, R.M. and Brent, R. (2005) Understanding student differences, *Journal of Engineering Education*, 94(1): 57–72.

Flanigan, J.E. and Amirian, S. (2006) ePortfolios: pathway from classroom to career, in A. Jafari and C. Kaufman (eds) *Handbook of Research on ePortfolios*. Hershey, PA: Idea Group Reference.

Fothergill, J. (2007) Profcasts: supporting online learning of campus-based students. Paper presented at the Learning Futures Conference, University of Leicester, 9 January. www2.le.ac.uk/projects/impala/presentations/impala_lfc0n_workshop (accessed 15 January 2008).

France, D. and Ribchester, C. (2004) Producing websites for assessment: a case study from a Level 1 fieldwork module, *Journal of Geography in Higher Education*, 28: 49–62.

Galloway, A. (2004) Intimations of everyday life: ubiquitous computing and the city, *Cultural Studies*, 18(4): 384–408.

Garrison, D.R. and Anderson, T. (2003) *E-learning in the 21st Century: A Framework for Research and Practice*. London: RoutledgeFalmer.

GCSU (Georgia College and State University) (2006) *iPods @ GCSU*. www.ipod.gcsu.edu/index.html (accessed 15 January 2008).

Gee, J.P. (1992) *The Social Mind: Language, Ideology, and Social Practice*. New York: Bergin and Garvey.

Gee, J.P. (1996) *Social Linguistics and Literacies: Ideology in Discourses*, 2nd edn. London: Taylor & Francis.

Gibbs, G. (2006) How assessment frames student learning, in C. Bryan and K. Clegg (eds) *Innovative Assessment in Higher Education*. London: Routledge.

Gibbs, G. and Simpson, C. (2005) Conditions under which assessment supports student learning, *Learning and Teaching in Higher Education*, 1: 3–31.

Giustini, D. (2007) How Web 2.0 is changing medicine, *British Medical Journal*, 333: 1283–4.

Glover, C. and Brown, E. (2006) Written feedback for students: too much, too detailed or too incomprehensible to be effective? *Bioscience Education e-Journal*, 7. www.bioscience.heacademy.ac.uk/journal/vol7/beej-7-3.htm (accessed 24 January 2008).

Goggin, G. (2006) *Cell Phone Culture: Mobile Technology in Everyday Life.* London: Routledge.

Grabe, M. and Christopherson, K. (in press) Optimal student use of online lecture resources: resource preferences, performance and lecture attendance, *Journal of Computer Assisted Learning.*

Gregg, M. (2006) Feeling ordinary: blogging as conversational scholarship, *Continuum: Journal of Media and Cultural Studies,* 20(2): 147–60.

Guertin, L.A. (2006) Integrating handheld technology with field investigations in introductory-level Geoscience courses, *Journal of Geoscience Education,* 54(2): 143–6.

Hake, R.R. (1998) Interactive engagement versus traditional methods: a six-thousand-student survey of mechanics test data for introductory physics courses, *American Journal of Physics,* 66(1): 64–74.

Hammersley, B. (2004) Audible revolution, *The Guardian Unlimited.* www.arts.guardian.co.uk/features/story/0,,1145758,00.html (accessed 14 January 2008).

Hardy, J.A., Antonioletti, M., Seed, T. and Bates, S.P. (2005) Integrating e-learning and on campus teaching II: evaluation of student use, in J. Cook and D. Whitelock (eds) *Exploring the Frontiers of e-Learning: Borders, Outposts and Migration.* Research Proceedings of the 12th Association of Learning Technology Conference, Manchester, 6–8 September.

Hargis, J. and Wilson, D. (2005) *Fishing for Learning with a Podcast Net.* www.unf.edu/dept/cirt/tech/podcast/HargisPodcastArticle.pdf (accessed 15 January 2008).

Hattie, J. and Jaeger, R. (1998) Assessment and classroom learning: a deductive approach, *Assessment in Education,* 5: 111–22.

Henwood, F., Kennedy, H. and Miller, N. (eds) (2001) *Cyborg Lives? Women's Technobiographies.* York: Raw Nerve Press.

Hestenes, D. and Wells, M. (1992) Force concept inventory, *Physics Teacher,* 30: 141–58.

Higgins, R. (2000) Be more critical! Rethinking assessment feedback. Paper presented at the British Educational Research Association Conference, Cardiff University, 7–10 September.

Higgins, R., Hartley, P. and Skelton, A. (2001) Getting the message across: the problem of communicating assessment feedback, *Teaching in Higher Education,* 6: 268–74.

Higgins, R., Hartley, P. and Skelton, A. (2002) The conscientious consumer: reconsidering the role of assessment feedback in student learning, *Studies in Higher Education,* 27: 53–64.

Hine, C. (2000) *Virtual Ethnography.* London: Sage.

Huann, T.Y. and Thong, M.K. (2006) *Audioblogging and podcasting in education,* Edublog.net www.edublog.net/astinus/mt/files/docs/ Literature%20Review%20on%20audioblogging%20and%20podcasting.pdf (accessed 15 January 2008).

Ice, P., Curtis, R., Phillips, P. and Wells, J. (2007) Using asynchronous audio feedback to enhance teaching presence and student's sense of learning, *Sloan-C Publications,* 11(2). www.sloan-c.org/publications/jaln/v11n2/v11n2_ice.asp (accessed 15 January 2008).

Ifinedo, P. (2005) Measuring Africa's e-readiness in the global networked economy: a nine-country data analysis, *International Journal of Education and Development using Information and Communication Technology,* 1(1): 53–71.

Innis, K. and Shaw, M. (1997) How do students spend their time? *Quality Assurance in Education,* 5: 85–9.

Institute of Physics (1990) *The future pattern of higher education in physics.* www.iop.org/activity/policy/Publications/file_6589.doc (accessed 22 January 2008).

Institute of Physics (2001) *Physics: building a flourishing future.* www.iop.org/activity/policy/Projects/Archive/file_6418.pdf (accessed 22 January 2008).

ISMA (Internet Streaming Media Alliance) (2005) *ISMA 2.0 specification.* www.isma.tv/specreq.nsf/TestSpecRequest (accessed 7 January 2008).

Jenkins, M. and Lynch, K. (2006) I want to tell you a story . . . Paper presented at the 23rd annual ASCILITE conference, Who's Learning? University of Sydney, Australia, 3–6 December. www.ascilite.org.au/conferences/sydney06/proceeding/pdf_papers/p74.pdf (accessed 15 January 2008).

JISC (2005) *Innovative Practice with e-Learning: A Good Practice Guide to Embedding Mobile and Wireless Technologies into Everyday Practice.* Bristol: Joint Information Systems Committee.

Jones, D. (2005) *iPod Therefore I Am: Thinking Inside the White Box.* London: Bloomsbury.

Jones, E.C.A. and Morris, A. (1998) *Cell Biology and Genetics.* London: Mosby.

Joseph, J. (1997) *When I am an Old Woman I shall Wear Purple.* London: Souvenir Press.

Josselson, R. and Lieblich, A. (1995) *Interpreting Experience: The Narrative Study of Lives.* California: Sage.

Kamel Boulos, M.N. and Wheeler, S. (2007) The emerging Web.0 social software: an enabling suite of sociable technologies in health and healthcare education, *Health Information and Libraries Journal*, 24: 2–23.

Kates, R. (1998) Tape recorders and the commuter student: bypassing the red pen, *Teaching English in the Two-Year College*, 25: 21–4.

Keegan, D. (1996) *Foundations of Distance Education*, 3rd edn. London: Routledge.

Kim, E. (2005) The effects of digital audio on social presence, motivation and perceived learning in asynchronous learning networks, PhD dissertation. www.archives.njit.edu/vol01/etd/2000s/2005/njit-etd2005-075/njit-etd2005- 075.pdf (accessed 15 January 2008).

Kirkpatrick, G. (2007) Meritums, spectrums and narrative memories of 'pre-virtual' computing in Cold War Europe, *Sociological Review*, 55(3): 227–49.

Knight, J. (2006) Investigating geography undergraduates' attitudes to teaching, learning and technology, *Planet*, 16: 19–21.

Knight, P. (1995) *Assessment for Learning in Higher Education.* London: Kogan Page/SEDA.

Koenen, R. (eds) (2002) *Overview of the MPEG-4 Standard*, International Organisation for Standardisation/Organisation International de Normalisation (ISO/IEC) White Paper, ISO/IEC JTC1/SC29/WG11 N4668.

Kolb, D. (1984) *Experiential Learning: Experience as a Source of Learning and Development.* New Jersey: Prentice Hall.

Kopomaa, T. (2000) *The City in Your Pocket: Birth of the Mobile Information Society.* Helsinki: Gaudeamus Kirja.

Kukulska-Hulme, A. and Traxler, J. (2005) Mobile learning and teaching, in A. Kukulska-Hulme and J. Traxler (eds) *Mobile Learning: A Handbook for Educators and Trainers.* London: Routledge.

Kukulska-Hulme, A. and Traxler, J. (2007) Design for mobile and wireless technologies, in H. Beetham and R. Sharpe (eds) *Rethinking Pedagogy for the Digital Age.* London: Routledge.

Kukulska-Hulme, A., Evans, D. and Traxler, J. (2005) *Landscape Study in Wireless and Mobile Learning in the Post-16 Sector*. Technical Report. Bristol: Joint Information Systems Committee.

Lally, E. (2002) *At Home with Computers*. Oxford: Berg.

Lane, C. (2006) *Podcasting at the UW: an evaluation of current use*. www.catalyst.washington.edu/research_development/papers/2006/podcasting_report.pdf (accessed 15 January 2008).

Lash, S. and Lury. C. (2007) *Global Culture Industry: The Mediation of Things*. Cambridge: Polity.

Laurillard, D. (2002) *Rethinking University Teaching: A Conversational Framework for the Effective Use of Learning Technologies*, 2nd edn. London: RoutledgeFalmer.

Laurillard, D. (2007) Pedagogic forms of mobile learning: framing research questions, in N. Pachler (eds) *Mobile Learning: – Towards a Research Agenda*. London: Institute of Education, University of London.

Lave, J. and Wenger, E. (1991) *Situated Learning: Legitimate Peripheral Participation*. Cambridge: Cambridge University Press.

Lee, M.J.W. and Chan, A. (2005) Exploring the potential of podcasting to deliver mobile ubiquitous learning in Higher Education, *Journal of Computing in Higher Education*, 18: 94–115.

Lee, M.J.W., Chan, A. and McLoughlin, C. (2006) Students as producers: second-year students' experiences as podcasters of content for first-year undergraduates. Proceedings of the 7th Conference on Information Technology Based Higher Education and Training. Sydney: University of Technology, Sydney.

Lee, M.J.W. and Chan, A. (2007a) Pervasive, lifestyle-integrated mobile learning for distance learners: an analysis and unexpected results from a podcasting study, *Open Learning*, 22(3): 201–18.

Lee, M.J.W. and Chan, A. (2007b) Reducing the effects of isolation and promoting inclusivity for distance learners through podcasting, *Turkish Online Journal of Distance Education*, 8(1): 85–104.

Lehtonen, T. (2003) The domestication of new technologies as a set of trials, *Journal of Consumer Culture*, 3(4): 363–85.

Leont'ev, N.A. (1978) *Activity, Consciousness and Personality*. New Jersey: Prentice Hall.

Levinson, A.J., Weaver, B., Garside, S., McGinn, H. and Norman, G.R. (2007) Virtual reality and brain anatomy: a randomised trial of e-learning instructional designs, *Medical Education*, 41(5): 495–501.

Lyotard, J-F. (1999) *La Condition postmoderne: Rapport sur le savoir* (*The Postmodern Condition: A Report on Knowledge*). Minneapolis: University of Minnesota Press and Manchester: Manchester University Press (Transl. G. Bennington and B. Massumi from *La Condition postmoderne: rapport sur le savoir*. 1979, Paris).

Maclellan, E. (2001) Assessment for learning: the differing perceptions of tutors and students, *Assessment and Evaluation in Higher Education*, 26: 307–18.

Manning, S. (2005) The promise of podcasting, *Pointers and Clickers*, 6(2). www.ion.illinois.edu/resources/pointersclickers/2005_03/Podcasting2005.pdf (accessed 15 January 2008).

Marquardt, M. (2005) *Leading with Questions*. San Francisco: Jossey-Bass.

Maskall, J., Stockes, A., Truscott, J.B., Bridge, A., Magnier, K. and Calderbank, V. (2007) Supporting fieldwork using information technology, *Planet*, 18: 18–21.

Mayer, R.E. (2001) *Multimedia Learning*. Cambridge: Cambridge University Press.

McDrury, J. and Alterio, M.G. (2003) *Learning through Storytelling in Higher Education: Using Reflection and Experience to Improve Learning*. London: Kogan Page.

McKillop, C. (2005) Storytelling grows up: using storytelling as a reflective tool in higher education. Paper presented at the Scottish Educational Research Association conference (SERA 2005), Perth, Scotland, 24–26 November. www.storiesabout.com/files/McKillop%202005%20SERA.pdf (accessed 23 January 2008).

McIntosh, S., Braul, B. and Chao, T. (2003) A case study in asynchronous voice conferencing for language instruction, *Education Media International*, 40: 63–74.

McLoughlin, C., Lee, M.J.W. and Chan, A. (2006). Fostering reflection and metacognition through student-generated podcasts. Paper presented at the Australian Computers in Education Conference, Cairns, 2–4 October. www.csusap.csu.edu.au/~achan/papers/2006_POD_ACEC.pdf (accessed 22 January 2008).

McLoughlin, C., Lee, M.J.W. and Chan, A. (2007) Promoting engagement and motivation for distance learners through podcasting, in A. Szucs and I. Bø (eds) *New Learning 2.0? Emerging Digital Territories, Developing Continuities, New Divides: Proceedings of the EDEN Annual Conference*. Budapest: EDEN.

Metcalf, D. (2002) Stolen moments for learning, *eLearning Developers' Journal*, 18–20 March. www.elearningguild.com/pdf/2/March02-Metcalf-H.pdf (accessed 21 January 2008).

Metcalf, D.S. (2006) *mLearning: Mobile Learning and Performance in the Palm of Your Hand*. Amherst, MA: HRD Press.

Michael, M. (2003) Between the mundane and the exotic: time for a different socio-technical stuff, *Time and Society*, 12(2): 127–43.

Microsoft (2004) *Advanced Systems Format (ASF) Specification*. www.microsoft.com /windows/windowsmedia/forpros/format/asfspec.aspx (accessed 10 January 2008).

Middleton, C. (2007) Illusions of balance and control in an always-on environment: a case study of BlackBerry users, *Continuum: Journal of Media and Cultural Studies*, 21(2): 165–78.

Millar, R., Leach, J. and Osbourne, J. (2001) *Improving Science Education: The Contribution of Research*. Buckingham: Open University Press.

Miller, D. and Slater, D. (2000) *The Internet: An Ethnographic Approach*. Oxford: Berg.

Moisander, J. and Eriksson, P. (2006) Corporate narratives of information society: making up the mobile consumer subject, *Consumption, Markets and Culture*, 9(3): 257–75.

Moon, J.A. (1999) *Reflection in Learning and Professional Development: Theory and Practice*. London: Kogan Page.

Moon, J. (2006) *Learning Journals: A Handbook for Reflective Practice and Professional Development*, 2nd edn. London: Routledge.

Moreno, R. and Mayer, R.E. (1999) Deriving instructional design principles from multimedia presentations with animations. Paper presented at the 1999 IEEE International Conference on Multimedia Computing and Systems (ICMCS'99), 1: 9720.

Mortiboys, A. (2005) *Teaching with Emotional Intelligence*. London: Routledge.

Mousavi, S., Lowe, R. and Sweller, J. (1995) Reducing cognitive load by mixing auditory and visual presentation modes, *Journal of Educational Psychology*, 87: 319–34.

Murray, C. and Sandars, J. (2007) Digital storytelling: forging identity through voice and three-dimensional reflection. Programme and abstracts of ALT-C 2007, 30–1, Nottingham, 4–6 September.

Mutch, A. (2003) Exploring the practice of feedback to students, *Active Learning in Higher Education*, 4: 24–38.

Naismith, L., Lonsdale, P., Vavoula, G. and Sharples, M. (2004) *Literature Review in Mobile Technologies and Learning*. Bristol: NESTA FutureLab.

Newnham, L. and Miller, C. (2007) Student perceptions of podcasting to enhance learning and teaching in an information systems course. Research proceedings of ALT-C 2007, 104–15, Nottingham, 4–6 September.

Nicol, D. and Macfarlane-Dick, D. (2006) Formative assessment and self-regulated learning: a model and seven principles of good feedback practice, *Studies in Higher Education*, 31: 199–218.

Nie, M. (2006) *The pedagogical perspectives of mobile learning*. www2.le.ac.uk/projects/impala/documents (accessed 22 January 2008).

Nygren, L. and Blom, B. (2001) Analysis of short reflective narratives: a method for the study of knowledge in social workers' actions, *Qualitative Research*, 1(3): 369–84.

Oblinger, D. (2003) Understanding the new students: boomers, gen-Xers, millennials, *EduCAUSE Review*, 38(4): 37–47.

O'Dowd, R. (2003) Understanding the 'other side': intercultural learning in a Spanish-English e-mail exchange, *Language Learning and Technology*, 7: 118–44.

O'Malley, C., Vavoula, G., Glew, J., Taylor, J., Sharples, M. and Lefrere, P. (2003) *Guidelines for learning/teaching/tutoring in a mobile environment*. Mobilearn project deliverable. www.mobilearn.org/download/results/guidelines.pdf (accessed 20 January 2008).

Pitts, S. (2005) 'Testing, testing . . .': how do students use written feedback? *Active Learning in Higher Education*, 6: 218–29.

Power, D.J. (1990) The use of audio in distance education, in S. Timmers (ed.) *Training Needs in the Use of Media for Distance Education*. Singapore: Asian Mass Communication Research and Information Centre. www1.worldbank.org/disted/Technology/print_recorded/aud-01.html (accessed 28 January 2008).

Prensky, M. (2001) Digital natives, digital immigrants, *On the Horizon*, 9(5): 1–6.

PSU (Pennsylvania State University) (2006) *About podcasts at Penn State*. www.podcasts.psu.edu/about (accessed 15 January 2008).

Quinn, C. (2000) mLearning: mobile, wireless, in your pocket learning, *LineZine*, Fall 2000. www.linezine.com/2.1/features/cqmmwiyp.htm (accessed 20 January 2008).

Race, P. (1999) *Enhancing Student Learning*. Birmingham: SEDA.

Race, P. (2005) *Making Learning Happen: A Guide for Post-compulsory Education*. London: Sage.

Ramsden, P. (1992) *Learning to Teach in Higher Education*. London: Routledge.

Ramsden, P. (2003) *Learning to Teach in Higher Education*, 2nd edn. London: Routlege.

Ramsden, A. (2007) Podcasting as a social network tool: is it a student reality? Programme and abstracts of ALT-C 2007: 117–18. Nottingham, 4–6 September.

Reeves, B. and Nass, C. (1996) *The Media Equation*. New York: Cambridge University Press.

Reynolds, M. and Trehan, K. (2000) Assessment: a critical perspective, *Studies in Higher Education*, 3: 267–78.

Richardson, I. (2007) Pocket technospaces: the bodily incorporation of mobile media, *Continuum: Journal of Media and Cultural Studies*, 21(2): 205–15.

Riedinger, B. (2006) Mining for meaning: teaching students how to reflect, in

A. Jafari and C. Kaufman (eds) *Handbook of Research on ePortfolios*. Hershey, PA: Idea Group Reference.

Riordan, M. (2007) M-learning and podcasting as an assistive technology. Proceedings of the 13th Online Educa Conference, Berlin, 28–30 November.

Robinson, J.A. and Hawpe, L. (1986) Narrative thinking as a heuristic process, in T.R. Sarbin (ed) *Narrative Psychology: The Storied Nature of Human Conduct*, New York: Praeger Publishers.

Romero-Gwynn, E. and Marshall, M.K. (1990) Radio: untapped teaching tool, *Journal of Extension*, 28(1). www.joe.org/joe/1990spring/a1.html (accessed 28 January 2008).

RSS Advisory Board (2007) *RSS 2.0 specification*. www.rssboard.org/rss-specification (accessed 8 January 2008).

Rust, C. (2007) Towards a scholarship of assessment, *Assessment and Evaluation in Higher Education*, 32: 229–37.

Rust, C., Price, M. and O'Donovan. B. (2003) Improving students' learning by developing their understanding of assessment criteria and process, *Assessment and Evaluation in Higher Education*, 28: 147–64.

Salmon, G. (2002) *E-tivities: The Key to Active Online Learning*. London and New York: Routledge.

Salmon, G. (2004) *E-moderating: The Key to Teaching and Learning Online*, 2nd edn. London and New York: Routledge.

Salmon, G. (2005) Flapping not flying, *ALT-J, Research in Learning Technology*, 13(3): 201–18.

Salomon, G. (1984). Television is 'easy' and print is 'tough': the differential investment of mental effort in learning as a function of perceptions and attributions, *Journal of Educational Psychology*, 76(4): 647–58.

Sandars, J. and Schroter, S. (2007) Web 2.0 technologies for undergraduate and postgraduate medical education: an online survey, *Postgraduate Medical Journal*, 83: 759–62.

Savel, R.H., Goldstein, E.B., Perencevich, E.N. and Angood, P.B. (2007) The iCritical Care Podcast: a novel medium for critical care communication and education, *Journal of the American Medical Informatics Association*, 14(1): 94–9.

Schlosser, C.A. and Burmeister, M.L. (2006) Audio in online courses: beyond podcasting. Paper presented at the World Conference on E-learning in Corporate, Government, Healthcare, and Higher Education 2006, Honolulu, 13–17 October. www.nova.edu/~burmeist/audio_online.html (accessed 15 January 2008).

Schunk, D.H. and Zimmerman, B.J. (1998) *Self-regulated Learning: From Teaching to Self-reflective Practice*. New York: The Guilford Press.

Scottish Council for Educational Technology (1994) Audio, in *Technologies in Learning*. Glasgow: SCET.

Sefton-Green, J. (2004) *Literature Review in Informal Learning with Technology Outside School* (Report 7). London: WAC Performing Arts and Media College, NESTA Futurelab.

Selwyn, N. (2002) Learning to love the micro: the discursive construction of 'educational' computing in the UK, 1979–1989, *British Journal of the Sociology of Education*, 23(4): 427–43.

Sharpe, R., Benfield, G., Roberts, G. and Francis, R. (2006) *The undergraduate experience of blended e-learning: a review of UK literature and practice undertaken for the Higher Education Academy*. www.heacademy.ac.uk/ourwork/research/litreviews/2005_06 (accessed 20 January 2008).

Sharples, M. (2000) The design of personal mobile technologies for lifelong learning, *Computers and Education*, 34: 177–93.

Sharples, M. (2002) Disruptive device: mobile technology for conversational learning, *International Journal of Continuing Engineering Education and Lifelong Learning*, 12(5/6): 504–20.

Sharples, M. (ed.) (2006) *Big Issues in Mobile Learning*. Nottingham: Kaleidoscope Network of Excellence, Mobile Learning Initiative.

Sheller, M. And Urry, J. (2006) The new mobilities paradigm, *Environment and Planning A*, 38(3): 207–26.

Shim, J.P., Shropshire, J., Park, S., Harris, H. and Campbell, N. (2007) Podcasting for e-learning communication, and delivery, *Industrial Management and Data Systems*, 107(4): 587–600.

Shin, M., Holden, T. and Schmidt, R.A. (2001) From knowledge theory to management practice: towards an integrated approach, *Information Processing and Management*, 37: 335–55.

Siemens, G. (2005) Connectivism: a learning theory for the digital age, *International Journal of Instructional Technology and Distance Learning*. www.itdl.org/Journal/Jan_05/article01.htm (accessed 20 January 2008).

Silverman, G. (n.d.) *A comparison between face-to-face focus groups, telephone focus groups and online focus groups.* www.mnav.com/onlinetablesort.htm (accessed 28 January 2008).

Smallwood, J.E. (2004) An anatomist's comments on learning and teaching, *Journal of Veterinary Medical Education*, 31: 79–82.

So, K.K.T. (2004) Applying wireless information technology in field trips: a Hong Kong experience, *Australian Educational Computing*, 19(2): 3–7.

Sobol, J. (2006) *Orality and Web 2.0.* www.thetalkingshop.ca/2006/12/ (accessed 30 December 2007).

SPLINT (2007) *Spatial Literacy: A Centre for Excellence in Teaching and Learning (SPLINT).* www.spatial-literacy.org (accessed 28 December 2007).

Sternberg, R.J. and Caruso, D.R. (1985). Practical modes of knowing, in E. Eisner (eds), *Learning and Teaching the Ways of Knowing: 84th Yearbook of the National Society for the Study of Education.* Chicago: University of Chicago Press.

Stevens, A. and Hewer, S. (1998) From policy to practice and back. Proceedings of the First LEVERAGE Conference, Cambridge, 7–8 January. www.greco.dit.upm.es/~leverage/conf1/hewer.htm (accessed 15 January 2008).

Stevens, A. (2007) *Text of podcasts used in this work.* www.ph.ed.ac.uk/~spb01/content/media/podcasts/stevens.html (accessed 22 January 2008).

Sun, L., Williams, S., Ousmanou, K. and Lubega, J. (2003) Building personalized functions into dynamic content packaging to support individual learners. www.ais.reading.ac.uk/papers/con41-building%20personalised.pdf (accessed 15 January 2008). Proceedings of the 2nd European Conference on e-Learning (439–48), Glasgow Caledonian University.

Sweller, J. (1999). *Instructional Design in Technical Areas*, Australia: Australian Council for Educational Research, Camberwell, Victoria.

Terranova, T. (2000) Free labor: producing culture for the digital economy, *Social Text*, 63: 33–57.

Thomas, C. (2006) Designing an online science lab around self-paced MP3 player-based field trips. Paper presented at the Philadelphia Annual Meeting, 22–25 October. www.gsa.confex.com/gsa/2006AM/finalprogram/abstract_108487.htm (accessed 15 January 2008).

Traxler, J. (2005) Mobile learning – it's here but what is it? *Interactions*, 9(1), University of Warwick.

Traxler, J. (2007a) Mobile learning in a mobile world – the practicalities of the social, ethical and legal environment, in T. Hansson (ed.) (2008) *Handbook of Digital Information Technologies: Innovations and Ethical Issues*. New York: IDEAS.

Traxler, J. (2007b) Managed mobile messaging and information for education. Proceedings of IST Africa Conference, Maputo, Mozambique, 9–11 May.

Traxler, J. and Kukulska-Hulme, A. (2005) Evaluating mobile learning: reflections on current practice. Proceedings of the MLEARN2005 4th World Conference on mLearning, Cape Town, South Africa, 25–28 October 2005. www.mlearn.org.za/CD/BOA_p.65.pdf (accessed 20 January 2008).

Tynan, B. and Colbran, S. (2006) Podcasting, student learning and expectations, in L. Markauskaite, P. Goodyear and P. Reimann (eds) *Proceedings of the 23rd ASCILITE Conference*. Sydney: University of Sydney.

Tysome, T. (2006) 'It's a rap, but not as we know it', *Times Higher Educational Supplement*: 3, 9 June.

Van Dijk, J. (2005) From shoebox to performative agent: the computer as personal memory machine, *New Media and Society*, 7(4): 311–32.

Vygotsky, L.S. (1978) *Mind in Society: The Development of Higher Psychological Processes*. Cambridge: Harvard University Press.

Watt, A. (2007) OK, so we got it wrong: how lessons from a disaster led to success. Proceedings of the 13th Online Educa Berlin: (139–41), 28–30 November.

Weaver, M. (2006) Do students value feedback? Student perceptions of tutors' written responses, *Assessment and Evaluation in Higher Education*, 31: 379–94.

Webb, E., Jones, A., Barker, P. and Schaik, P. (2004) Using e-learning dialogues in higher education, *Innovations in Education and Teaching International*, 41(1): 93–103.

Welham, K. (1999) Tape recorded feedback, in I. Moore and K. Exley (eds) *Innovations in Science Teaching*, 2: 35–9. Birmingham: SEDA.

Whitehead, D.E.J., Bray, D. and Harries, M. (2007) Not just music but medicine: podcasting surgical procedures in otolaryngology, *Clinical Otolaryngology*, 32: 3–6.

Winterbottom, S. (2007) Virtual lecturing: delivering lectures using screencasting and podcasting technology, *Planet*, 18: 6–8.

Woodward, J. (2007) *Podcasts to support workshops in chemistry*. www2.le.ac.uk/projects/impala/presentations/impala_lfc0n_workshop (accessed 22 January 2008).

Woolgar, S. (1991) Configuring the user: the case of usability trials, in J. Law (ed.) *A Sociology of Monsters: Essays on Power, Technology and Domination*. Oxford: Blackwell.

World Bank (2000) *Broadcast and computer-based: radio*. www1.worldbank.org/disted/Technology/broadcast/broad_radio.html (accessed 28 January 2008).

Yuen, S. and Wang, S. (2004) M-learning: mobility in learning, in G. Richards (ed.) *Proceedings of World Conference on E-Learning in Corporate, Government, Healthcare, and Higher Education 2004*. Chesapeake, Virginia: AACE.

Index

ONLINE LEARNING AND TEACHING IN HIGHER EDUCATION

Shirley Bach, Philip Haynes and Jennifer Lewis Smith

- What are the links between theory and practice in the area of online learning in higher education?
- What are the strengths and weaknesses of the online approach?
- How can online learning be used to enhance the student experience?

This book provides the first critical evaluation of theory and practice in online learning and teaching in higher education. It also provides a critique of online learning for all those working in a higher education setting. It examines the online approach in the context of the internet age and global higher education, examining changes in distance learning as well as how online learning is affecting mainstream mass higher education. Practical examples throughout the book allow the reader to:

- Understand quality issues with regard to online learning
- Design appropriate courses
- Create stimulating online learning environments
- Transform learning methods
- Adapt and develop strategies to enhance online teaching practice

Online Learning and Teaching in Higher Education is key reading for lecturers, managers and policy makers in the higher education sector.

2006   220pp
978–0–335–21829–5 (Paperback)   978–0–335–21830–1 (Hardback)